Teaching Comprehension

Teaching Comprehension

The Comprehension Process Approach

Cathy Collins Block
Texas Christian University

Boston ■ New York ■ San Francisco
Mexico City ■ Montreal ■ Toronto ■ London ■ Madrid ■ Munich ■ Paris
Hong Kong ■ Singapore ■ Tokyo ■ Cape Town ■ Sydney

Series Editor: Aurora Martínez Ramos
Editorial Assistant: Katie Freddoso
Senior Marketing Manager: Elizabeth Fogarty
Production Administrator: Michael Granger
Editorial-Production Service: Omegatype Typography, Inc.
Manufacturing Buyer: Andrew Turso
Composition and Prepress Buyer: Linda Cox
Cover Administrator: Kristina Mose-Libon
Electronic Composition: Omegatype Typography, Inc.

For related titles and support materials, visit our online catalog at www.ablongman.com.

Between the time Website information is gathered and published, some sites may have closed. Also, the transcription of URLs can result in unintentional typographical errors. The publisher would appreciate notification where these errors occur so that they may be corrected in subsequent editions.

Library of Congress Cataloging-in-Publication Data

Block, Cathy Collins.
    Teaching comprehension : the comprehension process approach / Cathy Collins Block.
      p.   cm.
    Includes bibliographical references and index.
    ISBN 0-205-32447-9 (alk. paper)
    1. Reading comprehension.   2. Reading, Psychology of.   3. Metacognition in children.   I. Title.

LB1050.45.B56 2004
372.47—dc21

2003044422

Printed in the United States of America
10   9   8   7   6   5   4   3   2   1   08   07   06   05   04   03

Contents

PART II   Domains of Comprehension and How to Teach Them

5 Developing Inferential, Predictive, and Interpretive Comprehension   102

6 Imagery: Looking Within and Up and Away without Moving Too Far from the Text   118

7   Metacognition: Monitoring One's Own Comprehension   133

PART III   Teaching and Assessing CPA Lessons across Curriculum, Media, and Cultures

8   Comprehension Instruction Is Not Generic—It's Genre Specific   156

9 Technological Comprehension and Reading Culturally Dominated Texts 183

10 Assessment of Comprehension 201

List of Comprehension Process Lessons

List of Figures

List of Tables

Preface

Teaching Comprehension: The Comprehension Process Approach presents newly developed, research-based methods that improve students' comprehension. This book is designed for practicing teachers and for graduate and undergraduate courses in elementary and middle school literacy methods, diagnosis and correction of reading problems, and content area reading instruction. Each chapter provides highly effective lessons that advance students' comprehension abilities. The book includes multiple methods of teaching specific comprehension processes. Every chapter ends with complete, ready-to-use lesson plans.

Many people contributed to this book. My mother and sister, JoAnn and Wanda Zinke, assisted me in this text's development. Rebecca Johnson, my graduate assistant, and Rachel Escamilla, my administrative assistant, enhanced its quality. My students provided the inspiration to write. I am indebted to countless educators and students who participated in the research. They worked diligently and shared valuable insights in the development of the comprehension process approach (CPA) to instruction. I deeply appreciate Aurora Martínez Ramos of Allyn and Bacon, the most positive editor with whom I have ever worked. She is one of the many dedicated professionals who made this book possible. Each person made excellent contributions to this text, especially Karla Walsh and the rest of the staff at Omegatype Typography. I am also grateful to the following reviewers who spent hours offering advice and suggestions. They improved this book immensely: Toni Bellon, North Georgia College & State University; Gregory Brooks, Nazareth College of Rochester; Melise Bunker, Palm Beach Atlantic College; Cherie A. Clodfelter, University of Dallas; Michael Graves, University of Minnesota, Twin Cities; Thomas Gunning, University of Minnesota, Twin Cities; Kathy Headley, Clemson University; Ellin Keene, Pennsylvania State University; Michael Moore, Georgia Southern University; Lynn Romeo, Monmouth University; and Michael Tanner, Pacific University. I also deeply appreciate all the hard work and examples created by Dionne Adkinson for Chaper 6 of this book.

CHAPTER 1

Teachers' Goals during Comprehension Instruction

Ms. Parks demonstrates the new responsibilities teachers can assume to increase students' comprehension.

TEACHERS' GOALS DURING COMPREHENSION INSTRUCTION

G
Goal 1: <u>G</u>iving choices during scaffolding and performing pivotal point scaffolding to avoid the slight rejection phenomenon

O
Goal 2: <u>O</u>mitting teacher dominated one-to-one conferences by holding more student-dominated discovery discussions

A
Goal 3: <u>A</u>voiding the tendency to merely give instructions by tilling the text, showing how, and storytelling

L
Goal 4: <u>L</u>eading students to initiate rather than merely contribute

S
Goal 5: <u>S</u>eeking students' increased understanding through respondent-centered questions, the power of three, and effective responses during discussions

Ms. Parks is dedicated to Demetria and Conrad. She is implementing research-based practices, presented in this book, which she learned through her work with the Institute for Literacy Enhancement. Ms. Parks and other teachers in the institute are striving to create effective comprehension lessons. By implementing the goal-oriented process, Ms. Parks is helping her students become successful, as attested to by Demetria when she stated: "Ms. Parks is the best teacher I've ever had. When I am in her class, I read better than I can without her. I wish I could live in our classroom."

Chapter Overview

What can you expect from this book? You can expect to develop an understanding of comprehension processes and realize the ability to implement highly effective comprehension lessons. Chapters 1 to 3 describe the responsibilities of teachers, curricula, and students in building comprehension. This book is based on the proposition that what students achieve depends greatly on the instruction they receive, the quality of past literary experiences, and the actions of their teachers (Block, Oakar, & Hurt, 2002). Highly effective comprehension instruction begins with effective literacy teachers that "have a privileged understanding of literacy instruction in part because their teaching is based on many decisions about what works in the classroom" (Pressley, Harris, & Guthrie, 1995, p. 365).

Comprehension instruction builds a strong interrelationship among teachers, students, and the comprehension processes needed to create meaning from a text. Teachers' goals include building a learning environment in which students can bring their natural energy and inclination for exploration to the study of new ideas in texts. Rather than considering comprehension as a series of isolated strategies, the Comprehension Process Approach puts students' cognitive processes at the center of the teaching process (Block, 1999).

This new approach is timely and important. The National Reading Panel (NRP, 2001) reviewed the body of data-driven studies concerning comprehension instruction and found that

- Reading comprehension is an active process. It is driven by intentional thinking that makes connections among thinking processes; textual content; and the reader's knowledge, expectations, and purposes for reading. Meaning was judged to reside in the "intentional, problem-solving, thinking processes of the reader that occur during an interchange with a text . . . influenced by the text and by the reader's prior knowledge that is brought to bear on it by the reader" (NRP, 2001, pp. 34–39); the teacher's direction; or, instructional goals.
- The goal of comprehension instruction is to build readers' thinking processes so they can read a text with understanding, construct memory and metacognitive representations of what they understood, and put their new understandings to use when communicating with others.
- During the past twenty years, the explicit instruction of reading comprehension focused on teaching individual cognitive strategies to students (NRP, 2001). Many curriculum programs have included multiple strategies for teaching reading, and researchers have begun to explore how professional development can help teachers learn how to teach comprehension in ways that they had not been taught themselves as students. This book seeks to address this contemporary need.
- Researchers acknowledge that because past instructional methods have been inadequate, many students have such weak literacy abilities that they cannot understand texts which were written for their grade levels (Chall, 1998; Durkin, 1978). Further, "it is clear that children who can not comprehend tend to fall fur-

ther behind their peers [in their comprehension abilities] by third grade, regardless of their decoding skill level" (Chall, 1998, p. 98).

■ Unstimulating and ineffective instruction must be stopped. The amount of time spent in highly interactive and engaging comprehension instruction must increase (Durkin, 1978/ 1979; Elley, 1992).

Studies have demonstrated that students who received the comprehension instruction presented in this book significantly outperformed schoolmates who were taught less systematically on measures of comprehension, vocabulary, decoding, problem solving, cooperative group skills, and self-esteem, as determined by the Iowa Test of Basic Skills, Harter Test of Self-Concept, informal reading inventories, and standardized reasoning tests (Block, 1999; Collins, 1991; Pressley, Goodchild, Fleet, Zajchowski, & Evans, 1989). This newly evolved Comprehension Process Approach to instruction contains print-rich, developmentally appropriate lessons, and actively engages students to initiate their own thinking processes to untangle the confusions and complexities in printed ideas.

These lessons also enable teachers to aptly explain how comprehension develops—how students and authors work artistically together to build understanding (Block, 1999; Leslie & Allen, 1999; Lipson & Wixson, 1997). These process-based lessons emphasize that during each meaning-making process, a reader's purpose, state of mind, knowledge of English, and background experiences are of equal importance to comprehension as are the printed words and the social, historical, and political contexts in which that text is read (Bakhtin, 1993; Bloome, 1986; Rosenblatt, 1978).

New comprehension process lessons value equally (1) individual interpretation and literal comprehension, (2) avid reading of fiction as well as nonfiction, (3) student reflection as well as direct instruction, and (4) both efferent and aesthetic responses to reading. Comprehension process lessons also demonstrate how readers can develop meaning by moving along a continuum of thoughts, bordered on one side by the author's intended message and on the other end by an application of the text to the reader's life experiences. Finally, these lessons are divided into three differentiated strands of instruction: (1) teaching students how to combine multiple thinking processes (Strand 1 of Comprehension Process Approach (CPA) instruction), (2) encouraging students to enjoy reading (Strand 2 of CPA instruction), and (3) increasing students' abilities to recognize their own comprehension weaknesses (Strand 3 of instruction).

Chapter 1 discusses five responsibilities teachers assume. It describes how reading comprehension teachers must go beyond merely "telling" students what to do. Teachers must not simply instruct, they must demonstrate. They must think aloud about how they select and initiate successful comprehension processes themselves, and model their own thinking processes in action. According to Laura Parks, reading specialist in Keller, Texas, "Everybody has a desire to have their needs met immediately. It is our job to meet students' needs *and* to ensure that they know that these needs are important to us. I have assumed the five responsibilities in this chapter, and as a result, for the first time, I am able to meet my students' needs the moment they are expressed" (Parks, personal communication, May 5, 2001).

By the end of this chapter, you will be able to answer the following questions:

1. With whom, in what situations, and in what ways, do artistic teachers teach comprehension explicitly and implicitly?
2. How can teachers go beyond providing think-alouds and assign the control for making meaning to students?
3. How can teachers encourage students to initiate their own comprehension processes?
4. What are the most important actions that teachers can take before, during, and after comprehension lessons?

New Responsibilities Teachers Bear: The Comprehension Process Approach

The **comprehension process approach (CPA)** involves teaching students (1) how to identify the thinking processes and meaning-making tools that they need to understand a text, and (2) how to initiate several thinking processes at points in a text when understanding is interrupted. CPA lessons establish goals for teachers, curriculum, and pupils during comprehension instruction. It is based on the following research.

Prior to 1980, many teachers taught comprehension by merely giving directions to students to "read carefully," assigning workbook pages, and asking literal questions after a text had been read. By 1997, in the second edition of the *Handbook of Reading Research*, Pearson and Fielding (1997) identified a shift away from these time-honored traditions. Teachers were beginning to teach comprehension strategies, which, in turn, required the demonstration and explanation of thought processes (what Paris [1986] calls "making thinking public"). Also, in the 1990s more teachers began to wonder how they could become better able to increase their students' abilities to make meaning. The new instructional roles described in this chapter can help teachers to answer this question.

CPA is also based on research studies in which the actions of highly effective comprehension teachers were studied (Block & Pressley, 2002; Block & Mangieri, 2003). Levin and Pressley (1981) divided teacher actions into two categories. Instructional episodes initiated before reading were labeled stage-setting activities; those taught during or after readings were labeled storage–retrieval activities.

In addition, Scott, Jamieson, and Asselin (1999) found that in 23 Canadian classrooms the amount of time that teachers were spending on teaching comprehension was 25.2 percent of the total time relegated to reading instruction. The instructional methods used were predominately small-group skill development lessons, think-alouds, guided reading, read-alouds, modeling, guided practice, brainstorming, and metacognitive explaining. These types of instruction appear to be a significant improvement over Durkin's (1978/1979) observations that less than 3% of classroom instructional time was spent in teaching comprehension. Although it is encouraging that today's teachers are devoting extra time to comprehension instruction, there is much work to be done before every child will be able to comprehend independently.

Moreover, while it has been proven that strategy instruction is more effective than isolated drill and practice on separate skills (Guthrie, 1981), recent data suggest that it is not explicit instruction per se but the quality of teacher–student interactions that significantly increases pupils' comprehension (Block, 2001c; Block, Gambrell & Pressley, 2002; Block & Pressley, 2002). When educators teach thinking processes, they increase students' involvement and control in making meaning, in large part through the rich conversations that such lessons contain (Applebee & Langer, 1983; Palincsar, 1986; Wood, Bruner, & Ross, 1976).

The type of cognitive demand, interventions, and questions teachers pose are also important. Several researchers have examined the most common type of question-and-answer sessions that occur in comprehension lessons. Usually the teacher asks a question, one or more students answer that question, and the teacher evaluates the response(s). There were no significant differences, however, between students' recall and literal interpretation of texts when their reading experiences were followed by this traditional questioning sequence or no discussion at all (see, e.g., Cazden, 1991; O'Flahavan, 1989). However, several significant differences were found in other aspects of students' comprehension when teachers' instructional discussions contained the qualities described in this chapter. These question and answer sessions did lead to increases in students' depth of attention to text, comprehension process knowledge, control over their own making of meaning, and positive self-perceptions of their important role in discussions about text read (Block, Schaller, Joy, & Gaines, 2001).

Further, according to Brown, Collins, and Duguid (1989) complex mental thinking evolves gradually during the process of reading authentic texts and not by teachers simply delivering procedural instructions to students prior to reading. Thus, in CPA lessons, the making of meaning is taught as a process—a process in which complex thoughts and comprehension tools are engaged when a text requires them. Moreover, to understand a text, students need teachers to help them participate in the whole act of comprehension until the students can carry out the entire thinking process independently. To do so, teachers must be careful to provide direct instruction as well as allow students independence. If teachers provide too much explicit instruction, they could limit students' self-initiated desires to read. Teachers may also hinder students' development of comprehension skill because students tend to over-rely on rote memory when all lessons follow the same sequence of actions. Over reliance on direct instruction can also reduce students' self-efficacy because teachers could be perceived as all-knowing. As a result, many students come to believe that they know little and cannot comprehend without assistance.

However, if teachers provide too little comprehension instruction or allow students to read with only peer assistance, they may reduce readers' abilities to transfer comprehension processes to new books. This would occur because peers, who are often equally weak in their knowledge of how to execute effective comprehension processes, can not describe to others how to think as they read. Unguided peer instruction that does not contain the characteristics of Strand 3 lessons, which will be introduced later in this book, often becomes similar to students teaching each other in a type of barter system. Each student brings only one half of a pair of shoes (a partially complete comprehension) for example, to share with peers. When students leave such "bartered" sharing sessions, they may take a different, single shoe back—having engaged in only a lateral shift in knowledge gain without attaining a growth in comprehension ability. Each student may take a different shoe back to his or her desk, but none will have attained a complete understanding (of one or more comprehension processes) that could be used effectively to make meaning with numerous texts. Moreover, without expert teacher-guided comprehension instruction, students cannot learn how to engage several processes consecutively when required in difficult texts. They simply will not have enough expert processes from among which to choose (Zecker, Pappas, & Cohen, 1998).

With these problems in mind, the next step to increase students' comprehension abilities is for us, as educators, to assume new responsibilities in teaching comprehension. These responsibilities can be remembered because the first word in each begins with the letters in the acronym GOALS, as depicted in the graphic at the beginning of this chapter.

Goal 1: <u>G</u>iving Choices during Scaffolding and Performing Pivotal Point Scaffolding to Avoid the Slight Rejection Phenomenon

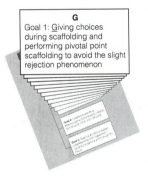

G

Goal 1: <u>G</u>iving choices during scaffolding and performing pivotal point scaffolding to avoid the slight rejection phenomenon

The **slight rejection phenomenon** occurs when students have a need, however slight, that a teacher does not address. Teachers can avoid the slight rejection phenomenon by (1) scaffolding, (2) giving students choices during comprehension scaffolding, and (3) pivotal point scaffolding.

Scaffolding occurs when a teacher demonstrates a comprehension process that is beyond a student's understanding (Means & Knapp, 1991). For example, Courtney was unable to read the directions for making an origami crane, but she could comprehend enough of *Making Origami Animals Yourself* to select the animal she wanted to create. To increase Courtney's ability to comprehend printed directions, Ms. Parks, her teacher, used scaffolding by asking Courtney to read aloud only one small part (i.e., one phrase at a time) of each instructional statement. Her teacher read and defined each unknown word and demonstrated how to fold each paper described in each phrase so Courtney could actually "see" the meaning that was carried in each phrase. Ms. Parks gradually reduced her scaffolding as she passed more of the responsibility for making meaning from each phrase to Courtney.

In scaffolding, teachers gradually reduce their support as students become more competent. This technique is similar to the temporary scaffolding used in building skyscrapers. Teachers place temporary scaffolds around students' comprehension until students can mimic their teachers' thinking processes as they create their own meaning from texts. Vygotsky (1978) was the first to teach teachers how to scaffold. He promoted learning by instructing teachers to scaffold students in their **zones of**

proximal development, which is defined as "the distance between the actual developmental level as determined by [students'] independent problem solving [abilities] and the level of potential development as determined through problem solving under adult guidance [scaffolding] and collaboration with more capable peers" (Vygotsky, 1978, p. 6).

Recently, researchers have developed new types of scaffolds. These scaffolds help students connect authors' intentions to the students' life experiences (Langer, 1991; Prawatt, 2001). The following types of scaffolds enable you to also eliminate the slight rejection phenomenon and address more of your students' comprehension difficulties.

Four Types of Comprehension Scaffolds

The four comprehension scaffolds are: (1) demonstrating a complete comprehension process before students begin to read; (2) inviting students to co-create a comprehension process with you by telling each other what you are thinking as you read; (3) beginning a comprehension process first and students join in when they understand how to think in that way (e.g., teacher begins to tell a summary of a story and tells how she is making the summary until students can tell the teacher how they are making their summaries); and (4) prompting with the name of a comprehension process to help students identify the process that would be helpful at a specific point in a text (e.g., teacher says, "I had to make a lot of *inferences* as I read this first page because ___. I am thinking that I will probably have to use my inference thinking processes a lot as I read the rest of the pages in this author's book because ___.").

For example, you could say, "Try using the 'pausing at the door of the dance and taking in all you know so far' image [a comprehension process] after you read the first two pages of a book to think about what the theme of each new book might be, like this [perform a think-aloud after you read the first two pages]" (a type 3 scaffold, described previously). Or you could say, "At this point in the text I am beginning to feel as if the author is relying on persuasion, rather than facts, to convince me of Hosea's valor. I must think about reading to detect propaganda techniques. I recommend that you "use detective thinking processes as you read this text and with future texts when you believe an author is using persuasive writing" (a type 4 scaffold, described previously).

Giving Students Choices during Scaffolding

A second way you can avoid the slight rejection phenomenon is by offering students choices while scaffolding. You can do this by providing two to three methods of engaging a specific comprehension process and asking students to select the one they prefer (Block, 2001b; Block & Mangieri, 1995/1996; Read & Roller, 1987). For example, Marcus asked Ms. Parks, "Would you help me? I can't think of how to put my main idea into a title for my story." Ms. Parks added choice to her scaffold by asking a question and then offering options to Marcus, as described below.

Ms. Parks asked, "What have you tried?"

Marcus answered, "I want a short title, but I don't want it to begin with the word *My* like all of my other titles do."

Marcus's answer told Ms. Parks that Marcus could use summarizing comprehension processes well. This was not the reason for his difficulty in generating a title. What he needed was a thinking tool that he can use in the future to increase his creative thinking. Ms. Parks scaffolded by saying, "When you want to stop and think about a main idea, or create a theme, such as a title, you could do two things. You could change some words to their synonyms, or you can choose words that tell about larger groups of thoughts or objects. For instance, if you don't want your title to be '*My Trip*,' you could change the word '*My*' by substituting a synonym, such as 'Marcus's,' 'our,' 'mine,' or 'the.' A second strategy you could use is to choose to put the one trip inside a larger group or theme, and write that larger idea first. For example, instead of making your title, '*My Trip*,' you can compare the trip to all others you've taken. '*This Trip Was the Best*,' '*The Trip That Most Took Marcus by Surprise*,' or '*The Most Important Trip*.'"

Once this scaffold was complete, Ms. Parks asked Marcus which thinking process he wanted to use to create his title: (1) selecting a synonym, or (2) creating a larger theme. Because she had demonstrated both to Marcus he could select the one he wanted to attempt on his first independent application of creative thinking for the first time.

Pivotal Point Scaffolding

Another action teachers can use to avoid the slight rejection phenomenon is pivotal point scaffolding. **Pivotal point scaffolding** is used to model a comprehension process at a specific point in a text where a child has difficulty, or at a point at which a particular comprehension process is necessary to attain a complete understanding. Pivotal point scaffolds can also enable you to identify a comprehension process that individual students need. Pivotal point scaffolds are think-alouds in which you describe a real-world analogy or visual image of a thinking process that a confused student(s) needs to make sense of a specific word, sentence, or paragraph in a text.

For example, Marcus was reading *Jubal's Wish* by Audrey and Don Wood to Roberto. Marcus had learned from Ms. Parks to conduct pivotal point scaffolds when tutees looked puzzled or seemed confused during tutoring sessions. According to the theme of *Jubal's Wish*, dreams often come true only after hardships have been endured. When the boys reached the point in the story when it appeared that Jubal's dream was not going to come true, Roberto asked, "I thought the wizard was going to grant Jubal's dream. Why did he trick Jubal?"

Marcus answered by identifying which comprehension process Roberto needed. This process involved comprehending details carefully to avoid inserting one's own desires for what an author *should* say into one's interpretation. Marcus took the first step in the pivotal point scaffold by turning back three pages prior to the point at which Roberto's question was raised. He showed Roberto how to reread details and to use images that depicted two directions this story's plot could take. Marcus said, "Here is a difficult point in this book. You may find similar difficult parts in other texts. When you come to paragraphs that tell you about two different directions a story could take, pay close attention to the author's choice of words in the next few sentences and to the images used to make the point. This will help you more quickly understand which of the two directions the author wants to take. For instance, in *Jubal's Wish*, the author said dreams 'sometimes work, and sometimes they don't. You never know how they'll turn out in the end.' At this point, you can pay attention to the next words and images of rain to predict that the next event will not be that the wish will come true. Audrey and Don Wood had used sunshine to denote happiness on past pages, and rain to denote sadness so we know that the dream is not going to come true in the next few pages."

Then, Marcus performed the second part of pivotal point scaffolding. He created a real-world analogy. He said, "When I come to a sentence in a book where the author writes that two different things could occur, I pretend I am a bird, perched high in a tree, looking at a fork in a dirt road. I use the comprehension process of remaining slightly detached so I can see the big picture the author is painting. I pay close attention to how all the details tie together in my mind as I read the next sentences, just like I would look all across the horizon to see everything I could if I were a bird trying to decide which direction to fly."

Because of this pivotal point's timeliness, six pages later, Roberto used the rain and sun images to correctly identify the direction that Audrey and Don Wood were taking the story. Through Marcus's teaching skill, Roberto rapidly learned how to use the comprehension processes of paying attention to details and imagery thinking. He proved it, because he made an accurate prediction as to the story's conclusion before the story ended.

The power of pivotal point scaffolding is derived from its timeliness. It can catapult students into significantly higher levels of understanding because a specific, relevant thinking process is modeled and projects students' thought processes forward immediately to overcome specific confusion while those students are in the process of trying to make meaning from a text.

Another pivotal point scaffolding example describes how authors develop characters. For example, instead of asking, "Who was your favorite character and why?" tell students, "This character is the most important because [pivotal point scaffolding here]. In your judgment, am I correct?" You can include in this pivotal point scaffolding how you selected the most important points that you liked about a selection.

When pivotal point scaffolding is complete, you can ask students to paraphrase what they learned so that they can perform this (or these) comprehension process(es) in the future when a text requires it. The best books to use in pivotal point scaffolding are high-quality fiction and nonfiction works that present universal themes, real-world issues, and common, human conditions written at a student's instructional level (Galda, 1998; Pardo, 1997; Raphael & Au, 1997).

In summary, to avoid the slight rejection phenomenon, you can (1) differentiate the types of scaffolds that you deliver, (2) provide choices during the scaffolding process so students can select the particular thinking process they want to use to remediate a comprehension difficulty, and (3) use pivotal point scaffolding. In scaffolding, your responsibilities include diagnosing the depth of comprehension processing that individuals are already engaging and analyzing which part of a text's content or format became an obstacle for that student.

Goal 2: Omitting Teacher Dominated One-to-One Conferences by Holding Student-Dominated Discovery Discussions

Goal 2: Omitting teacher dominated one-to-one conferences by holding more student-dominated discovery discussions

In **discovery discussions,** students meet alone with their teacher to discuss how they improved their reading abilities, what they depend on to read well, and what they need to comprehend better. Such self-knowledge is essential because the students themselves are the ones who are most aware of the level of effort (and are most sensitive to the level of drive) that they are willing to expend to become more successful comprehenders.

Discovery discussions improve teacher one-to-one conferences in several ways. First, they can be scheduled by students or teachers. Second, their purpose is to discover something that is blocking a student's comprehension. Third, they provide individualized time for teachers to listen to students' stories about their comprehension—Ms. Parks has a chart in her classroom where students can sign up for discovery discussions with her. Three students can sign up each day. If Ms. Parks wants to meet with an individual, she places that student's name in one of the three slots designated for a meeting that day. Fourth, discovery discussions differ from one-to-one conferences because they are not top-down interrogations (that is, teachers are not asking all the questions). Students do most of the talking and ask most of the questions.

Discovery discussions are intended to increase the level of effort and drive that students expend to become better readers (Block & Mangieri, in press b). Discovery discussions are much like days of old, when knowledge grew through fireside family conversations and by-the-bench mentoring. Teachers and students ask more questions of each other. During these conversations, students tell specific stories about their reading abilities, learn intensely in their zones of proximal development, and communicate the next step they want to take to become better readers. As a result, students can ensure that they do not have to spend much time in the "zones of their already known."

Discovery discussions do not always have to be formal, long meetings. **PAR (praise-ask-raise)** is one type of an impromptu discovery discussion. It provides individual feedback to students when they implement comprehension processes successfully. Praise-ask-raise is based on research confirming that teachers who significantly help their students increase their comprehension do so by providing more than simple praise when they interact with readers (Block, Schaller, Joy, & Gaines, 2002).

PAR is defined as a three-step praise cycle. It begins when students ask their teachers if they have done something correctly. Teachers respond by acknowledging a segment of the comprehension process that the student has executed well. Teachers praise (P) the student for the immediate growth he or she has accomplished. Then, the teacher adds a separate statement asking (A) the student what he or she was thinking to accurately complete that segment of the comprehension process. After the student answers this question, the student's abilities are raised (R) by posing a challenge that will assist that individual to use the comprehension process with more difficult texts in the future.

For example, Michelle asked Ms. Parks if she knew of any other books that had characters like Grace in *Amazing Grace*. Ms. Parks (P)raised Michelle for finding so many good qualities in a character in a book. Then, she (A)sked Michelle why she liked Grace. Michelle answered that she had imagined herself as Grace. Ms. Parks (R)aised Michelle by asking why she thought she was able to do so with this book. Michelle answered that it was because the main character was her age and felt the same way that she did. Ms. Parks continued by asking which type of character she wanted to identify with next. Did she want to learn about different children her own age, or would she prefer to read a book about a child who was older or younger than herself? Ms. Parks told Michelle that she could continue to improve her comprehension process of identifying with a wide variety of main characters by remembering what she was like at a younger age, or by predicting how she might feel when she was older. She can also place herself in a character's shoes by applying the values that she currently holds to problems that she has yet to face. After Michelle decided how she wanted to proceed, Ms. Parks found a book that accommodated her choice and did a think-aloud using the first paragraph in the book to demonstrate how Michelle could relate to that character.

In summary, the purpose of discovery discussions and the praise-ask-raise method is to help students apply what they have learned about comprehension processes on their own. According to Alec MacKenzie, a prominent social psychologist, "Most problems result from actions taken without thought. Those who know what to do succeed once. Those who know why they succeeded will succeed again and again" (1972, p. 17). Discovery discussions and praise-ask-raise methods enable students to tell you why they comprehended a book, and why they know that they can do equally well or better in the future.

Goal 3: <u>A</u>voiding the Tendency to Merely Give Directions by Tilling the Text, Showing How, and Storytelling

A
Goal 3: <u>A</u>voiding the tendency to merely give instructions by tilling the text, showing how, and storytelling

"**Tilling a text**" involves previewing a text. It teaches students how to (1) use content, authorial, and textual clues to discover meaning; (2) become aware of subtleties in authors' choices of words and writing styles to increase comprehension; (3) use subheadings, print features, paragraph lengths, and amount of white space to establish reading goals and determine a text's conceptual density; and (4) use background knowledge so as not to interfere with but expand one's understanding. In CPA, students learn how to continuously prepare their minds before they read (just as farmers fertilize and plow to nurture the soil before they plant).

To teach these tilling the text processes, you can model how it is useful to stop reading from time to time to process meaning. You pause at difficult points in a text where children could have problems interpreting an author's textual features. To illustrate, in Ms. Park's classroom, a lesson began with the following "till-ing the text" think-aloud:

> The author gave his characters strange names and I think he did so for a reason. He used the names of his characters to set a mood and communicate implied meanings. The names Alice in Wonderland, the Mad Hatter, the Queen of Hearts, and so on, denote imagination. I ask myself: "Why would the author give characters names of places and things? Is he trying to tell me something about the character?" Maybe I should attach the emotions associated with dreams, playing card games, and events that occur in this book with the characters to discern underlying meanings. For example, when the Queen of Hearts plays croquet, she has fun while following the rules because she truly enjoys the people with whom she is playing. I think the author is trying to suggest life princi-ples by giving his characters names with which most of us can associate emotions and experiences from our lives. What does "Mad Hatter" connote to you? What did the au-thor want us to think about this character?

The power of tilling processes is that they make textual features of specific gen-res salient to students, and as Blair-Larson and Williams (1999) demonstrated, tilling the text activities can become increasingly advanced as students mature. Schmitt (1988) was among the first to document the effects of tilling a text on students' comprehen-sion. When taught how to till a text, third graders gradually assumed responsibility for previewing textual features without prompting. In so doing, they activated their prior knowledge. Blair-Larson and Williams (1999) and Block (1999) also found that when students were taught to make connections between their tilling of texts and their prior knowledge, they comprehended texts more completely. Tilling the text also helped stu-dents interpret subtle symbolisms, imageries, and foreshadowing.

Once you have completed a tilling the text lesson, you can ask students to prac-tice using the series books (i.e., *Clifford, Frog and Toad,* and other series texts listed in Table 1.1). In this way, the same authorial writing styles can be reread. This reduces the difficulty of tilling a text and increases the speed with which such comprehension processes become automatic. Using this method of instruction, each student has an in-creased chance of successful comprehension.

In summary, before a reading begins, you can teach students to "till a text" by identifying difficult sections, attending to authors' writing styles, and considering the functions of paragraphs. Each time they read independently in the future, they should remember these suggestions. More specific information about how to teach authorial writing styles and paragraph functions follows.

Attending to Authors' Writing Styles

You can help readers to recognize the logic that an author followed when he or she di-vided the text into chapters and subtopics. By skimming a text, you can show pupils how to identify dense sections of a text that may require more concentrated thinking. You can teach attending to author's writing style by showing students how to skim or scan a full text for 1 to 3 minutes before they begin attentive reading. During this scanning, show students (by talking aloud) how they can think silently to themselves, before they

TABLE 1.1   Text Sets to Practice Tilling the Text

Reading Level	Series with Same Book Characters	Author
First and second grade	Clifford, The Big Red Dog	Norman Bridewell
	Jullian Jiggs	Phoebe Gilman
	Arthur books	Lillian Hoban
	Frog and Toad	Arnold Lobel
	George and Martha	James Marshall
	Little Critters	Mercer Mayer
	Little Bear	Else Minarik
	Amelia Bedilia	Peggy Parish
	Curious George	H. F. Rey
	Henry and Mudge	Cynthia Rylant
	Mr. Putter and Tabby	Cynthia Rylant
	Marvin Redpost	Louis Sachar
	Harry (The Dirty Dog) books	Gene Zion
	Nonfiction books	Eric Carle
Second and third grade	Amber Brown	Paula Danzinger
	Pee Wee Scouts	Judy Delton
	Kids of Polk Street School	Patricia Reilly Giff
	Horrible Harry	Suzy Kline
	Kids on Bus 5	Marcia Leonard
	Junie B. Jones	Barbara Park
	Nate the Great	Marjorie Sharmat
	Boxcar Children	Gertrude Warner
	Peter Cottontail	Beatrice Potter
	Magic School Bus	Scholastic
	Encyclopedia Brown	Donald Sobol
	Nonfiction All about _____	Scholastic
	Ask a Question about Nature	Scholastic
Fourth and fifth grade	Harry Potter	J. K. Rawlings
	Nancy Drew	Carolyn Keene
	The True Confessions of Charlotte Doyle	Avi
	Nothing but the Truth: A Documentary Novel	Avi
	What Do Fish Have to Do with Anything?	Avi
	The Summer of the Swans	B. Byars
	The Pinballs	B. Byars
	Cracker Jackson	B. Byars
	The Wretched Stone	C. Van Allsburg
	Just a Dream	C. Van Allsburg
	Sleeping Ugly	J. Yolen
	Julie of the Wolves	J. C. George
	Sounder	W. H. Armstrong

(continued)

TABLE 1.1   Continued

Reading Level	Series with Same Book Characters	Author
Sixth grade	Maniac Magee	J. Spinelli
	Roll of Thunder, Hear My Cry	M. Taylor
	Hey, Al	A. Yorinks
	Shiloh	P. R. Naylor
	Mrs. Frisby and the Rats of NIMH	R. C. O'Brian
	Hatchet	G. Paulsen
	Number the Stars	L. Lowry
	A Single Shard	L. Parks
	Bud, Not Buddy	C. Curtis

read, about the connections between subheadings that they think the author is making. For example, you could say: "I see that the author is beginning with the history of San Antonio, then moving to the present activities, and concluding the chapter with a description of three major tourist attractions."

You can conclude your think-aloud by teaching students that such overview tilling of texts can establish a framework that can be completed as they read. It also enables students' comprehension to move in the direction that most closely adheres to the main idea chains that the author created, which has been demonstrated to increase retention (Beck & Dole, 1994; Mangieri & Block, 1994). Such think-alouds "show students how to" think while they read, which is as powerful an instructional tool as story telling and sharing examples that tie to students' life experiences are to build comprehension abilities.

Story frames, diagrams of the connections between subsections in a text, can also increase students' comprehension abilities (Loxterman, Beck, & McKeown, 1994). In teaching story frames, you can provide partial outlines of a chapter's key points and tell students how you recognized that these were the main points. Then, ask the students to complete the remainder of the outlines as they read. Students share their outlines, the rationales for the key points they chose, and the connections between key points they made after the story has been completed. An example of a story frame created by Connor, a third grader from *The Butterfly* by Patricia Polacco, appears in Figure 1.1. Before Connor completed this story frame, Ms. Parks had demonstrated how she created a story frame using a different Patricia Polacco book. She taught how to analyze Ms. Polacco's authorial writing style and how to use story grammar to improve comprehension. Connor learned well and rapidly, as shown in Figure 1.1. A blank story frame for you to photocopy and use in your classroom appears in the Appendix at the end of this book.

Predicting the Functions of Paragraphs

When students anticipate the likely function of upcoming paragraphs, they can execute a valuable thinking process to assist them to make meaning (Kintsch, 2001). Although authors do not always order their paragraphs as denoted in Table 1.2, you can help

Setting: (When and where does the story take place?) _The story takes place during the war with the Nazis in France._

I know this because the author uses these words: _"Choisi-le Roi, just outside of Paris."_

Main characters: (Who are the important people in the story?) _Monique, Sevrine, Marcel (Monique's mother)._

I know they are important because: _The whole story is about them._

The problem starts when: _Monsieur Lendormy sees Monique and Sevrine in Monique's bedroom window._

or

The main character's goal is: _Monique is trying to be a friend to Sevrine and keep her safe from the Nazis._

The plot: (What happened?)

Event 1: _Monique and Sevrine let a butterfly go out the window and Monsieur Lendormy saw them._

After that . . .

Event 2: _Sevrine and her mother and daddy had to leave Monique's house where they were hiding._

Next . . .

Event 3: _Sevrine's mother and daddy went with Pere Voulliard. Sevrine left with Monique and her mother._

Then . . .

Event 4: _Sevrine, Monique, and Monique's mother walked a long distance until a car came to help Sevrine._

Turning point: (How I know the plot is reaching a solution)

The resolution: (How did it end?) _Monique and her mother finally made it to the train station and returned home safely._

I know this because the author uses these words: _Finally_

Author's moral or purpose (or, purpose for me): _It is important to help other people._

I think this is the moral because: _The story was about how Monique and her mother helped keep Sevrine and her parents safe from the Nazis. Sevrine and her parents were Jews._

FIGURE 1.1   Sample Story Frame for _The Butterfly_

TABLE 1.2   Tilling the Text by Teaching Students to Recognize Paragraph Functions

- Introductory: Introductory paragraphs provide an overview for an entire text; they tell readers the goals of the paragraphs that follow.

- Descriptive: Descriptive and explanatory paragraph give reasons for events, outcomes, positions, and authors' ideas. They delineate features and individual points after a main idea has been introduced. These paragraphs frequently can be identified by the words *for example, specifically, for this reason, in addition, moreover,* and *another.*

- Effect: Effect and cause paragraphs present the results of one or more causative agents or actions that led to a specific event. Key words in these paragraphs include *because, since, so that, so, if,* and *as.* These paragraphs can begin with a question and the remainder of the sentences answers the question. These paragraphs also specify what would happen if something else occurred or state the limits of an idea presented in a previous paragraph. Key words in these paragraphs include *if . . . then, unless, although, only,* and *if.*

- Arrange: Arranged by time, by sequence, or spatially relate the order in which particular events or ideas occur. They give the arrangement of things. Frequently, these paragraphs can be recognized by the words *first, second, third, then, next, before, after, during, while, another, also, in addition, when, until, meanwhile, always, following, finally,* and *initially.*

- Last: Last paragraphs are concluding paragraphs that summarize the most important points from previous paragraphs. Key words in these paragraphs include *hence, therefore, in summary, as a result, thus, in conclusion, accordingly, consequently, finally,* and *to sum up.*

students remember these functions by using the acronym IDEAL. In an ideal writing, the order of paragraphs follows the order shown in Table 1.2. You can teach the functions by showing sample paragraphs from a text that students are about to read on an overhead projector. You can demonstrate how you recognize the function of a few paragraphs, and then ask students to perform think-alouds to demonstrate how they recognized the functions of subsequent paragraphs.

Goal 4: Leading Students to Initiate Rather Than Merely Contribute

L
Goal 4: Leading students to initiate rather than merely contribute

At times when you change the role that you assume during CPA lessons, you enable students to become the initiator of improving their own comprehension. For example, you can act as a contributor to, rather than the initiator of, a lesson's goal by preparing surprises or congratulatory instructive statements the day after students demonstrate a comprehension process without your prompting. These surprises become visible displays of how much you value pupils' self-initiated comprehension. To do so, on the next day after student(s) have initiated a comprehension process without your prompting, add something to the ideas that the student(s) expressed the previous day, or surprise them with a concrete object that you brought that highlights the comment that was made. Such surprise actions, teaching tools, and congratulatory statements communicate to the students that they will be acknowledged and supported when they attempt to comprehend a text alone.

For example, Brooke asked Ms. Parks if the class could demonstrate how much they had learned from their nonfiction readings by staging a television news broadcast. She agreed and the next morning Ms. Parks surprised them by displaying a banner with a printed television logo that she had made for them and giving each student an individual name tag of the TV figures that each pupil was to become that could be worn on the broadcast. Because she had visibly shared in their initiative, the enthusiasm for the project mounted and the students read three more books on the topics of their individual broadcasts, by their own suggestion, to ensure that their speeches were accurate and interesting.

As a second example, if students asked to write and enact a sequel to *The Little House on the Prairie* series, you could surprise them with a box of vintage clothes from which they could select costumes to enhance their performance.

To review, students' engagement in making meaning increases when you initiate a surprise on the day after they take the initiative, without your prompting, to demonstrate their comprehension. Your surprise relates to the initiative the students took, and concretely demonstrates your support and value for their voices. Surprising students also develops students' initiative to increase their own comprehension and volition (Block & Beardon, 1997; Block & Mangieri, 2003).

Being a "sage at students' sides" after they have initiated goals can also come in the form of analogous statements. You can provide explanations through analogies that relate to students' lives and interests. For example, in preparation for the news broadcast, Ben was trying to understand how the speed of a tornado accelerates. This was an important objective for him because he was to be the television meteorologist. When he asked Ms. Parks to explain this phenomenon, instead of using technical terms Ms. Parks created an analogy. She related the motion of tornadoes to the momentum that emerges on a spinning bicycle wheel as pedaling increases.

A third way to help students develop initiative during CPA lessons involves asking them to try something in a special way that uses their special talents. For example, Brooke wanted to be the leader of the previously described news broadcast. She had exceptional leadership skills. Her instructional reading level was below grade level. Ms. Parks surprised Brooke by allowing her to use her reading and leadership skills together. After Brooke had demonstrated the initiative to learn more about news broadcasting by writing to the newscaster from the local television station, Ms. Parks became a contributor by volunteering to read several drafts of Brooke's letter of introduction, making suggestions for improvements.

Individual comprehension lessons also increase in creativity when students are encouraged to set their own comprehension goals for each lesson (Block & Beardon, 1997). In so doing, students will also communicate their preferred learning methods. For instance, to prepare for the broadcast Kendall asked to watch TV and write down all the words spoken in a list that he could use in writing the script he would speak. He also wanted to complete a grid that he could share with the class so everyone could learn newcasting terminology. In contrast, Brooke made an outline of key points about which she would speak, and turned it in as her demonstration of her comprehension of the trade books that she had read. Kristen asked to complete a report that was more than twice the teacher's minimum requirements. Sean asked if he could write one page of his interpretations instead of using half a page to summarize information in the book and half a page to write his own interpretations.

Lance asked if he could paraphrase the book. Sunshine asked if Ms. Parks could correct what she wrote on the first page of her formal report before she continued on with her second page. Eric wrote only a half page summary of six books, but during the presentation, he became so inspired and confident that he decided not to read the half page. Instead, he read six summaries that he had written from nonfiction books he had borrowed (self-initiation) from his neighborhood library to prepare for his speech.

Goal 5: Seeking Students' Increased Understanding through Respondent-Centered Questions, the Power of Three, and Effective Responses during Discussion

Goal 5: Seeking students' increased understanding through respondent-centered questions, the power of three, and effective responses during discussions

"When children give a wrong answer it is not so often that they are wrong as they are answering another question, and our job is to find out what question they are in fact answering" (Bruner, 1985, p. 34).

Respondent-centered questions, the "power of three" technique, and handling inaccurate answers to questions effectively significantly increase students' depth of comprehension (Block, Schaller, Joy, & Gaine, 2002). **Respondent-centered questions** are those that do not have only one correct answer and that require students' precise, elaborate thinking to answer. Respondent-centered questions enable students to (1) explain details, sequence, main ideas, and themes; (2) generate problem–solution sequences, (3) assimilate dissimilar events into their own lives; (4) express affective responses and insights; and (5) justify and defend their positions. Sample respondent-centered questions that generate each of these types of thought appear in Table 1.3. Teachers have found it helpful to select one question from each category to practice for one month's time. At the end of that month, you could select another question to practice, and continue in this way throughout the school year. If you photocopied Table 1.3 and placed it on your desk, you could easily refer to, and continuously use, these questions.

Pearson and Johnson (1978) were among the first to demonstrate that students understand and remember ideas better when they transform those ideas from one form to another. Asking respondent-centered questions is an effective way of engaging such transformation. These questions actively engage students in comprehending because they have to create a mental image, elaborate on a point, or justify a position to answer them (Allington, 2001; Au, 1993). Moreover, when you ask respondent-centered

TABLE 1.3 Four Categories of Respondent-Centered Questions

Elaboration

Does this selection make you think of anything else you read?
Would you like to be one of the people in this selection? Who? Why?
Did you like this selection more or less than the last thing you read? Why?
What parts of this selection did you especially like or dislike?
What did you mean by _____? Can you give me an example?
If _____ happened, what else could happen?
Does this story remind you of any other one? Why? What specific characteristics do they
   have in common?
Did the author make you feel any specific emotion?
Can you describe the _____?
How could you advertise this book?
If you had a chance to talk to this author, about what would you speak to him or her?
Why do you suppose the author used this title? Can you think of another appropriate title?
Why is this an important story to share?

Metacognition (Thinking about Thinking)

How would you feel if _____ happened?
What were you thoughts when you decided whether to _____ or _____? How did you decide?
Why did you choose this selection to read?
Do you think this story could really happen? Explain.
After reading this story, has your perception or view of _____ changed? Explain.
Can you describe your thinking? Give more details.
What makes you think he or she _____? How do you know this?
What do you know that you did not know before this reading?
Did your thoughts and feelings change as you were reading? How and why?
Did you have to remember what you already knew?

Problem Solving

What do you need to do next?
Can you think of another way we could do this?
How did you solve this problem?
What did you do when you came to difficult words?
What do you do when you get stuck?
What do you do when you do not understand the content or context?
How did you discover _____ and what helped you the most?
How could you determine whether _____ is true?

Supporting Answers

Why is this one better than another?
Yes, that's right—but how did you know?
What are your reasons for saying that?
What do you (or the author) mean by _____?
Why does this go here instead of there?
Do you have good evidence for believing that?
How did you know that?

TABLE 1.4   Effective Responses to Students' Incorrect Answers

If a wrong answer is given, use one of the following strategies, depending on the student who has answered.

1. *Supply the question the student was answering.* Try to let the student down easily permitting him or her to retain dignity. If you recognize why the answer was wrong, you could supply the question for which the student's answer would have been correct. For example, if the question was, "What is the capital of the United States?" and the student answered "Sacramento," you could respond, "Sacramento would be correct if I had asked for the capital of California, but I am asking for the capital city of the entire 50 states."

2. *Allow time for the student to think.* Use this strategy when the student who gave the incorrect answer has the background to answer the question and you determine that he or she would be able to give the correct answer if allowed enough time to think about it. To illustrate, a student gave an incorrect answer to a question about the subject matter you emphasized yesterday in class. You respond by saying, "I know you know the correct answer. You just need a minute to think." Then allow the 6-second wait time and implement strategy 3, 6, or 8 as follows. This response works best with older students because younger students tend to lose their train of thought and become frustrated with additional time allotted.

3. *Prompting.* Use this strategy when students have a partial answer or when a student needs the teacher's guidance or structure for thinking. Structure creates a sense of comfort and the additional reassurance needed to be able to perform. All prompts should be related to the content and not to incidental clues. For example, if the question concerns a mathematical problem prompt the names of geometric procedures with aspects within the procedure rather than using words that rhyme with that name.

4. *Use differential reinforcement.* Use this strategy when you determine that part of the answer was correct. Use it to reinforce a student's first attempt to contribute to class discussions. This is another form of prompting; however, it

reduces the student's temptation to guess. It gives the student information with which to modify his or her thinking. For example, you could say, "You almost have the idea. The first part was exactly correct. There was an error in your second part. Do you want me to lead you through the second part, or do you think you can get that part yourself?" "That was correct. It sounds as if you have been doing some original thinking. How would _____ fit in with your conclusion?" "That's almost 100 percent accurate. Consider this and then tell me what you think: _____."

5. *Paraphrase the question.* Use this strategy when an irrelevant answer has been given or when students begin to ramble. This strategy is also effective if the question you have asked is a long one. This strategy helps students rethink the answer they have given. Many times this strategy affords the student an opportunity to recognize his or her mistake before the teacher points it out to him or her. To illustrate, you might say, "I'm sorry, I wasn't clear"; "Let me clarify my question"; "Let me give another example"; or "I wasn't as specific as I wanted to be in my question."

6. *Expand on the answer.* Use this strategy when you are not clear why the student answered the way he or she did. This strategy asks students to tell the teacher why they answered as they did or why they believed their answers were correct. This strategy is used when an answer is partially correct or when the answer is completely incorrect.

7. *Tell the student the answer and express the need for him or her to remember it.* This strategy could be labeled "making the student accountable" because you will tell the student the correct answer and then return to the student and reask the same question again before the period is over. For example, "The correct answer is Washington, D.C. Now, I know you will remember it. I will ask you to tell me what the capital of the United States is before this period is over. Be prepared."

TABLE 1.4 Continued

(You might then also wink, just to add a light touch to the response.) You cannot forget to return to the student, however, because if you do, the strategy will lose its effectiveness in the future for other students. This strategy gives the student the responsibility for making a successful contribution, and the incentive to remember the information, but the risk to achieve success is not great.

8. *Ask a fellow student to give clues.* Use this strategy with strong groups that have good rapport. This strategy works well because of the support students give each other. When other students assist one another, the pressure and fear of failure is alleviated.

9. *Give examples of the possible answer.* Use this strategy at the close of a unit or lesson or as a review. This strategy assists students in focusing on material in which many types of content could

be present. For example, you could ask, "What type of imports do we receive in the United States?" Then you could give an oral multiple-choice answer of plausible choices but with only one correct answer. Students select the correct answer from the choices. As a second example, if you ask the question, "Who discovered the "fountain of youth," and no one gave a correct response, you could then say, "_____ discovered the fountain of youth—Balboa, Cabasa De Vaca, Ponce de Leon."

10. *Use nonexamples or opposites of the answer.* In using this strategy, you tell what the answer is not. It is used effectively when no student raises a hand to answer a question. Other students can use this strategy by calling on students who raise their hands first to tell classmates what the answer is not, allowing other students time to think.

questions, students tend to mimic you and ask these questions of themselves silently while they read (Block, 2001c). Respondent-centered questions raise the ante on thinking by asking students for the thinking that lies behind their personal comprehension.

Another step toward increasing students' comprehension involves responding effectively to students' incorrect answers. Ten helpful responses to students' incorrect answers appear in Table 1.4. The variety of responses is necessary because students answer incorrectly for a wide variety of reasons. When you diagnose the reason why a student responded as he or she did, you can select the appropriate response. For example, if a student understood the concept but either misheard the question or misread a detail, you could use the first strategy in Table 1.4, "Supply the question the student was answering." This response allows the student to regain dignity before his or her peers. For instance, if the question you asked was, "What is the capital of the United States?" and a student answers "Sacramento," you could respond, "Sacramento would be correct if I had asked for the capital of California, but I am asking for the capital city of the entire 50 states." With this "supplying the question that the student was answering" response, a student who knows the answer can quickly provide it and regain a strong self-concept, and if the student does not know the answer, the class can quickly understand how an error could have occurred, enabling the student to retain dignity.

Power of three is a teaching technique that uses three distinct examples of a comprehension process through modeling, demonstrations, and think-alouds. These three examples can be concrete, pictorial, or symbolic, as shown in Figure 1.2. The three examples can include three different pictures of a concept being taught, or model one method of thinking through a comprehension process, then a second way, and finally a third distinctive method. When you use three highly engaging but different examples of comprehension processes in action, students have a greater likelihood of understanding that process before they must do so in the course of reading. After repeated use of this strategy, students develop the ability to explain why they engaged a particular set of comprehension processes and their interrelationships.

At first, some students may not be successful even after four prompts of different examples. In time, however, when contrasting examples are given, many students become enthusiastic about new realizations that these examples stimulate. In addition, as demonstrated in a recent study of 647 exemplary elementary teachers from eight English-speaking countries, the responses they gave to students during discussions increased student comprehension significantly (Block & Mangieri, 2003; Block,

Concrete

Pictorial

Symbolic

FIGURE 1.2   Example of "The Power of Three" Teaching Strategy

Oakar, & Hurt, 2002). These responses appear in Table 1.5 and demonstrate how they asked students to explain their answers, gave choices to contribute or not, kept single students from dominating or withdrawing from comprehension discussions, and how they assisted students to lead discussions.

TABLE 1.5   Ways Teachers Can Increase Comprehension during Discussions

- Ask students to explain how they successfully comprehended and decoded (e.g., after a student reads a word correctly, the teacher says: "You just read 'school' correctly. How did you know that word?").

- Allow up to (but usually not more than) six students to express their answers to questions (e.g., "Why do you think this author picked this title?"). Then ask a student to summarize the group's thinking before proceeding.

- Give students the choice whether to contribute during discussions (e.g., "Do you want to pass, think about it for a minute, or 'call a friend' for a clue?"). When the teacher determines that a student knows an answer but needs a few moments to recall it, a statement similar to the following can be made: "Let's give Brian a moment to write and when he is finished we will move on. [Silence.] As soon as Brian finished writing a note on his paper, Brian said, "OK," and this was the signal that the discussion was ready to move on. Brian knew that the time to formulate his ideas was important enough for the class to pause for a moment.

- Reward a student's rapid thinking while increasing other pupils' time for reflection (e.g., when a student raises a hand first in a discussion, the teacher could say, "Great, [student's name]! I have one idea that is ready to be shared! As we give others a little more time to think, improve on your idea and how you want to say it."

- Do not allow students to "piggy back" on someone else's comments without thinking. As a result, students will not repeat the same concept during classroom discussions (e.g., "Now, we are all stating sports ideas, so we know that we can add any sport we want to our stories. You can write 'They played football. They played soccer, and so forth.' So, it's time to change our thinking. What other topics do you want in our stories?").

- When a student gives a partially correct answer, teachers can reward that student enabling him or her to learn which aspects of the answer were correct, by immediately turning to the group and saying, "Tell me what [student's name] did right in his/her thinking to arrive at that answer."

- When students notice discrepancies between themselves and other students' abilities, the teacher could indicate that the differences they observed occurred because someone had less practice with the concept to be learned, and not that some were less able than others. The teacher assures that this child can practice with her and with other classmates.

- Allow students to first make comments or ask questions about the material read. Usually, teachers should not begin reading response sessions by posing their own questions to students. They should pause after an oral or silent reading experience, and if no comments are made, ask questions that enable students to initiate their own relationships to the reading (e.g., "What question do you think I would ask about this book/story? Why?"; "Which of these words from this list on the board do you know, and how do you know them?").

Source: Adapted from Collins Block, Cathy. (2000). Handout from Preconvention Institute 16, annual meeting of the International Reading Association.

In Summary

Chapters 1 through 3 describe the types of student support for comprehension that (1) teachers can furnish (Chapter 1); (2) the instructional process must provide (Chapter 2); and (3) students themselves must supply (Chapter 3). When these components are engaged simultaneously, the synergy they produce creates a depth and breadth of meaning that cannot occur when any of these components is missing (Block, 2002b). When you assume the GOALS (teaching roles) described in this chapter, you take the responsibility to (1) maximize students' comprehension competencies, and (2) assist students to employ numerous comprehension processes independently, at points of need. The roles that you perform include (1) giving students choices during scaffolding, (2) using pivotal point scaffolding to avoid the slight rejection phenomenon; (3) orchestrating one-to-one conferences so that they become discovery discussions; (4) encouraging, showing, storytelling, and tilling the text; (5) leading students to take the initiative to learn by assuming the role of contributor rather than initiator; and (6) increasing students' understanding through respondent-centered questions, the power of three technique, and sustaining highly effective discussions. These goals enable you to provide support for students before, during, and after reading.

Chapter 2 describes the role and responsibilities that instruction and curriculum must assume if all students are to succeed. For pupils to execute comprehension processes successfully, instruction must be differentiated and unite three distinct strands of lessons in a school year, much as a cord coils three wires to create an electrical current. It takes three distinctive types of comprehension lessons in a reading program before all students can attain their highest levels of comprehension abilities.

REFLECTING ON WHAT YOU HAVE LEARNED

1. Rank your present level of ability in each of the actions described in this chapter. A ranking of 1 means that information was completely new to you, a ranking of 2 means that you have tried the action at times but do not use it as regularly as you could, and a 3 means that you do the action daily. For the action you ranked lowest, develop an action plan to increase your abilities.

2. Read the following excerpt. It requires one of the actions discussed in this chapter as a response. Decide your response. Then, you can read about the action Ms. Parks took in this situation and why. The answer key is on page 25, after you have decided on your own action.

> Marcus said, after Ms. Parks had given three examples, "I have so many ideas in my head, but by the time I get up the courage to speak them out loud the discussion has moved on."

3. How many respondent-centered questions can you instantly recall? How many strategies have you mastered to respond to students' incorrect answers? Which new ones do you want to learn or practice? To implement the five goals, it is important to review

them at the beginning of each grading period. As you review, write specific actions that you will take to implement each. Write down these actions now.

4. *Your Professional Journal: Summarizing Journal.* In this section at the end of each chapter you will have the opportunity to create many types of journals. These journal activities can be modified and used with students. This first one increases the summarization comprehension process.

   Describe new roles teachers must perform to ensure that all students develop the ability to comprehend. After you have made this journal entry, share it with two colleagues; discuss points that you have in common, and values that conflict.

5. *Making Professional Decisions.* Suppose that you are preparing to introduce this chapter to your students. Till the text. After you have selected the aspects of the chapter that you will preteach, describe how you will do so and why.

6. *Field Applications and Observations.* Try using one of the teaching actions described in this chapter with one or more elementary or middle school children. Reflect on your performance. Compare it to the information in this chapter and discuss it with a colleague. Explain why you were successful or less successful in the goal you attempted.

7. *Multicultural Applications.* What are the benefits of the power of three for students who come from diverse cultures and language backgrounds?

8. *Key Terms Exercise.* Following are new concepts introduced in this chapter. If you learned seven of these terms on your first reading, congratulations. These constructed meanings add to your professional knowledge base.

   _____ comprehension process approach (CPA) (p. 4)

   _____ slight rejection phenomenon (p. 6)

   _____ scaffolding (p. 6)

   _____ zone of proximal development (p. 6)

   _____ pivotal point scaffolding (p. 8)

   _____ discovery discussions (p. 10)

   _____ PAR (praise-ask-raise) (p. 10)

   _____ tilling a text (p. 11)

   _____ respondent-centered questions (p. 18)

   _____ power of three (p. 21)

9. *Answer Key.* Question 2: Ms. Parke used PAR because Marcus had successfully initiated a comprehension process and she wanted to increase and reward his success.

10. *Comprehension Process Lesson 1: Teaching Students the Process of Thinking Metacognitively As They Read by Holding Discovery Discussions.* The following comprehension lesson demonstrates how to implement goal 2 of the new responsibilities that teachers hold in teaching comprehension. This lesson contains five questions that you can ask when you meet with students in one-to-one settings. You can use this lesson in your classroom to improve conversations about comprehension. Students' answers to these questions will also help them become active participants in increasing their own comprehension abilities.

C O M P R E H E N S I O N   P R O C E S S   L E S S O N   1

Teaching the Process of Asking for Help: Conducting Discovery Discussions

1. Create a chart for students and you to sign up for discovery discussions.
2. Create a folder in which you can record the information discussed in discovery discussions.
3. Explain to students how to sign up for a discovery discussion. Specify that they can sign up for one every week if they want to discuss new discoveries that they are making about their reading abilities.
4. Hold no more than three discovery discussions a day so you are not depleted of the energy to stay intensely focused on each student's story about his or her abilities and progress.
5. Allow the students to open the discovery discussions. If he or she does not begin with a question, some suggestions are as follows:
   - What have you discovered about your reading abilities?
   - What are you learning about comprehension?
   - What do you want to learn to comprehend better?
   - What bothers you about your reading abilities?
   - What do you need me to do to help you improve your comprehension?
6. When students share an insight, paraphrase it and ask if you heard them accurately. If you observe that a student has increased his or her comprehension in a specific way, ask the student if your observation is accurate. Then, the student can demonstrate that comprehension process and describe how he or she knows to use it.
7. To become a trusted mentor, do not rush from one student to the next. Rather, provide undivided attention to each student. The most important part of discovery discussions often occurs at the end. It is at this latter point when many students gain the confidence to risk asking a very important question and sharing an insight about their reading weaknesses. Without discovery discussions, many students will never describe their weaknesses from their perspective.

CHAPTER 2

Curriculum and the Comprehension Process Approach

The Case for Differentiated Instruction

Joshua and Mario are learning how to make meaning and choosing what they want to learn about reading.

CURRICULUM AND THE COMPREHENSION PROCESS APPROACH: THE CASE FOR DIFFERENTIATED INSTRUCTION

Strand 1 Lessons: Integrating two comprehension processes

Strand 2 Lessons: Time to "live within books"

Strand 3 Lessons: Students choose what they want to learn

I taught the lessons in this chapter once a week to Ms. Beardon's fourth-grade class at Bell Manor Elementary School, Hurst-Euless-Bedford Independent School District (Texas). On April 7th, I watched Sara lead a teacher–reader group. This was a Strand 2 lesson. Students met to learn how to detect facts and opinions. Sara demonstrated how to avoid propaganda techniques. She showed a second and third example. I smiled inside as I observed. She was using the "power of three" teaching strategy! Everyone in the group eagerly raised their hands to participate. Reid turned to me and predicted: "The next one's going to be testimonials!"

Enthusiasm was high and students were learning. Sara did not tell them what was right or wrong; instead she asked why they reasoned as they did. The students respected her teaching and literacy strengths. Her leadership facilitated their ability to recognize unsubstantiated opinions. A discussion began about how to improve comprehension processes to detect propaganda. Next, Sara asked Kristin to summarize what they had learned; the group had agreed previously that Kristin was a good summarizer. Last, they made a chart and selected John to report what this teacher–reader group had discovered. He was chosen because he was very talented in generating examples and explaining key points when classmates asked questions. ■

Chapter Overview

The preceding lesson is one strand in the CPA differentiated comprehension instructional process. It assists students to diagnose their weaknesses and generate methods of overcoming them. The purpose of this chapter is to demonstrate how differentiated instruction maximizes students' comprehension. Comprehension process lessons (strand 1), stop and ask as well as student share lessons (strand 2), and teacher–reader lessons (strand 3) are presented.

Unfortunately, unlike students in the lesson portrayed in the chapter opening vignette, many pupils are reluctant to exert extra effort to understand without prompting. When comprehension instruction is not differentiated, struggling readers flounder as they try to read texts above their reading levels. As a result, many pupils retreat to "good enough reading" (Block, 2001b; Mackey, 1997). "Good enough reading" is pressing on while reading, saying word after word haltingly, and making compromises to create only a general understanding, hoping that clarity will somehow magically emerge. Other readers, of necessity, implement ineffective reading processes, which interfere with complete comprehension. They guess at answers to questions, memorize information, and move their eyes across the text as their minds wander. They skip too many words, gloss over (rather than ferret out) meaning in long sentences, and accept the reality that some ideas will become only confused images in their minds. These readers fail to integrate enough details to interpret upcoming events and fill gaps in a text's meaning with their own personal experiences rather than an accurate interpretation of the printed words.

By the end of this chapter, you will be able to answer the following questions:

1. Why do we need differentiated comprehension instruction?
2. What are the three strands of differentiated comprehension instruction?
3. What types of instruction eliminate students' comprehension challenges at the point of need?

4. How do comprehension process lessons (strand l) develop students' comprehension before they have trouble understanding what they are reading?
5. What are stop and ask and student share lessons (strand 2), and how do they provide students with more time to appreciate books and reading?
6. How can teacher–reader groups (strand 3) help students to diagnose and overcome their comprehension weaknesses?

Why Differentiated Comprehension Instruction Is Needed

Increasing students' reading comprehension is a priority at the elementary and middle school level. Unfortunately, this is not an easy task. It is difficult to create daily, effective activities that serve the multiple intelligences, varied personalities, and literacy needs of a full classroom of students. To teach children to develop their own comprehension processes, you can differentiate lessons, which have proven to result in significant gains for students (Block & Johnson, 2002). These lessons teach students how to (1) engage multiple meaning making processes (strand 1 of comprehension instruction), (2) come to appreciate reading and grow as human beings in the course of reading comprehension instruction (strand 2), and (3) diagnose their comprehension weaknesses (strand 3).

CPA is based on the tenet that comprehension occurs on several distinctive levels. One method of instruction cannot cut a path to all levels simultaneously. Before students can comprehend completely, reading programs must differentiate the goals and formats of their comprehension instruction. Just as students use a variety of strategies to decode new words, they must also experience numerous comprehension lessons interactively. When comprehension is taught as a continuous thought process that ebbs and flows to meet the changing demands in a text, the making of meaning can come more directly under students' control (Beck & Dole, 1994; Block & Pressley, 2002).

CPA instruction provides three distinct instructional foci and is more than richly enhanced teacher-directed strategy lessons or highly elaborated think-alouds. It moves beyond telling students how to find main ideas to showing them how to relate details until main ideas become evident (main ideas anchor thoughts as they read, as discussed in Chapter 6). One study of the effects of these three strands of differentiated instruction was conducted from 1996 to 1998. It involved 1,424 sixth graders who attended 17 elementary and middle schools in two, southwestern U.S.A. school districts (Block, 2001c). Twenty percent of the students lived in economically disadvantaged homes, 70 percent came from mid- to low-socioeconomic backgrounds, and l0 percent resided in high-socioeconomic environments. Moreover, twenty-three percent of these students were from highly mobile families. The ethnic representation was 17 percent Hispanic, 21 percent from African American, 12 percent from Asian American, 2 percent Native American, and 47 percent Anglo-American.

Students were randomly assigned to experimental and control groups. Experimental subjects were taught the lessons from this chapter and Chapter 6 for 7 months; students in the control group followed a basal reader, or literature-based program. Following instruction, the experimental group outperformed control subjects on the reading subtest of the Iowa Test of Basic Skills Comprehension Subtest ($t = 65.666, p < .027$). Descriptions of these lessons and illustrations of their implementation in the first through sixth grades follow, and are summarized in Table 2.1.

TABLE 2.1   Lessons in Three Strands of Differentiated Comprehension Instruction in CPA

Strand 1: Integrating Comprehension Process Lessons (Instruction before Point-of-Need)	*Strand 2:* Stop and Ask Lessons (Instruction at Point-of-Need)	*Strand 3:* Teacher–Reader, Mock Book Report or Review Lessons (Instruction after Point-of-Need)
Step 1. Identify two comprehension processes that students need.	Step 1. Have students select a book and read silently.	Step 1. Divide students into small groups based on students' needs and interests.
Step 2. Give a 2-minute introduction including at least three distinct examples of these processes in action and interacting as you read a text.	Step 2. Help students who raise their hands when they encounter a comprehension problem with a two sentence response.	Step 2. Work with a small group. Allow each student to use his or her individual skills as assets to the entire group.
	Student Share (STAR) Lessons	
Step 3. Allow at least 30 minutes of silent or oral reading time, performing Whisper Reads using the Whisper Read Record Form.	Step 1. Read a book aloud.	Step 3. Report back to the class what the group learned about improving their use of comprehension processes in the future.
	Step 2. Stop to allow student comments as they arise.	
Step 4. Ask questions about how the process helped the students and how they applied it to their reading.	Step 3: Ask students what they want to learn about crafting a thorough understanding of this book.	
Step 5. Have students develop a plan for using these processes together as they read in the future.		

Source: Adapted from material created by Erin Barre, masters of elementary education candidate and BS in Spanish, Texas Christian University, Fort Worth, Texas. Used by permission.

Strand 1 Lessons: Integrating
Two Comprehension Processes

Strand 1 Lessons: Integrating two comprehension processes

Instruction before the Point of Need.   Strand 1 lessons teach comprehension processes *before* students experience confusion. The goal of strand 1 lessons is to teach how to make meaning through the use of more than one comprehension process through stories that teachers tell about how they, and other readers, process text. Teachers also explain how to use the **teachers-within** (students' metacognitions, prior experiences, and personal goals) and **teachers-without** (peers, teachers, textual clues, and other print, visual, or oral media tools) when lack of prior knowledge about the subject matter creates comprehension difficulties (Cain-Thoreson, Lippman, & McClendon-Magnuson, 1997; Pressley & Afflerbach, 1995). Teachers demonstrate how students can (1) build intertextuality; (2) comprehend on literal, inferential, and applied levels simultaneously; (3) add depth and breadth to their knowledge base; (4) link efferent and aesthetic thinking processes; (5) make connections between words, facts, and concepts and the historical or political context in which they are written; (6) fill the gaps in narrative and expository trajectories (Golden & Rumelhart, 1993); and (7) till a text. Strand 1 lessons teach students how to use more than one of the following thinking processes simultaneously:

1. Flashbacks and savoring special sections of a story
2. Flash-forwards and making predictions about what they think will happen next
3. Unusual points of view and mental images
4. Process poetry, slogans, and advertisements
5. Rhymes, alliterations, figures of speech, and interpreting abstract word choices and images
6. Metacognition and overcoming confusion
7. Text sensitivities, such as recognizing inconsistencies concerning an author's goal

Teaching Students to Integrate Comprehension Processes.   **Integrating-comprehension-processes lessons** and the **TRIO teaching cycles** are the two most powerful lessons that can be used to teach students to interrelate two comprehension processes as they read. These lessons teach pupils how to discover meaning by employing thinking processes in conjunction with the unique clues authors give in their texts. Their purpose is to introduce new processes and to demonstrate how the new processes can be integrated with one or more that were previously learned.

Integrating-comprehension-processes lessons teach two comprehension processes that will be valuable to understanding a particular text. These lessons begin after you have identified literary processes, such as those mentioned previously, that students will need to comprehend a particular text. Next, you prepare a 4- to 5-minute description of two thinking processes, using the power of three techniques for both. During each 2-minute introduction, you can present at least three highly distinctive graphics, models, examples, or think-alouds so students can think about the new strategy integratively with those taught previously. These graphic organizers are designed as unique icons, models are relayed as processes in action, and think-alouds are performed during the oral reading of a paragraph from the text that students will read. After the introduction and discussion of the process, students read silently from a text for 10 to 20 minutes, depending on grade level. When the silent application period ceases, you do not ask literal, interpretative, or application questions. Rather, you ask

- How did these two processes help you as you read?
- How did they help you think ahead, image, or remember?
- How did they help you stay involved in the story?
- How did they help you overcome distractions in the room?
- How did they help you overcome confusion in the text?

These questions have one characteristic in common. They cannot be answered unless students comprehended the reading passage. Alternatively, asking "What did you like about this selection?" can be answered regardless of whether the student understood a text, and it does not improve students' ability to use two comprehension processes to make meaning. The next step is to ask students to volunteer to read a paragraph aloud to classmates and to pause when they can describe the processes that they are using to comprehend. When students are ready to have their abilities to relate processes assessed, you can listen to them individually as they read from a text, stopping them periodically to ask for a description of the comprehension processes they are using. Texts for these lessons can be found in *Reason to Read* (Block & Mangieri, 1995/1996) and *Qualitative Reading Inventory—III* (Leslie & Caldwell, 2001). The passages in these books are marked at points at which fruitful think-alouds could be delivered if students are comprehending successfully.

The following example demonstrates such a Strand 1 lesson. Ms. Turner decided to teach her sixth graders (1) how to infer how characters feel, and (2) how to make connections between an author's meaning and the historical and political context presented in a text. She selected a paragraph from a history textbook. She displayed the first paragraph on the overhead and told students that many thinking processes work in their minds as they try to comprehend (Kintsch, 1998). She described the processes previously discussed and underlined words on the overhead that illustrated characters' emotions and the text's historical and political context.

Next, she demonstrated how the mind decodes words and joins the meanings of the words into sentences to determine the historical context conveyed. Then, she demonstrated how to generate a gist (to hold an overall general meaning in mind as one reads), and organize historical contexts to determine a global meaning when three paragraphs are read consecutively. She concluded that she used inference to instill human emotions in events as they unfolded. Together, Ms. Turner and her students read the following opening paragraph in the textbook.

Their stomachs churned with fear and emotions. The old man and woman clasped each other's hands and looked up and down the enormous gray bank. There was no way to enter. They were paralyzed by fear, and all their lives' dreams flashed before them in an instant.

After reading this extract, they discussed how they felt and what they thought as they inferred the historical context that the paragraph portrayed. Students discussed how they felt and what they thought as both processes related together to generate a deep meaning. Students considered the processes they used to (1) infer something about the bank that must have frightened the people and (2) extract the gist of the historical context in which the paragraph was written. Then, the teacher demonstrated how the historical and political context in which a text is written influences the text. She described two different historical contexts that existed in 1929. These contexts included the facts that in the 1920s rivers swelled often, few bridges existed to cross them, and the U.S. economy declined, creating the most disastrous depression that this country had ever experienced. Next, Ms. Turner asked the students to relate the paragraph to the 1929 context in which it was written. They were to infer how the characters felt if the following sentences had appeared right before the paragraph they had just read:

> The old man and woman raised their heads and saw the bear at exactly the same instant. He was running toward their riverbank camp at top speed. Their stomachs churned with fear and emotions. The old man and woman clasped each other's hands and looked up and down the enormous gray bank. There was no way to enter. They were paralyzed by fear, and all their lives' dreams flashed before them in an instant.

Then she asked students to read with a new historical context and to infer emotions of the characters simultaneously as if the next set of sentences had appeared immediately before the paragraph that they read previously. She asked them to pay attention to how the two processes' interrelationships changed their mental images and inferences because the historical context had changed.

> It was October 29, 1929, Black Tuesday. As they heard about the stock market crash, the old man and woman drove all night from their New Hampshire farm to reach New York City's World Bank at dawn. Their stomachs churned with fear and emotions. The old man and woman clasped each other's hands and looked up and down the enormous gray bank. There was no way to enter. They were paralyzed by fear, and all their lives' dreams flashed before them in an instant.

At the end of each Strand 1 lesson, you can conclude by saying, "Whenever you come to points in a text like this in the future, I suggest that you call upon both of these processes simultaneously, and think something like this to develop the deepest, most fulfilling meaning."

Here is a second example. Mr. Mackey, a third-grade teacher, taught the comprehension processes of tilling the text and using the sea of thoughts surrounding a story as context clues. He demonstrated how individual words reveal the sea of thoughts that an author wants to convey, which can be enhanced and more easily identified if readers till the text in advance. Then, he demonstrated how to till a text and use an author theme (sea of thoughts) to comprehend as the class read the following sentence: "The characters have strange names—Arsenic, Venom, and Hemlock."

Mr. Mackey said, "I know that hemlock is a tree with a poisonous berry or leaf. Why would the author give characters names that mean poison? I think he is trying to tell us something about the characters. This makes me think about how carefully I must till this text as I read, because the author is very subtle in his choice of words. I think we should pay close attention to subtleties in this author's writing style. I think this author will depend on us to infer a lot from individual words to identify his theme and apply it to our lives."

Through Strand 1 lessons, students can learn how to (1) build background knowledge through comparisons between two texts; (2) comprehend on literal, inferential, and applied levels simultaneously; (3) add depth and breadth to their knowledge base through summarizing and inferring; and (4) make connections between the concepts they read and the historical or political context in which the words were written and read. Such lessons also help students overcome their fears of developing their own interpretations as they read. They encourage students to take risks and to become deeply involved in the stories that they read. Strand 1 lessons enable more students to reach their highest levels of comprehension than would be possible without them because comprehension processes are taught explicitly and reinforced repeatedly. In this way, more students learn how to initiate the processes unprompted and can explain why they used a particular set of processes as they read a particular text.

These types of lessons are also learned more easily by some students when graphics are used to depict comprehension processes. These graphics are called "thinking guides," and they illustrate *the direction students' thoughts can take* to attain a complete interpretation as they read. Examples of two thinking guides appear in Figures 2.1 and 2.2. These graphics have assisted students in independently integrating both the process and outcome of strategic thinking (Block & Mangieri, 1995/1996; Schraw, 1998). Moreover, when such graphics are included in the comprehension program, teachers no longer have to depend on all students reaching a deep level of comprehension simply by reading without instructional support. Students at all grade levels can learn strategies that are particularly valuable in comprehending a wide range of genres and content domains (e.g., they learn how to sequence details using mental timelines when reading historical texts). These lessons also enable students at all grade levels to learn how to critically analyze and make valid inferences from text and visually displayed information.

At the end of this chapter is a lesson plan that can be used when teaching Strand 1 CPA lessons.

The TRIO teaching cycle is the second type of lesson that increases students' abilities to relate two cognitive processes together. TRIO stands for teach-reteach-individualize-other. This teaching style can be used in many organizational plans, including guided reading schedules, block grouping plans, and literacy anthology groups. TRIO teaching cycles teach comprehension processes to the entire class. Then, you reteach, pulling students who could not relate two processes after your introduction together in a small group and reteaching the processes in a new way.

What does this
remind me of?

I'm picturing this in my mind
because _____ .

**FIGURE 2.1   Thinking Guide
for Making Connections**

**FIGURE 2.2   Thinking Guide
for Making Mental Images**

For instance, as Mr. Mackey said, "If several students had difficulty learning the two comprehension processes that I had just taught, I gather these pupils together the next day and work with them until they understand how to make that relationship. Students who had learned the processes during my introduction chose to read books in pairs, silently wrote, or went to centers while I retaught the processes to those who needed it."

Third, you individualize instruction. This involves one-to-one discovery discussions in which you provide personalized, individualized scaffolding. You use a particular book and example that you create specifically for each individual as you and that student read together. If, after this interaction, a student still does not interrelate the comprehension processes independently, others are asked to join the instructional team. Those invited include peer teachers, parent volunteers, and specialized teachers or materials.

TRIO lessons are learned more easily by some students than others because CPA thinking guides are used to depict the comprehension processes being taught. After these graphic thinking guides are presented, students can read silently with two of these thinking guides on their desks. When these thinking guides (e.g., Figures 2.1 and 2.2) are included in the TRIO teaching cycle, teachers no longer have to depend on students reaching a deep level of comprehension simply through relying on rote memory.

In summary, Strand 1 lessons do not let students struggle alone but rather teach processes before a reading selection stumps and frustrates them. Teachers talk students through their first applications of comprehension processes using personal stories and think-alouds. Students learn how to perform all of the processes discussed in this chapter and to (1) connect text to their background knowledge, (2) infer, and (3) integrate information across paragraphs. Without Strand 1 lessons, many students simply store literal information in incomplete, often inaccurate, paraphrases, a practice that is negatively correlated to comprehension achievement (Block, 1997; Pressley, 1998).

Strand 2 Lessons: Time to "Live within Books"

Strand 2 Lessons: Time to "live within books"

Instruction at the Point of Need.   The goal of Strand 2 lessons is to provide time for students not merely to read books but also to "live within them." To do so, students need privacy and large blocks of uninterrupted time that presently are not allotted in many classrooms. Strand 2 lessons are prefaced by students selecting how, what, and where they will read, as well as how their reading will contribute to the themes in classroom topics under study. The books which students select are exceptionally high quality fiction and nonfiction. These books often keep students thinking and talking about what they have discovered in them long after their reading has ended. Before they begin to read, students are reminded to establish their reading goals and initiate the comprehension processes that expert readers use to make meaning, surmise, and reengage motivation when it wanes. During Strand 2 lessons, students can relax and read. They can feel assured that they will not have to perform a task relative to the information that they learn, unless they choose to share something.

In the past, in teachers' attempts to use SSR (sustained silent reading periods) and "choose your own library book and read until everyone returns to the room" as means to increase comprehension, they often inadvertently decreased students' perseverance as well as the breadth and depth of literary taste (Block, in press a). Strand 2 lessons improve sustained silent reading experiences by advancing students' volition and risk-taking abilities. Using Strand 2 lessons enables students to move more frequently to higher levels of understanding because their teachers become personal coaches, at their sides if they experience confusion. Second, reading challenges are monitored in conjunction with individual student goals. You scaffold individually so each student can understand deep, broad concepts at the points in a text when an author's theme emerges or when the students' interests are piqued for topics in which they had prior knowledge. Third, students' abilities to set their own purposes and develop meaning on several levels simultaneously are increased.

Strand 2 lessons are distinct from homogeneous group instruction and guided reading experiences. First, they do not teach processes and then ask children to demonstrate them as they read. Second, strand 2 lessons often culminate in personal meanings, which are broad-minded (and often only tangentially related to the text's original intent). Students think about texts in ways that authors likely are never to have imagined. Many pupils report that Strand 2 lessons also help them to understand that authors have to be selective and, as a result, leave gaps in stories. Therefore, texts are only glimpses into the messages and lives that writers want to share. Furthermore, many pupils realize that had they written the stories, they would have selected different words to describe events and communicated different meanings than a particular author did. Thus, Strand 2 lessons help students to realize why a complete comprehension can not occur if they simply accept authors' condensed reflections of reality. Students must add their own personal reflections to achieve full, rich meanings.

In summary, Strand 2 lessons (described in Table 2.2) teach children how to

- Respond to print uniquely;
- Care deeply about authors' messages;
- Enhance their self-worth as valid crafters of meaning; and
- Acquire control over their comprehension, especially for second-language learners (Weaver & Kintsch, 1996), emergent readers (Purcell-Gates, 1996), and less able readers (Block, 2001a).

Incorporating Strand 2 Lessons in a Weekly Reading Program. Strand 2 lessons follow two formats: "stop and ask lessons" and "student share lessons." **Stop and ask lessons** occur when students listen to stories read by teachers, peers, or in pairs, or when they read silently, and stop to ask questions as the reading unfolds. These lessons differ from unmonitored sustained silent reading periods because in the former lesson students raise their hands when they come to a point in a text when comprehension is interrupted because of an unknown meaning or because their minds were wandering. When students' attention is interrupted, teachers (and adult volunteers) kneel down and listen as students explain a misunderstanding or ask a question. These questions

TABLE 2.2 Strand 2 Lessons: "Time to Live within Books"

Student Share (STAR) Lessons	Stop and Ask Lessons
Step 1. Read a book, selected by the students, aloud to the whole class.	*Step 1.* Have students select a book and read silently.
Step 2. Stop to allow student comments as they arise or have a recorder list them for later discussion.	*Step 2.* Aid students who raise their hands when they encounter a comprehension problem by providing a two-sentence response to the question posed by the student.
Step 3. Have a student lead a discussion about the book.	*Step 3.* Student returns to independent silent reading.
Step 4. Ask students to select what strategy they want to learn about crafting comprehension.	

Source: Created by Erin Barre, masters of elementary education candidate and BS in Spanish, Texas Christian University, Fort Worth, Texas. Used by permission.

should be answered in two sentences as often as possible, rather than reteaching a comprehension process in depth. Teachers can answer in one sentence exactly what the meaning was that the student needed. Then, in a second sentence, a statement can be added revealing the comprehension processes used to gain that meaning. This way, students' crafting processes are only disturbed momentarily. Then students can be quickly transported back into the setting and actions of the book. When students resume their silent reading, teachers can make appropriate notations on charts they use to record the questions that students ask during "stop and ask lessons." These notes denote the thinking processes that need to be taught in future Strand 1 lessons, through small, guided reading groups composed of students who need to learn more about that process.

Before beginning a "stop and ask lesson," teachers remind students to (1) set their own goals, (2) recall what they learned in Strand 1 lessons as they read, and (3) raise their hands and keep reading until their teacher (or another personal coach) arrives to assist them with comprehension difficulties. For example, Mr. DeAngelo began his fourth graders' "stop and ask lesson" by reviewing the qualities of expert readers that he wants his pupils to emulate. He posted these qualities permanently around his classroom on charts. New comprehension processes are added to these charts all year as new traits of expert readers are studied in Strand 1 lessons. On October 12, the processes posted on the chart were: "Take risks to infer so your reading becomes informative and enjoyable simultaneously; reread when you become confused or your mind wanders; and stay engaged by adding to your purposes and committing to use this time to improve your knowledge." His next introductory comment asked students to complete a sentence on a note card. They referenced a second classroom chart that contained sample purpose-setting sentences and students established their own goals before they began to read. The statements from which students could select were: "I want to become a better reader by _____ ; I want to learn more about _____ ; I don't know _____ ; I'm curious about _____ ; or I'll ask these questions: _____ ."

As the students finish writing, they place the note cards at the sides of their books so that they and Mr. DeAngelo can reference them throughout the "stop and ask lesson." If any student finishes his or her book before the "stop and ask lesson" ends, that student can add ideas to tell classmates about the reading and thinking he or she did to comprehend to the front of his or her note card. On the back of the cards, students can write questions that they want answered and describe how they would like to answer the questions. These cards can be turned in at the end of the period and be used to form Strand 3 lessons.

To close "stop and ask lessons," pupils read to their classmates what they have written on the front of their note cards or ask what they have penned on the back. For example, Ms. Campbell responded to first grader Michelle's hand, told her the reason that the author was repeating the question "Brown Bear, Brown Bear, what do you see?," and told her how the word "parakeet" is pronounced and what it meant by pointing to the picture in the book. Michelle immediately resubmerses herself in making meaning and returned to continue her book. Ms. Campbell noted the questions Michelle asked on her "stop and ask lesson" grid. She concluded this Strand 2 lesson by asking students how they had selected the books they want to read, and tilled the text to ensure that they would enjoy reading them. After 20 minutes, her students were so engrossed in reading that they were unaware that it was recess time.

The second type of Strand 2 lessons, **student share lessons,** are defined as whole shared reading experiences in which reading is temporarily stopped so students can share how they made meaning or the results of their comprehension. Student share lessons can occur during the oral reading of books to a whole class or small group. These lessons are distinct from traditional shared reading experiences in that teachers pause their oral reading *only* (1) if children want to report how they made the author's story their own or (2) to answer students' questions about how to make meaning. In student share lessons, teachers do not have the first word after the reading. Students do. This is necessary because whoever manages the dialogue and does most of the talking during discussions controls the crafting of understanding. In student share lessons, students begin and sustain conversations about (1) a surprise that reverses the book's plot; (2) an action-filled segment; (3) a character who repeats an attempt to resolve a problem, or says or does something insightful; or, (4) an event that triggers a change in the usual order of things that happens normally in students' lives.

To illustrate, we can contrast Ms. Martin's second graders' "student share lesson" with a traditional shared reading. In the "student share lesson," the first difference occurs in that students select the book to be read and decide if they want to stop the reading periodically to make comments, the "student share lesson," or if the reading is to be completed without anyone adding his or her ideas, the "silent thinking until the end and then share" method. Because the latter was chosen in Ms. Martin's reading, students raise their hands when they have something to share, but no one speaks out. An adult volunteer (or, in other classrooms, an older schoolmate) listed students' names in order and recorded the page numbers that triggered each thought. This list determined who began the book conversation when the oral reading was completed.

In summary, Strand 2 lessons encourage students to read good books at school. Stop and ask lessons and student share lessons become windows in which students read books and see the world anew; the books act as mirrors by which students can quietly reflect and make new discoveries about themselves by reading someone else's insights (Block & Mangieri, 1995/1996; Block & Cavanagh, 1998; Galda, 1998; Gaskins, Gaskins, & Gaskins, 1991; Pressley et al., 1995). Students have a master reader (a teacher or an adult volunteer) at their side to coach them at points of need. Moreover, because Strand 2 lessons are prefaced by instruction in how to set goals, students learn how to establish their own purposes for reading and to turn to books to learn more about topics that they value. These lessons are based on the premise that the best teaching often occurs through a learning community in which the sharing of inside jokes, personal insights, and laughter assist students and their teachers to bond together as a group and with reading. Strand 2 lessons increase the number of questions students ask about the reading process, which, in turn, expand their comprehension abilities. Students who pose questions score higher on standardized comprehension tests than do students who simply discuss the materials that they read (Block, in preparation, 1992, 1997; Graham & Block, 1994; King, 1994).

Strand 3 Lessons: Students Choose What They Want to Learn

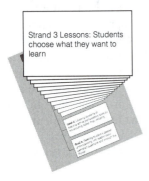

Strand 3 Lessons: Students choose what they want to learn

Instruction after the Point of Need.   The goal of Strand 3 lessons is for students to identify their own strengths and weaknesses and to increase their drive to solve problems in their reading abilities. Strand 3 lessons extend the benefits of book clubs, literature circles, and reading response groups because they allow students to choose what they want to learn *about the reading process and not simply what they want to read.* These lessons allow students to apply both the cognitive and affective powers of choice and challenge *to the comprehension process itself.* As students improve their capabilities as readers, they experience more positive feelings and knowledge about their comprehension strengths and weaknesses (Caine & Caine, 1997). Such self-knowledge is essential because the students themselves are the people who are most aware of the level of effort (and are most sensitive to the level of drive) that they are willing to expend to become better readers. The purpose of Strand 3 lessons is to increase the level of effort and drive that they want to expend to become better readers.

Because optimal internal motivation emerges when individuals operate at their highest capability, Strand 3 lessons can strengthen students' desire to read by increasing the number of insights pupils realize about their own reading processes. Similarly, in order to avoid boredom, they self-initiate more effort and drive when they recognize that unleashing their own intuition about the reading process builds understanding at all levels, even in grasping literal facts, as also reported in Greene (1998).

One quality of effective comprehension teachers in the future will be that they are more skillful in the art of sharing responsibilities for instructing comprehension processes with students. They will see each new class of students not only as a group of different readers who reach different understandings but also as potential comprehension teacher–reader group leaders. Many teachers report that this is the more difficult strand to teach. Students apply more of what they have learned in Strands 1 and 2 when these are followed by Strand 3 lessons (Block & Johnson, 2002), which teach students how to think strategically and apply processes appropriately.

Strand 3 lessons elicit students' (1) intentional and deliberate thoughts; (2) flexible and adaptable, free-flowing understanding; (3) reasoning to select and combine appropriate comprehension processes continuously when new needs arise in texts, and (4) metacognition, or the conscious thinking of one's own processing before, during, and after comprehension is engaged. Recent studies have demonstrated that although good and poor comprehenders use similar comprehension processes, good comprehenders are willing to persist in using and adapting them until they attain meaning. Alternatively, without Strand 3 lessons, poorer readers tend to reuse only a very few processes, and dive into every text with the same set of comprehension processes so that reading, after time, becomes boring. Their abilities to discover and savor subtle meanings are dulled, which in turn limits their capacity to enlighten their senses, emotions, drive, and desire.

"Please, Ms. Block, would you tell me what I did right when I read this story so that I can do it again tomorrow?" A third type of strand 2 lesson involves creating time in the reading curriculum to discuss new methods students use to make meaning, and to find out what they want to learn next to comprehend better. In these lessons, teachers schedule time to listen to students' stories about their lives as readers, their present level of reading abilities, and their literacy goals so teachers can incorporate these insights into their comprehension goals for future instruction. In these lessons, students tell their teachers what they depend on to read, as well as what they need to comprehend completely. These lessons enable teachers to ask more questions of students, such as

- In what new ways are you thinking as you read?
- What are you learning to do to comprehend better?
- What is bothering you about your reading abilities?
- What thinking processes do you recommend that we use at this point in a text?

If this type of lesson is neglected, *students' ideas* about *how they can* become better readers can be disregarded. When these metacognitions are expressed, many students experience new insights that they discovered themselves about the reading process. Subsequently, by using Strand 3 lessons, many students increase their desires to improve their comprehension because they learn new insights to meet more difficult comprehension challenges (Block, in preparation).

Incorporating Strand 3 Lessons in a Weekly Reading Program.   Strand 3 lessons follow three formats: teacher–reader groups, group officers, and mock book report or review leaders. **Teacher–reader groups** can begin by using the note cards written at the end of Strand 2 lessons in which students told you what they wanted to learn next. Then, students select a group where that aspect of the reading process will be taught and discussed in a more focused way than in any other strand of lessons. During these group meetings, students discuss how they accomplish this aspect of the reading process. Students and teachers also offer suggestions for overcoming specific reading problems within that domain of comprehension, as Sara illustrates in the vignette that opens this chapter. Students are required to stay with the same group for at least two meetings but can, and most do, remain in the same group for four or more lessons, electing not to change after the mandatory time has elapsed.

Between meeting times, students practice the suggestions they learn. In the second week's student-initiated literacy learning meetings, peers teach what they have learned about that aspect of making meaning. Because a teacher meets with only one teacher–reader group at a time, other groups either meet at a different time that day (so that the teacher will also be present) or on different days. Such lessons are conducted most effectively if no more than three teacher–reader groups meet each week so that students can have three choices of comprehension processes for which they can learn more. For example, the groups created by Ms. Nichols' sixth graders are described in Figure 2.3. These choices are posted on a chart where students signed up to become members. As teacher–reader groups meet, they discuss the comprehension processes

FIGURE 2.3   Teacher–Reader Groups

Meaning Makers	We want to learn how to understand better, make more in-depth responses to material read, and learn how to interrelate new thinking processes to craft understanding.
Transformer Titans	We want to learn how we can more rapidly apply what we read to our lives.
Word Wanters	We want to learn more decoding strategies. We will bring a book we are reading to group meetings to model how we decoded a difficult word. We will ask classmates to find similar words and try out these strategies in their books.
Speed Mongrels	We want to increase our speed of oral and silent reading.
Memory Menders	We want to find ways to retain more of what we read.
Critical Analyzers	We want to learn how better to connect what we read to other readings and our lives. We also want to learn how to reflect more on what we read.

that they used. At the end of the lesson, each person in the group answers the questions outlined in Figure 2.4. The answers are recorded so teachers can assess students' level of understanding of processes that were discussed.

These lessons can open guided reading sessions. For instance, Tyler, a second grader, came eager to share "something new that she was doing to comprehend better." Tyler began her group's discussion by telling how she was using her story's main idea to learn new vocabulary words. She said, "Ms. Block told us to put two thoughts together when we don't understand something. I do that now. When I come to a word I don't know I think about the main idea of the paragraph I'm reading. You know, like the other day I came to the word *Indians* and I didn't know it. Just "sounding it out" didn't fill my mind enough. So, I thought about what word the author would want to write for the main idea he was telling me. He was telling me about the first Thanksgiving and who the people were he wanted to invite. Then the word just came to me. Because the word began with *I* and the people at the first Thanksgiving wanted to invite Indians to eat with them, I learned that word. I'll never forget it either!"

The second lesson in Strand 3 involves students becoming **mock book report** or **review leader.** Before students present the comprehension processes that they have used in their favorite books, they write about them on newspaper sheets. These newsletters are distributed before the mock book report is presented. Students enjoy these Strand 3 lessons because they can creatively describe the processes that they have learned in Strand 3 lessons using both in these oral and written descriptions of their independent application in mock book reports and reviews (of comprehension processes used to read a book) before the class. An example of a news bulletin that students created to critique several books is illustrated in Figure 2.5.

FIGURE 2.4   Chart to Record Teacher–Reader Groups' Thinking

Name of the Book _____

Author of the Book _____

Strategy Taught _____

"What was your mind telling you?"

1.
2.
3.
4.
5.
6.

"How did the strategy help you comprehend better?"

1.
2.
3.
4.
5.
6.

In Summary

It is an exciting time to be educators. Teachers are discovering that comprehension instruction is most effective when it contains different types of lessons designed to strengthen distinct cognitive, emotional, and literacy processes so that students can attain rich understandings. They are learning how to graphically depict comprehension processes so readers can picture how to direct their own thinking processes. They are also increasing the amount of time spent answering students' individual questions at the exact point in a text when confusion arises, and while students read silently. Teachers have learned how to model, give examples, provide think-alouds, and monitor guided practice sessions when strategies are introduced.

To enhance success, future comprehension instruction should (1) include more opportunities for students to learn how to use two processes before the need to use them arises in a text; (2) provide more time for students to "live within books," become enthralled with reading, and depend on the individualized support of their teachers in "stop and ask lessons" to eliminate confusion exactly when it occurs; and, (3) involve students in decisions about what reading difficulties they want to learn about next.

In 17 classrooms when comprehension was differentiated, students' reading abilities significantly increased. Students felt safe to take risks, and no one was belittled. In addition, by using Strand 1, 2, and 3 lessons students discovered the power of (1) using

UNUSUAL UNBELIEVABLE UNREAL

April 1998	Literature at its best	Free

Tailor Kills Seven at a Blow

The Brave Little Tailor

Readers can meet new friends both real and imaginary within the section **Unbelievable Characters**. Titles include: Lou Gehrig: The Luckiest Man, The Most Beautiful Roof in the World: Exploring the Rainforest Canopy, Willy's Silly Grandma, The Ghost on Saturday Night, Dancing With Great Aunt Cornelia, The On-Line Spaceman and Other Cases, The Brave Little Tailor, and Happily Ever After.

Girl Makes Flying School Bus

Junk Pile

Characters found in the section **Coping With Adversity** struggle with adverse situations requiring unusual talents or unbelievable experiences. Titles include: Junk Pile, Breath of the Dragon, Travels with Rainie Marie, Moving Mama to Town, Spaceman, and The Heart is Big Enough.

Horse Helps Man Become Tsar of Russia

The Little Humpbacked Horse

The fantasy of fairy tales and traditional folklore is appealing for its invitation for readers to transcend reality and experience **Unreal Tales From Real Places**. Titles include: The King of Ireland's Son, The Cricket's Cage, The Gold at the End of the Rainbow, Little Folk: Stories From Around the World, and The Little Humpbacked Horse.

Fish & Frogs Fall from Sky

Strange Mysteries From Around the World

What may seem unreal to many might actually be a mysterious natural phenomenon. Titles in the **Unreal Phenomena** section include: Strange Mysteries From Around the World, The Moon Book, Batwings and the Curtain of Night, A Drop of Water, Eye of the Storm: Chasing Storms With Warren Faidley, Flood, and Disappearing Lake: Nature's Magic in Denali National Park.

INSIDE

Unbelievable Characters
Coping With Adversity
Incredible Accomplishments
Unreal Tales From Real Places
Unusual Plants and Animals
Unreal Phenonmena
Transformations
Too Good to Miss

Healthy Looking Girl Can't Get Out of Bed

Westminster West

The **Transformation** section has a trio of fascinating times and places where mysterious changes occurred. Titles include: Westminster West, The Orphan of Ellis Island, and Blue Lightning.

Desert Trees From Sprouting Twig

The Never-Ending Greenness

Incredible Accomplishments of characters real and fictitious, contemporary and historical are highlighted in this section's books. Titles include: If Sarah Will Take Me, The Neptune Fountain: The Apprenticeship of a Renaissance Sculptor, The Never-Ending Greenness, A Distant Enemy, Hell Fighters: African American Soldiers in World War I, You Must Remember This, Spike Lee: By Any Means Necessary, Danger Along the Ohio, Mississippi Mud: Three Prairie Journals, and Journey to Nowhere.

Toothless Whale

Big Blue Whale

Books in this section are sources of information about **Unusual Plants and Animals**. Titles include: Katya's Book of Mushrooms, Chameleons on Location, Komodo Dragon on Location, Animals You Never Even Heard Of, Big Blue Whale, and An Extraordinary Life: The Story of a Monarch Butterfly.

Mysterious Footprints Found on Shore After Fatal Shipwreck

Ghost Canoe

Some books are just **Too Good to Miss**. Such is the case for the last section. Titles in this section include: Seedfolks and Ghost Canoe.

Special thanks to W. Quinn White, Franklin Elementary School, Van Wert, Ohio, USA, for creating this graphic.

FIGURE 2.5   Sample Newsletter with Which Students Describe Comprehension Processes to Parents

Source: Freeman, Evelyn B., Lehman, Barbara A., & Scharer, Patricia L. (1998, April). Children's books: Unusual! Unbelievable! Unreal! *The Reading Teacher, 51*(7), 558–597. Reprinted with permission of the International Reading Association.

several processes continuously, (2) experiencing high-quality literature, and (3) gaining more information about themselves as readers. As a result, making meaning came more directly under their control, and "good enough reading" was no longer as good as it got for these students.

REFLECTING ON WHAT YOU HAVE LEARNED

1. In your opinion, what is the most important lesson for students at the grade level you teach (or will teach) in each of the three strands of differentiated comprehension instruction that were presented in this chapter? Why?

2. List five important principles about instruction that you learned in Chapter 2.

3. *Field Applications and Observation.* Teach or observe someone else teach one of the lessons in this chapter. How did this experience enhance your understanding of differentiated comprehension instruction? Discuss your observations with a colleague who taught the same lesson. What caused the differences, if any, in your observations?

4. *Your Professional Journal: Goal Journals.* Describe the first step you would like to take to differentiate the instruction that you deliver. Why did you choose this step?

5. *Making Professional Decisions.* Write a concise one-paragraph description of the following: (a) your fondest memory of a comprehension lesson that was similar to a strand 1, 2, or 3 lesson and how it increased your understanding of a text; (b) a learning principle that caused your growth; (c) your teacher's best efforts in a lesson; or (d) the reason this lesson was so memorable for you.

6. *Multicultural Application.* When instruction is differentiated, it is important to select appropriate books for students that speak languages other than English as their first language. Reflect on the available children's literature that can help students learn idioms and common English sentence patterns (a list of these books appears in Chapter 9). Read one of these books to a child whose first language is not English as you implement a Strand 1, 2, or 3 lesson. Follow the procedures outlined in this chapter for that strand of differentiated instruction. Note how children react to your selection and teaching. Share your experience with colleagues.

7. *Key Terms Exercise.* Following is a list of concepts introduced in this chapter. If you have learned the meaning of a term, place a checkmark in the blank that precedes that term. If you are not sure of a term's definition, increase your retention by reviewing the definition of the term. If you have learned six of these terms on your first reading of this chapter, you have constructed many meanings that are important for your career.

_____ teachers-within (p. 31)	_____ stop and ask lessons (p. 37)
_____ teachers-without (p. 31)	_____ student share lessons (p. 39)
_____ integrating-comprehension- processes lessons (p. 31)	_____ teacher–reader groups (p. 41)
_____ TRIO teaching cycle (p. 34)	_____ mock book report and review leaders (p. 42)

8. *Comprehension Process Lesson 2: Teaching Students to Think about Two Comprehension Processes While They Read.* The following comprehension lesson describes the steps in performing think-alouds to demonstrate how students can initiate two or more processes when sentences in a text are misunderstood. The lesson contains five steps that you can take in assisting students to become more active strategic readers when confusion occurs during reading.

COMPREHENSION PROCESS LESSON 2

Teaching Students to Think about Two Comprehension Processes While They Read

This comprehension process lesson is an example of how you can teach students to think about more than one comprehension process as they read. The steps in this lesson can be followed with any two comprehension processes that you want students to think about as they read. The five steps in this example illustrate how you can help students set their own purpose prior to reading and inference while they read.

- Step 1. Explain to the students how to set their own purposes prior to reading and to use inferencing while they read. Explain how the processes will help them become better readers.
- Step 2. Read two pages and do a think-aloud that shows how you set your own purpose for reading. Ask students to explain what their purposes are.
- Step 3. Put an adhesive note (see accompanying diagram) on the bottom right side of page 3. Describe the inferencing process to students. Demonstrate how to inference. Explain that you were able to inference because you recognized clues in the way the author wrote the first three pages. Tell the students what these clues were. Move the adhesive note to page 4.
- Step 4. Repeat the think-aloud and move the adhesive note of step 3 two more times (to pages 5 and 6).
- Step 5. After reading page 6 together, ask students to inference and tell you how they made their inference.

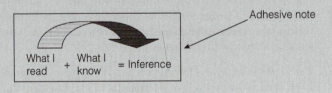

CHAPTER 3

Students' Responsibilities in CPA

Voices and Choices Strengthen Their Competencies

Reader of the day increases students' active participatory role in reading comprehension when students write respondent-covered questions to ask classmates after they finish reading a book to them.

STUDENTS' RESPONSIBILITIES IN CPA: VOICES AND CHOICES STRENGTHEN THEIR COMPETENCIES

- Empowering students' voices

- Empowering students' choices

- Increasing students' abilities to become active participants in the comprehension process

Ms. Ford had implemented many of the lessons in this chapter throughout the year. One day in early May, Conrad told Ms. Ford, "Talking about what I read with my friends helps me comprehend. I know you have to do a lot of planning so we can talk together about books. I've also learned how hard it is to lead good discussions. Sometimes we argue and talk too much. Today, in my buddy reading group, Chad told me that I was a good group leader! Thank you for teaching us how to comprehend better through giving us choices and buddy reading groups."

Chapter Overview

Teachers and curricula perform two important functions in developing students' comprehension. Pupils' active participation is the third component in effective comprehension development. In this chapter, you will learn how to boost students' engagement by moving beyond merely giving and regiving procedural directions. In addition, instead of teaching and repeating the same comprehension processes year after year, requiring the same level of difficulty, you can learn how to teach increasingly more advanced comprehension processes at the intermediate and middle school levels. This chapter introduces lessons to help students (a) express more empowered voices, (b) make better choices during reading instruction, and (c) hoist their own comprehension abilities to comprehend at higher levels.

By the end of this chapter, you will be able to answer the following questions:

1. How can you help children become active partners in the comprehension process?
2. How does comprehension improve when children express their voices, make wise choices, or strive for higher comprehension abilities?
3. What methods enable children's voices to become more powerful?
4. Which choices can you offer students that can increase their comprehension?
5. How can you help readers to hoist their comprehension abilities higher?

Students' Roles in CPA

In recent years, attention has focused on students' performing more active roles in the comprehension process. As Norman (1981) summarized:

> It is strange that we expect students to comprehend yet seldom teach them about the comprehension process. We expect students to solve problems as they read yet seldom teach them about problem solving and, similarly, we sometimes require students to remember a considerable body of material yet seldom teach them the art of understanding (p. 97).

Research suggests that there are two paths students can follow to reach comprehension success. The first involves relying on only a few strategies. These comprehenders approach every text with the same set of thinking processes. The second path involves becoming cognizant of the metacognitive joy that can result from the mental flow experienced when numerous comprehension processes interact to synergize a deep personal understanding. When students make personal investments to initiate their own comprehension processes, the second path becomes possible (Alexander & Murphy, 1998a, 1998b). Empowering student voices and offering choices are the keys to entering this second path (Calkins, 1997; Daniels, 1996).

CPA follows the second, more fruitful path. When learners become empowered to voice their understanding, to make intelligent choices, and to increase their own levels of achievement, they can comprehend at several levels concurrently. This occurs because, when they are mentally active (on a metacognitive level), students no longer view themselves as objects to be scripted, or as empty vessels to be filled with knowledge. They become mature individualistic sculptors, chiseling their personal meanings onto their own mental slates. The activities discussed in this chapter enable them to do so.

Empowering Students' Voices

Empowering students' voices

Many young children are frequently told to keep quiet and "not to speak unless spoken to." As a result, when they enter school, some find it hard to speak up in class and join group discussions. Often, a few pupils sit in the back of a class with their heads down afraid to answer a question. Children need to know that their opinions are important and should be known (Miller, 1999). As teachers, it is important to stress to students that they should defend their statements and be bold when necessary. Students need to become equal partners in the comprehension process because of the novel, individualized worldviews they use to interpret texts.

For more than 100 years, psychologists and educators have recognized the import of this personal view. In the words of William James (1890), "millions of items of the outward order are presented to students' senses which never properly enter into their experiences. Why? Because they have no interest for students. My experiences are what I agree to attend to. Only those items which students notice will shape their mind" (p. 402). By increasing students' abilities to voice their own interpretations of what they comprehended, they can more ably enter into discussions of text. This sharing motivates learners to execute and explain their internal comprehension processes.

Structured turn taking is a lesson that facilitates all voices being heard equally, and is presented as Comprehension Process Lesson 3 at the end of this chapter. In it, students learn how to ask better questions. They write queries about confusions they had while they read. Structured turn taking empowers students to alter their energy allocations as they read and to more productively organize their metacognitions as they progress through a text (Ames, 1992; Wigfield, Eccles, & Rodriguez, 1999).

A variation of structured turn taking involves having students write questions that arise as they read on note cards. Then, in small teacher- or student-led group discussions, cards are drawn and peers relate the comprehension processes that they used to answer the question on that card for themselves as they read.

The second method of empowering children's voices involves allowing them to write **mock book reviews.** One-sheet newspapers can be shared with other children at their grade level; it could be entitled "Literature at Its Best." In these news bulletins, students can analyze several books with the same genre, author, or topic, as was illustrated in Figure 2.5. By increasing the options that students have available to respond to a book, their voices become authentic and genuine. After demonstrating mock book

reviews in Figure 2.5, you can distribute copies of Figure 3.1 and allow students to select the next format that they want to use to express their ideas about books.

Research also indicates that children gain the courage to speak when they are
allowed to write their comments prior to speaking (Gray, 1999). Another courage-
building method involves allowing them to submit their compositions for publication. To that end, *Stone Soup* (a magazine) has published more than 3,000 selections
of children's writings. It recently celebrated its twenty-fifth anniversary, and has a cir-
culation of more than 20,000 readers. Information that can be used to submit your
students' writing appears at the end of the chapter.

A fourth method of increasing students' ability to express their own interpretations of books (and to recognize the importance of doing so) is the **10-minute write**

FIGURE 3.1   Communicating Responses to Books: Book Review Selections

Name _____ Date _____

Title of Book _____

Author _____

I chose this book because _____

I want to present my review;

_____ In writing only

_____ Orally to small group on [date].

_____ Orally to entire class on [date].

Choose the way you want to respond to this book.
Attach your response to this form if it is written.

Your Book Critic's Rating is:
*   *   *   *   *
1   2   3   4   5
Poor   Ok   Really
book   book   need to
read the
book.

Write the first chapter for a sequel to this book.

Conduct a discovery discussion with my teacher

Summary

Timeline of major events

Letter to a character as another character

Taking a position on an issue in the book

Letter to the author with suggestions for
improvement

Book jacket as poster

PowerPoint presentation

Venn diagram to compare this book to another to
resolve a difficult concept

Letter to a friend about the book

Skit, play, song, or poem

Describing an experience from the perspective of
a character or thing in the book

Become a show host with someone in the book,
dressed in costume of the period.

Other _____.

Source: Designed by Rachel Escamilla, administrative assistant, Texas Christian University, Fort
Worth, Texas.

activity. Developed at Benchmark School, Media, Pennsylvania, readers are allotted 10 minutes to write their response to a book. After sharing the responses, children write about what they learned concerning how their metacognitive processes worked as they listened to or read about other people's voices. For this activity, children fold one sheet of paper horizontally. On the top half, they write, "Expressing my voice about [title of piece they selected]." They write on the first half, and if they have more to write, they can turn the page over, essentially completing a full page of writing in a 10-minute period. Students and the teacher share their writings. (Teachers' writings should be read about halfway through the exercise so as not to intimidate children or allow them to perceive that the teacher's interpretation is always the last, and correct, voice.) After a selected number of children have shared, everyone writes on the second half of the page. They describe what they learned by hearing so many interpretations and the importance of expressing their voices.

As an example, Ms. Carey, a fourth-grade teacher, and Ashlee, a fourth grader, read the book *The Lazy Bear* together and completed a 10-minute write to predict how the story would end (see Figure 3.2). After sharing their writings and then reading the author's ending, Ms. Carey and Ashlee wrote what they learned from performing the activity. As you will notice, Ashlee was unable to express what she learned. This is an indication that she needs additional instruction in strand 1 to improve her metacognition. Ms. Carey used this 10-minute write to increase Ashlee's voice, and as a diagnostic

FIGURE 3.2   Two-Part 10-Minute Write Lesson

1st 10-Minute Write

I think that the bear is going to jump in the pile of leaves. He will probably go home with some leaves on his body and his mom will find out. He might get in trouble, but I don't know. Maybe somebody else will see him and tell him to get out of the leaves that he had just raked, and then send him home.

2nd 10-Minute Write

Everybody can interpret the story differently. A story can have many different meanings. This is important to me because it makes me feel like I can write an ending to any story or even write a whole story. The ending to this story surprised me, and I would have never guessed what the author said.

Ashlee

He is going to have something in his hand's. His mom will say that is neet. Were did you get that it will be a cup. The will be rich to. The will tall everybody. The will say neat. Someone will still it.

2nd 10-min Write

What we remibed and we read good we read good to it was long and we read it.

tool to increase Ashlee's comprehension. As a result, she implemented three of the strand 1 lessons in Chapter 9 of this book and Ashlee's comprehension increased significantly, as demonstrated by her scores on the Stanford Achievement Test Comprehension Subtest.

To review, 10-minute writes require students to write for 2 to 10 minutes after you or a peer has read a book aloud. You will also write. Each writer should explain what was most important about the book, the most important thoughts he or she gained from it, or what the concluding episode is likely to be and which strategies were used to make this prediction. When writings are complete, ask students to read their work to others. You can read your writing about halfway through the sharing experience. When all who wish to read their writings have shared, discuss differences among the thoughts, comprehensions, and metacognitions of the group. Another positive aspect of this and all activities to enhance students' voices is that students are exposed to different interpretations for a single text.

If students do not recognize the differences between two or more interpretations, you can identify several salient differences and demonstrate how a detail in the reading possibly held more meaning for one person than another, which could have led to different personal responses. Similarly, if readers do not write their most important thoughts or prediction, ask if they would like to hear a think-aloud about how you make decisions about what is most important to you as you read. Books that have proven highly successful for 10-minute writes include *Frederick* by Leo Lionni, *Leo the Late Bloomer* by Leo Lionni, *Alexander and the Terrible, Horrible, No Good, Very Bad Day* by Judith Viorst, *The Lazy Bear* by Brian Wildsmith, *Sylvester and the Magic Pebble* by William Steig, and *The Giving Tree* by Shel Silverstein.

The fifth activity to build students' voice is based on the principle that students must have an internal drive to reach for understanding. To this end, teachers can ask children to write to people they value. They can ask these people why comprehension is important to them and other questions as well. A letter written to President George W. Bush demonstrates the power of this CPA lesson and is shown in Figure 3.3.

Empowering Students' Choices

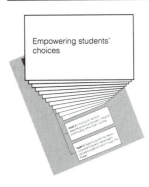

Empowering students' choices

It is equally important to provide reading choices as to empower students' voices. One nerve cell (of the 100 billion cells in the brain) can receive input from as many as 20,000 others simultaneously (Diamond, 1999). Because so many cells are in action at the same time, children make conscious choices about which stimuli to attend to. When they are taught how to select comprehension processes, they can effectively choose which features within words should be attended to as individual words are entered. According to the direction their thoughts take, effective comprehenders can construct meaning based on the stimuli intertwined with their own experiences and culture.

Further, by providing choices, teachers can avoid the common pitfall of too much teacher direction. If we, as teachers, insist on doing

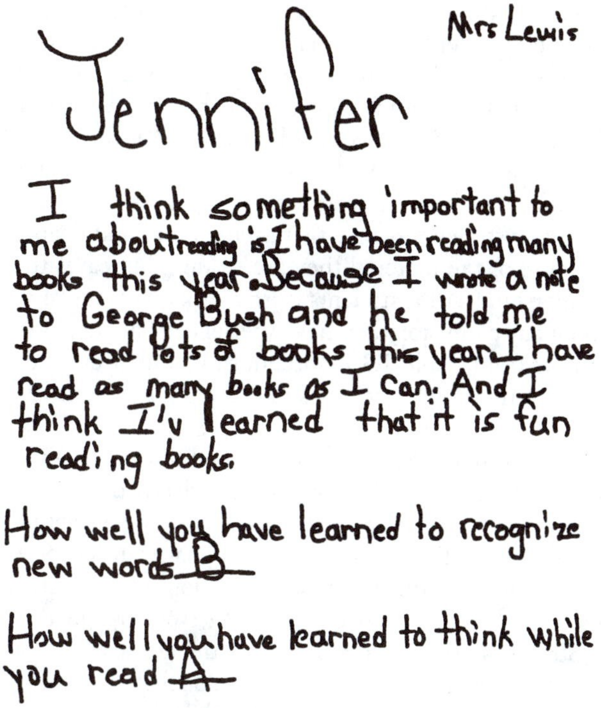

Mrs Lewis

Jennifer

I think something important to me about reading is I have been reading many books this year. Because I wrote a note to George Bush and he told me to read lots of books this year. I have read as many books as I can. And I think I'v learned that it is fun reading books.

How well you have learned to recognize new words B

How well you have learned to think while you read A

FIGURE 3.3   Writing a Letter to an Admired Person Improves a Student's Voice

all of the thinking for our students and if they interpret this as meaning that everything has to be done according to the teacher's way, then what have we left for our students to turn to with pride concerning their own comprehension? In CPA, students are taught to commit themselves, to take chances, and to get involved in making meaning to the very limits of their capabilities. Through the lessons described next, students can overcome the fear that they are incapable of comprehending.

Authors do not need to rely on seductive details to spice up their books before students will choose them. It is not necessary for catastrophe, danger, power, or death to occur in a text for it to become interesting. To be engaging, information must relate to the interests of students (Way, Buxton, & Kelly, 1999). Even if a text conflicts with readers' prior experiences, as long as a text is plausible and convincing, students can use it to become better comprehenders. When students learn how to recognize texts that will be of interest to them personally (and how to do so is described in a comprehension process lesson later in this book), comprehension increases significantly (Block, 2001a).

A second method of increasing students' power of choice is to teach them how to ask provocative questions before, during, and after reading (Meichenbaum & Biemiller, 1990). As Albert Einstein is credited to have stated, "The most important thing is to never stop questioning." The lesson described next enables students to elicit a full range of questions, a horizon of possibilities, in their minds as they read. This variety, in turn, provides opportunities for students to gain knowledge, feel successful, and monitor their reading. The subsequent positive affect increases the amount of time that students practice reading. This volume of reading experiences, in turn, increases their access to and familiarity with books, which enhances the likelihood that they will choose wisely in the future. Each of these cause-effect chains enables students to submerge deeper and deeper into the layers of meaning in comprehending a text.

In the process, many students realize that asking more and deeper questions of themselves as readers and of the material they are reading increases their enjoyment and their ability to understand. After students learn to ask questions, they should learn how to tell stories about any confusion that they experience. They can do so as they read by posing two questions from Table 1.3 before, during, and after reading. Students' choices of and answers to their own questions indicate their present level of comprehension competence.

For example, students should be taught to stop and reflect: "I don't understand. I need to stop and explain what I just read to myself more clearly or ask my teacher to explain why I misunderstood this point in the text. Was the sentence structure too complex, did an unknown word appear, or did an event occur that I have never experienced?" Once students have been taught how to stop and ask such questions of themselves in a Strand 1 lesson, and have practiced doing so in three Strand 2 lessons, readers can exercise the choice during future Strand 2 lessons of stopping to ask themselves questions as they read and verifying with their teacher if their answers to personal queries were correct, or to raise their hands and ask their teachers to deliver a mini lesson when they misunderstand a page of text. By the third experience of posing two types of questions before, during, and after one reads, students can also be taught the activity described next which enables them to monitor any confusion they may experience as they read.

Students are taught how to use the strategy of writing a checkmark or a question mark in the margin of photocopied pages as they read silently. Alternatively, they can use a sheet of paper and write the page number, paragraph number, and the following symbols to denote points of understanding and confusion while they read:

✓   I know that I understand this paragraph

?   I know that I don't understand this paragraph

For variety, students can read and write the appropriate symbol beside each paragraph on acetate that covers a page in a book to indicate how well they understand it. After students mark 10 paragraphs, they bring their books to you for a discovery discussion. You and this student analyze what the misunderstood paragraphs had in common. If students have difficulty detecting similarities, you can describe the textual patterns that you see that may be causing comprehension difficulties.

These interactions can raise students' levels of comprehension because they help them become internally guided readers. To identify difficulties that are interfering with their comprehension, they must (1) till the text before they read, (2) make meaning while they read, (3) reflect after they read, and (4) select processes interactively. However, providing choices about what book to read and which questions one can ask while reading in and of themselves is not enough. Choices must be challenging (Ames, 1992).

When choices are challenging, students build a driving commitment to comprehend. This emotional elicitation increases volition, persistence, and motivation.

Thus, through the quality of choices that you provide, students can come to understand that comprehension is not merely terminating confusion but also selecting appropriate thinking processes to remediate that confusion. Successful remediation of a misunderstanding does not guarantee that comprehension will take its place, however. Students must add active voices and choices, and they must develop their own abilities to detect the fact that incoming stimuli are coherent or incoherent. This process of making something one's own also means transforming meaning into a larger reference set of experiences so relevance can increase. When choices and challenges intertwine, children become strongly engaged in literacy (Cameron & Pierce, 1994), assuming this control rewards students by promoting deeper levels of personalized comprehension (Cameron & Pierce, 1994; Lion & Betsy, 1996).

Another crucial task of educators in the twenty-first century is to promote curiosity and adventurous choices as goals for children to strive toward as they read. When highly-engaging, interesting choices are available, creativity is fostered and a deep level of personal commitment is fostered. Both of these effects enhance students' abilities to learn main idea, and respond to higher-level comprehension questions (Schmitt, 1990).

To sum up, the reason having challenging choices about what to read and how to think as one reads is a key component in comprehension development is because it develops self-regulated readers. Such learners have three important characteristics. First, they regulate their comprehension processes, and learn continuously as they intertwine facts in the text with their own purposes. Second, the challenging choices that their teachers extend lead them to believe that they are capable of deriving meaning from any text that interests them. Third, the challenging choices that their teachers extend to them to question texts in their own unique manners enable them to set numerous goals for themselves before, during, and after reading. As a result, such students most often monitor their own comprehension, evaluate how well they perform compared to their own standards, and voice their understandings uninhibitedly (Zimmerman & Bonner, 2000).

Increasing Students' Abilities to Become Active Participants in the Comprehension Process

As students learn to make challenging choices in reading content and voice their understanding, they need you to teach lessons that increase their self-efficacy as readers. Students' efficacy can increase when they teach other students, or become group officers, book buddies, or the "reader of the day."

In a study of 637 children from kindergarten to grade 3 who were asked what they do to improve their own comprehension, they could not cite any methods that they used to teach themselves. The only thing that they knew to do to boost their comprehension was "to read more" (Block, 2001d). We, as teachers, can develop students' self-efficacy as comprehenders by assisting them to work through the confusions of life with characters in books. When students are taught to understand how a character resolved right and wrong, for instance, readers augment their ability to comprehend what other characters do relative to other large issues and human conditions (Lehr & Thompson, 2000).

A second method of helping students to boost their abilities involves making them group officers. In a recent study by Orellana (1995), when students were allowed to collaborate and select their own book groups for reading based on interest, their reading significantly improved at every grade level. When teachers continually allow students to group and regroup themselves, and to elect an officer to lead their small-group discussion, students realize that they are more alike than different in their reading abilities, regardless of the reading level from which they entered the group's discussion. For this reason, it is important for everyone to become a group officer rather than simply to meet in cooperative groups. There are several ways that students can become officers, shown in Figure 3.4.

Block (1997) demonstrated a side benefit of this lesson. Students who became group leaders reported that they no longer felt a need to hide their faults from fellow group members. They more freely admitted their errors in comprehension because they were group officers, which meant they had the responsibility of telling their peers when they did not comprehend something well. This admission tended to increase students' abilities to diagnose when they had comprehension problems.

After students complete their responsibilities in a teacher–reader group, (Group Leaders or Reader of the Day, described later in this book), they and their peers can evaluate themselves using a form similar to that appearing in Figure 3.5. Moreover, when students become group officers, they learn to work cooperatively in groups by using the information shown in Figure 3.5.

Book Buddies Program

A third method of building self-regulated comprehenders is to implement a book buddies program. In book buddy sessions, two students are engaged 100 percent of the time. **Buddy reading,** or "book buddies," involves pairing underachieving readers with older, more advanced students from classes that are a few grade levels above their own. Book buddies can also be formed from among students in the same classroom of different reading levels. The typical format is for more able students to select books at their partner's readability level and then to share them with their "buddy" once a week for 30 minutes. Most often, during these sharing periods the older or more able book buddy holds the book so that the younger reader can follow along silently as it is read aloud. Both book buddies ask and answer questions about the content. Primary-grade teachers meet with intermediate-grade teachers to schedule time for their teams of book buddies to read. They also identify locations on the school campus where buddy interactions can occur in a relaxed atmosphere.

The benefits of buddy reading are well documented (for a review of the research see Block & Dellamura, 2000/2001; Johnston, Invernizzi, & Juel, 1998). The tutor, the early reader, and the teacher benefit from this program. Even as early as grade1 benefits are apparent as Suzanna, a six year old, suggested, "I liked it too day [sic] cus [sic] it

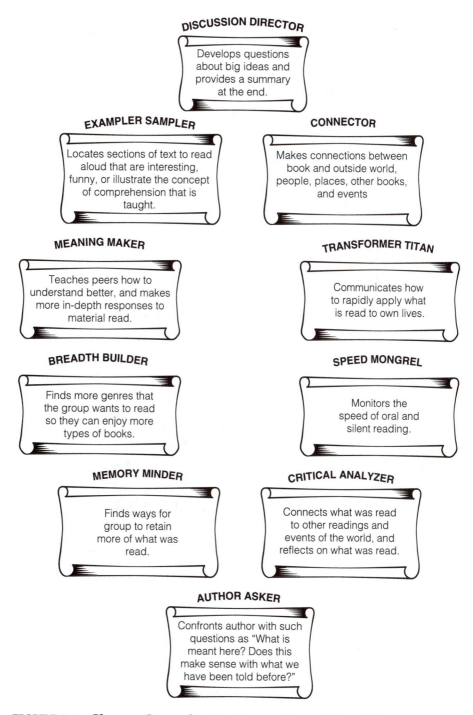

DISCUSSION DIRECTOR

Develops questions about big ideas and provides a summary at the end.

EXAMPLER SAMPLER

Locates sections of text to read aloud that are interesting, funny, or illustrate the concept of comprehension that is taught.

CONNECTOR

Makes connections between book and outside world, people, places, other books, and events

MEANING MAKER

Teaches peers how to understand better, and makes more in-depth responses to material read.

TRANSFORMER TITAN

Communicates how to rapidly apply what is read to own lives.

BREADTH BUILDER

Finds more genres that the group wants to read so they can enjoy more types of books.

SPEED MONGREL

Monitors the speed of oral and silent reading.

MEMORY MINDER

Finds ways for group to retain more of what was read.

CRITICAL ANALYZER

Connects what was read to other readings and events of the world, and reflects on what was read.

AUTHOR ASKER

Confronts author with such questions as "What is meant here? Does this make sense with what we have been told before?"

FIGURE 3.4   Choose a Comprehension Process Group Officer Role

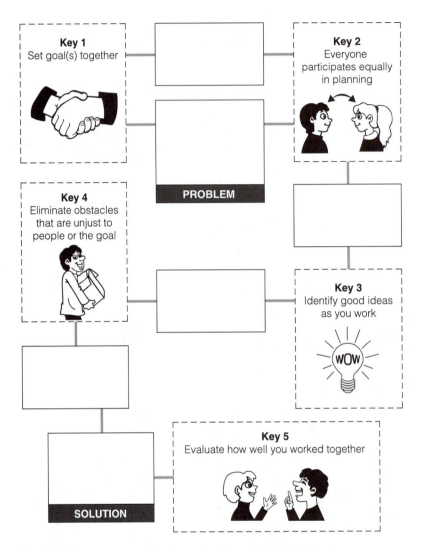

FIGURE 3.5   Cooperative Learning Lesson Plan for Students

Source: Reason to Read, Volume 1 by Dr. Cathy Collins Block and John Mangieri. Copyright © 1995 by Pearson Education, Inc., publishing as Dale Seymour Publications. Used by permission.

was fun. I red [sic] One hole [sic] book I like my reader because She is nice and it is fun I lik [sic] reading with my reader She likes me and I like her." Tutors also quickly develop dramatic modulations and inflections in their oral reading abilities. They also learn to use other vocal qualities to sustain their younger readers' interests, such as pronouncing individual words with wide-ranging pitches, using variant paces, and creating distinct voices to depict different characters in a story.

In addition, by choosing a book to share, tutors gain a sense of accomplishment. They realize that their own reading ability has progressed when they choose books for their buddies and recognize how much easier it is for them to read the books than it was in their recent past. This value of realizing how far they have come as readers disperses positive affects and leads to growth in other subject areas as has been documented through testimonials and retelling forms (see Figure 3.6) of more than 100 book buddies programs (Block & Dellamura, 2000/20001).

FIGURE 3.6   Retelling Form for Use in Book Buddy Programs

Name _____ Date _____

I listened to _____ retell the book _____.

1. Ask your partner to retell the book. As he or she talks check what is said. Write one sentence after each comment.

2. Check the comprehension processes your partner did well and write a sample sentence he or she said after each process you checked.

   My partner told about:

   _____ The characters _____

   _____ The setting _____

   _____ The events in the story or several facts from the book _____

   _____

   _____ The beginning _____

   _____ The ending _____

   _____ Applied it to his/her life _____

   _____ Told why he/she did or did not like it _____

   _____ The main ideas _____

   _____ The details _____

Describe the process your partner did best.

_____

_____

_____

Describe the process with which your partner needs more help.

_____

_____

_____

A book buddies program helps tutors verbalize comprehension processes. Such explanations enable tutors to realize that many times they have used these same processes in their own reading. After several book buddy sessions, tutors purposely seek books for their tutees in which they can teach their buddies how to apply specific comprehension processes to the books that they will read together. For instance, David, a fifth-grade student, contemplated and considered many books for his buddy before selecting *The Stinky Cheese Man* by Jon Scieszka. This was his "all time favorite book" and he was excited about his choice. Then, he decided to search for a second book. He reasoned thus. The goal that his teacher had established for this particular book buddies' session was to increase Sam's (his buddy's) prediction abilities. After carefully surveying several titles, he added *If You Give a Moose a Muffin* by Laura Numeroff to his buddy's reading plan. According to David, "For a kindergarten child, this book will be better for me to show how to make a prediction. That's what I want to teach today." After this book buddy lesson, David reported that being required to examine this process of prediction and apply it to *If You Give a Moose a Muffin*, he increased his abilities to make predictions when he read. Verbalizing the predictive thinking process by teaching with think-alouds and repeated examples made this expert reading process more automatic for him.

Tutees realize many benefits from buddy reading as well. First, they are assigned an older student in the school who befriends them. In Sam's case, he had come to enjoy David's visits almost as much as his recess periods. He would see David in the hall, wave, and proudly announce to anyone within earshot: "That's my buddy!" Not only did Sam's esteem, belongingness, and pride increase, his literacy abilities grew at a rapid pace. This acceleration was marked not only in measurable rises in readability levels but also in Sam's deep, internalized value for literacy in his life. One measure of the impact of the book buddies program on his affective literacy growth was evidenced when he presented David with a treasured Christmas present. Sam walked into the library with his beloved gift hidden behind his back in a paper sack that he had decorated. Before he handed it to David, he whispered in Ms. Carey's ear that he had selected this present with special care because he wanted David to have the very best present in the world. When David opened his package, he saw Sam's treasured gift: a book for David to keep forever! Having a book of one's own was something that Sam had come to value, which is a published goal that almost every reading program strives to achieve.

The third person to benefit from a buddy reading program is the classroom teacher. Instruction of an expert to a novice reader, for an extended period of time at least once a week, translates into significant literacy gains for students who are in most need of one-to-one instructional time. Such person-to-person tutoring would not be possible for a classroom teacher to deliver weekly to numerous students without a book buddy program in action. Time would not permit it. If a single teacher were to share a book for 30 minutes with every student (in a class that contained 23 pupils) it would require that teacher to do nothing else except "buddy read" every minute of the school day for two full days every week.

Second, book buddy activities enable teachers to provide less able readers opportunities to receive the benefits of exclusive attention, interesting reading experiences, and personalized instruction from people other than their teachers. Third, book buddies enable younger readers to pose more questions and hear literacy strategies explained in words that are more closely attuned to their own oral vocabularies. Elementary-aged tutors create examples to communicate difficult concepts through words that are only privy to the rapidly changing, colorful, everyday vernaculars of children.

Traditionally, individual book buddy sessions unfold by a tutor reading a story aloud and then asking questions in an oral format. Then, the younger buddy in each pair shares his or her thoughts and responses to the book. Most often, these exchanges are not documented with written records of the questions asked and answers given. As a result, it is difficult for teachers to chart the specific progress of each child. I recommend the following types of writing activities, which can eliminate these deficiencies and significantly increase the effects of buddy reading. The lessons are easy to implement, which is an important factor for teachers who manage buddy-reading programs.

Studies have shown that when buddy reading is coupled with writing activities, writing abilities, comprehension, and reading retention increase (Block & Dellamura, 2000/2001; Invernez, Mendon, & Juel, 1999). For this reason, book buddies are more successful when book buddy journals are kept. A journal can be a file folder, which contains single sheets of notebook paper. Each tutor's and tutee's name is written on the folder's label and cover. Prior to each book buddy session, on single sheets of notebook paper, tutors can record the date of the session, titles of books to be read, and questions that they want to ask about the book or activities they want to engage using the book. Following each question, the tutor leaves space to write the answers given by the tutee. As a closing activity, on the back of each page, tutors can write the free response answers that their tutees gave to one or more of the following questions (or questions that their teachers use to assess individual tutees' reading progress): (1) What did you learn today that helped you read better? (2) Is there anything else that you would like to share or say about this book? (3) What do you want to learn at the next book buddy session?

The second writing application uses the **book buddy journal reflection sheet,** as shown in Figure 3.7. After six sessions, tutors (and tutees if they are old enough to write independently) record descriptions of all that they (and their tutees) have learned during this grading period. If tutees cannot write independently, tutors can read what they wrote and tutees can voice their agreement or disagreement with the written statements. Tutees can also answer each question on Figures 3.7, 3.8, and 3.9 orally and tutors can write these on a separate form for tutees. After such one-page descriptions are finalized, tutors (and tutees) can grade their growth by referring to the criteria in Figure 3.10. These objectives can change each grading period to reflect the goals that have been taught in a specific 6-weeks' work. Through these shared reflections, tutors and tutees can assist each other to improve their literacy, and discuss ways that the next 6-weeks' work together can be strengthened.

A third type of writing activity is the buddy reading record on which tutees can list the titles of all the books that they have shared (**buddy reading record** in Figure 3.8). At the end of each book buddy session, tutees can rate each book on a 5-to-1 scale. The rating is similar to that used by critics in their ranking of new movies. This

FIGURE 3.7   **Book Buddy Journal Reflection Sheet**

Name _____

Buddy's Name _____

Directions: When you and your partner have completed 6 buddy journal entries, you and your partner can discuss and grade them. If you agree with the grade, check "yes" and write why. If you disagree, check "no" and write why.

Buddy's Evaluation	**Partner's Response**	
	Yes	*No*
1. Reading lessons were clear, interesting, and helped me improve my reading abilities. Grade _____ Specific examples:		
2. Opening and closing discussions were captivating and increased my comprehension. Grade _____ Specific examples:		
3. I increased my vocabulary. I now use and can read more vivid words, including adjectives, nouns, and verbs. Grade _____ Specific examples:		
4. I do not repeat words or ideas unnecessarily when I read orally, write, or share my responses. Grade _____ Specific examples:		
5. I can comprehend difficult sentences. Grade _____ Specific examples:		
6. I can decode better. Grade _____ Specific examples:		
Additional comments and things I would like to add about our buddy readings:		

FIGURE 3.8   Buddy Book Reading Record

Name: _____

Date started	Title	Author	Date completed	Rating
				★ ★ ★ ★ ★
				★ ★ ★ ★ ★
				★ ★ ★ ★ ★
				★ ★ ★ ★ ★
				★ ★ ★ ★ ★
				★ ★ ★ ★ ★
				★ ★ ★ ★ ★
				★ ★ ★ ★ ★
				★ ★ ★ ★ ★
				★ ★ ★ ★ ★
				★ ★ ★ ★ ★
				★ ★ ★ ★ ★
				★ ★ ★ ★ ★

reading record documents tutees' depth and breadth of reading interests. This form can assist tutors and teachers to select more advanced books within an individual tutee's interest, appreciation, and skill.

The fourth type of writing activity is used when tutors and tutees read orally; it is the **strategies check form** (see Figure 3.9). This form encourages decoding and comprehension strategies that can be used when difficult words or ideas are presented. Strategy names can be spaced on the paper so that tutors have room to write the specific words or sentences that gave them trouble during a buddy reading session. This record provides teachers with knowledge of individual students' frequency of use and effective application of each strategy. Tutors can place a checkmark whenever they prompt their tutees with a particular strategy during a buddy reading lesson. Tutors enjoy this form because it provides a record of all the strategies that were taught. Emergent readers profit by having a sheet to read of the numerous strategies to use when difficulties arise.

FIGURE 3.9   Buddy Reading Strategies Checklist

Name _____

Buddy's Name _____

Directions: When your partner needs your help with a hard word, suggest one of these strategies. Check whether your suggestion worked.

	Yes	No
1. Think of what makes sense.		
2. Sound it out.		
3. Look for chunks in the word.		
4. Look at the picture.		
5. Look for endings you know.		
6. Look at another page where you saw the word.		
7. Go back and get a running start.		

Comments on my buddy's retelling of the part that was read:

Comments on my buddy's use of the strategies:

This form adds variety to book buddy sessions. For example, tutors can ask tutees to read orally. As tutees read, tutors can check each decoding strategy on the form that tutees demonstrate or report they use. When used in this way, the form enables tutors to stay thoroughly engaged as younger students read. It sharpens tutors' writing skills, and abilities to document how much their buddies' comprehension processes have improved.

A fifth writing activity is a spinner game called the **Readers' Million Dollar Game** (illustrated in Figure 3.10). In this activity, a blank copy of the spinner game board can be enlarged to fill an 8 × 11 cardboard paper. It is laminated and affixed with a brad or metal spinner in the middle of the game board. Questions, based on a book to be read, are written in each quadrant of the board by the tutor, a teacher in the book buddies program, or a school librarian. After the reading, the tutee spins and answers the question on which the spinner lands. If the answer is correct, the tutee receives the total number of points designated for that quadrant. Next, the tutor spins and receives the designated points for a correct answer to the query posed in the quadrant in which the spinner lands. If a pair of book buddies wants more than two spins each, they can

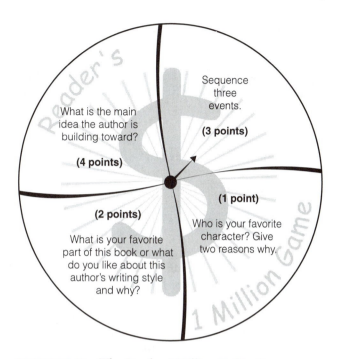

FIGURE 3.10   The Readers' Million Dollar Game

Source: Designed by Rachel Escamilla, administrative assistant, Texas Christian University, Fort Worth, Texas.

request that up to four questions be written in each quadrant. In this way, both students can receive eight turns each until all questions are answered. At the end, the student with the most points wins. Before students write questions for peers on the quadrants, they have to have comprehended well the material read by all Million Dollar Game players.

To vary this activity, writing assignments can be designated in each quadrant. When used in this manner, during the reading of a chosen book, tutor and tutee can stop after reading approximately 10 pages and take turns spinning. Each participant then engages in the writing activities in the quadrant where the spinner landed. After writing, book buddies could read and discuss their answers. The activities in each quadrant can vary according to the specific literacy abilities taught in a particular grading period. For example, students can write (or draw depending on the skill level of prekindergarten through first-grade tutees) (1) about the student's favorite character thus far in the story; (2) a summary of the story's unfolding plot; (3) the cause–effect relationships that occurred to that point in the story; (4) what will happen next; or (5) a "mystery question." The mystery question is an opportunity for tutors or tutees to ask their partners something about the reading material thus far about which they want their partner's opinion. This spinner game has been demonstrated to enhance the pleasure and retention of material read during book buddy sessions.

The final step in a book buddy program is to chart progress using **goal books.** Book buddy teams design these booklets to depict progress on their own self-selected literacy goals. They reflect students' creativity and personalities (e.g., Chan, an eight year old, cut his goal book out in the shape of a football; and Shandra, a six year old, drew a picture of *Clifford*, the big, red dog, which is her favorite book friend, on the cover of her goal book). Inside goal books, young readers note their daily progress, and tutors praise and validate the goal books when these self-initiated goals are attained. Stickers can also be placed on daily sheets to denote the completion of each day's work and to enhance each tutee's sense of accomplishment. Figure 3.11 is an example of a page from Shandra's goal book.

To sum up, a book buddy program encourages tutors and tutees to reach new heights in comprehension. By incorporating record keeping and writing activities, teachers can significantly increase the program's benefits. Book buddy journals, book buddy journal reflection sheets, buddy reading records, strategies check forms, the Readers' Million Dollar Game, and goal books have been demonstrated to significantly increase tutees' and tutors' literacy abilities (Block, 2001b; Block, Schaller, Joy, & Gaines, 2001). Sometimes change is slow in coming. The following quotation is similar to one that appeared in the early 1800s. This quotation came from a program that was written less than 30 years ago (Bereiter & Bird, 1985):

FIGURE 3.11   A Child's Book Buddies Goal Sheet

Once the alphabet has been mastered, the work focuses upon drill with spelling patterns and upon the reading of sentences and stories containing such words. When this stage is reached, a gradual transition is carried out from reading material presented on the chalkboard to reading from printed sheets and finally to reading from book. (p. 292)

In addition to students teaching each other, group officers, and book buddies, a fourth way of helping students advance their own comprehension skills is to assign a **reader of the day.** The reader of the day is a student who opens a class meeting as shown in the accompanying picture. When class begins the student leader begins to describe something that is important about the project on which he or she has been working and something that will be taught this day that this student has prepared in advance

for peers. This method of allowing each student to create comprehension activities that teach peers and to start the school day develops a partnership and ownership between teacher and students in the classroom (Block, 2001c; Horne, 2000). After these teaching episodes as reader of the day, program charts are posted of their work and students sign up for a day when they have something that they would like to teach and share about comprehension processes, rather than teachers appointing who is to be the reader of the day. When students become reader of the day, their choices, voices, and abilities improve their comprehension. Their words begin the day's community conversation. They control the dialogue in that classroom and are in charge of that classroom's literacy growth for those few moments.

In Summary

There may be several reasons why students' simple requests are not met in all classrooms. The first is that teachers do not take enough time to teach comprehension processes in depth. Many teachers feel pressured to cover content. The second reason is that teachers have not built a long tradition of allowing students to establish their own direction in comprehension development. When teachers are able to implement the lessons in this chapter more frequently, student-initiated activity will become more commonplace. Students should meet together and decide what they need to learn more about, and they should be encouraged to teach others how they can boost their meaning making to higher levels, and control their own comprehension in groups.

It is important to remember that students' voices, choices, and hoists must occur throughout the day. As you integrate comprehension instruction into other subject areas, remember that integration is not something you plan and implement. Rather, it is a process that occurs in learners. When curricular units are framed by broad, real-world problems, and begin with students' voices and choices, students make comprehension process connections more readily. These connections link students and literacy with the world.

In closing, there are several methods of adding power to students' voices, choices, and control of their own comprehension abilities. Among these are the abilities to write (do a 10-minute write activity), select books that they will enjoy, join teacher–reader groups, become group officers, become better book buddies, and become readers of the day. In Chapters 4, 5, and 6 you will learn how to enhance students' literal, inferential, and metacognitive comprehension processes.

REFLECTING ON WHAT YOU HAVE LEARNED

1. List five important principles you learned in Chapter 3.

2. *Your Professional Journal: Record-Keeping Journal.* Make a chart listing each activity in this chapter. In the right column, write the titles of children's or adolescent literature you

want to use for students to express their voices, choices, and decision about their own interests and comprehension needed. Fill in as many as possible now, and add to it throughout your teaching career.

3. *Making Professional Decisions.* In approximately one paragraph, describe your fondest memory of a comprehension lesson that was designed to (a) increase your students' voice; (b) increase your students' choice; or (c) enable students to hoist their own comprehension abilities higher. How did it increase your students' comprehension?

4. *Field Applications and Observations.* Interview students about choices, voices, and hoists that they have exerted in their own reading lessons. Compare these students' abilities with the benefits that can accrue from the lessons in this chapter. To obtain forms to submit your students' writing for publication, you can contact: *Stone Soup,* at P.O. Box 83, Santa Cruz, CA 93063, USA; telephone: 408-426-3337 or 800-447-4369; Fax: 408-426-1161; e-mail: editor@stonesoup.com; Web site: www.stonesoup.com/ or access the International Reading Association Web site at www.reading.org and download the application to the Paul A. Witty Outstanding Students' Writing Award.

5. *Multicultural Application.* Perform a case study by visiting with a student for an hour in which he or she shares a favorite book, lesson, and writing sample. Chose a student who is older than youth with whom you have had frequent experiences and one who is from a heritage other than your own. After the visit, write about what you learned from the experience that will assist you in adapting the lessons in this chapter to enhance students' learning who are from that heritage to make better choices, express more courageous voices, and hoist their comprehension abilities higher.

6. *Key Terms Exercise.* Following is a list of concepts introduced in this chapter. If you have learned the meaning of a term, place a checkmark in the blank that precedes that term. If you are not sure of a term's definition, increase your retention by reviewing the definition of the term. If you have learned nine of these terms on your first reading of this chapter, you have constructed many meanings that are important for your career.

_____ structured turn taking (p. 49)   _____ buddy reading record (p. 61)

_____ mock book reviews (p. 49)   _____ strategies check form (p. 63)

_____ 10-minute write activity (p. 50)   _____ Readers' Million Dollar Game (p. 64)

_____ buddy reading (p. 56)   _____ goal books (p. 66)

_____ book buddy journal reflection sheet (p. 61)   _____ reader of the day (p. 67)

7. *Comprehension Process Lesson 3: Teaching the Comprehension Process of Asking Questions While Reading.* Comprehension Process Lesson 3 is one of the most basic lessons. It can lead students from becoming passive decoders to active, questioning, idea-seeking students who want to take advantage of the new responsibilities that teachers can provide teaching comprehension. This lesson contains two different methods. You can also modify it in several ways. Its core is that the more we ask students to write and answer questions

while they read, the more they will do so metacognitively without prompting. Comprehension Process Lesson 3 assists students in becoming active participants in making their own meanings from text.

C O M P R E H E N S I O N P R O C E S S L E S S O N 3
Increasing Students' Abilities to Ask Questions through Structured Turn Taking

This CPA lesson encourages students to ask questions about what they need. Structured turn taking can be implemented in a variety of ways to reach this objective. The following procedures are basic steps which can be enhanced through a variety of options.

1. Students read a story (either to themselves or aloud with the teacher).
2. Students are each given a note card with a number on one side. (There must be enough note cards for each student to have one and they should all have different numbers on them.)
3. Students are asked to write down a question they have about the story or an idea they would like to discuss with the class. This should take only a few minutes.
4. The note cards are retrieved and redistributed to different students who then take a few minutes to read their question and think of a way to start a group discussion about the topic.
5. The student with card number one reads his or her question or topic aloud and then begins the discussion for the class. Members of the class raise their hands and respond. This process continues until all the questions or topics on the cards have been discussed.

There are many pros to this activity. Using note cards gives the students time to consider their answers and how they want to present them to the class without having to experience on-the-spot pressure. Students also know when they will be called on to answer their questions so they are not taken by surprise and placed in situations in which they may feel embarrassed. The note cards also give students the ability to ask a question anonymously. Many times this is easier for children because they will not fear being ridiculed by their classmates.

The note cards can also be used with partners or in small groups where a few children can discuss what they think and then share with the class by telling or writing to express their answers. The note cards can also serve to encourage students to get to know one another and become comfortable speaking in front of other students and those they do not know. Because this is a discussion session, children need not fear being wrong. They can express their feelings, and whether they agree or disagree with others.

The following example shows a modification of Comprehension Process Lesson 3. In this procedure of structured turn taking, students write a story on numbered note cards or sheets of notebook papers. Classmates draw randomly from numbered peer reaction sheets. The student who selects Peer Reaction Sheet 1 offers suggestions to improve the story written on the notebook paper labeled number 1. Suggestions are then shared in paired groups or in writing with the author.

Why is this story called
"Frisky Feet"?

The sight of that long hallway seems to have a dire influence on my feet. It was not I who was racing pell-mell through the hall, but I was merely the victim of exceptionally mischievous feet. They play dual roles. Usually, they play the role of friends, walking me quietly within the buildings. But at the sight of the long hall they turn into "frisky feet." With a dash and a slide, they sail through the hall. After I get blamed, they just dangle out of sight under my desks, probably planning another scramble from the room, a dash down the hall, and a leap through the door, and so goes the cycle of the normal child against abnormal frisky feet.

Peer Reactions: Suggested Improvements for Note Card 1

Paper's Title _Frisky Feet_   Author's Name _Meisong_

Peer Reactor _Allison_

The writing describes the mischief the feet create. Your ending is so good I want readers to have a big build up to the ending.

Additional Questions (for older students)

What is the best sentence (or word)? "racing pell-mell"

What is the strongest aspect of this piece? Your excellent choices of words

What do you like about it? The idea is creative.

What don't you understand? The title doesn't fit for me.

Are there words inappropriately used, or words that could be stronger? 1st sentence

Does the message have a clear beginning, middle, and end? yes

Does the story make sense? yes

Which part of the paper needs more specific descriptions? middle

Can you find a good example of a writing strategy we've recently learned in a minilesson, learning center, or writing work?
    How to write with personified elements

Crafting Accurate Literal Understandings

Sean, Ricardo, Alisha, and Mariah have learned to ask questions of themselves while they read, establish their purposes before they read, and take notes to increase their retention of literal comprehension.

CRAFTING ACCURATE LITERAL UNDERSTANDINGS

Crafting accurate literal understanding at the sentence level

Crafting accurate understanding at the paragraph level

Attending to authors' writing styles

Establishing a purpose

Overcoming word-calling

Expanding content specific vocabulary

Instead of building background, teach students how to let background build

Instead of finding the main idea, teach students how main ideas find them

Using comprehension processes synergistically

It was the first day of school! Ricardo, a precocious second grader in Ms. Johnson's Grapevine-Colleyville, Texas, classroom, listened intently to his new teacher. Ms. Johnson was asking her students to write reasons why they needed to go to school, and she suggested possibilities. As she wrote items on the board, she reassured her new class that they could describe any idea that they wanted. She said, "There are no right or wrong answers." Instantly, Ricardo raised his hand and said with the greatest desire to assist his teacher, "Ms. Johnson, it's OK. You can look in your book. In first grade, our teacher had a really big book in her lap and it had all the right answers in it!"

Chapter Overview

After only one year in school, Ricardo, like many students, has deduced that everything he reads is to be interpreted literally. Teachers know all the answers, or if they don't, they can read them in the "teacher's manual." If students become confused, they try to read their teacher's expression and guess the correct answer. Unfortunately, these deductions limit students' comprehension in two ways: Students do not learn how to construct accurate literal interpretations, and they refrain from thinking beyond a literal level to apply readings to their lives.

In this chapter, you will learn research and instructional methods that facilitate students' abilities to construct accurate literal understandings. These procedures develop students' abilities to comprehend single sentences and interpret meaning, between sentences, paragraphs, with a full text, and with multiple texts. The discussion includes increasing students' abilities to ask themselves questions while they read and increasing their recall. This discussion is intended to ensure that students build accurate, factual bases, from which they can draw inferences and images. Throughout the discussion, the focus is on activities that enable students to become actively involved in the construction of sentences, paragraphs, and multiple texts at the literal level. Once students understand what an author intended, they are better able to make valid translations to their lives.

By the end of this chapter, you will be able to answer the following questions:

1. What are the problems that students encounter when they read individual sentences?
2. How can teachers increase children's abilities to understand how sentences within paragraphs link together?
3. How can children be taught to use an author's "sea of thought" (Beck, McKeown, Hamilton, & Kucan, 1997)?
4. How can students build macrostructures to tie chapters together in fiction and nonfiction reading, and build bridges between books related to similar topics?
5. What is tilling the text and how can students learn to till a text?

Crafting Accurate Literal Understanding at the Sentence Level

Crafting accurate literal understanding at the sentence level

One of the most difficult problems in teaching literal comprehension is to get past skills, drill, and kill. Of the multitude of methods and programs for teaching comprehension that were developed prior to the 1980s, most were not designed to train the brain in pattern recognition. As a result, every new sentence is viewed by children as an obstacle for literal comprehension. For many years, teachers taught many different methods to help students. They taught them to use phonics, letter names, phonemic awareness, chunks within words, word parts, word meanings, foreign language clues, context clues, syntax, picture clues, structural analysis, sentence meanings, and the flow of ideas represented in the author's sea of thoughts.

In the 1990s, teachers began to teach students to comprehend through thinking guides, to diagram thinking processes that taught children to recognize relative levels of importance between individual sentences within paragraphs, to teach children the different functions that paragraphs serve, and to teach students to recognize other similar types of macro structures in print. Only then were children able to comprehend literally with less effort. By the turn of the century, teachers and researchers were beginning to design more methods by which children could be taught literal comprehension as a process and not as individual skills or strategies.

Skill can be defined as anything children can think or do that can be answered with *yes* or *no*. For example, you can ask children to underline a main idea. This is a skill because students can simply ask if a particular sentence *is* or *is not* the one that they think is most important. Yes, they can underline it correctly, or no, they cannot. **Strategies,** however, are defined by the state of ongoing mental processing, not by whether something can or cannot be done. For instance, decoding and comprehension strategies are tools that are used during the process of making meaning. Strategies construct processes that create something new. Thus, strategic thinking initiates comprehension processes that make meaning. Students are either strategic at times, for example strategic throughout the reading of a sentence, or strategic decision makers about how future events in a plot are likely to unfold. Students regulate their strategic thinking and how many strategies they apply as they read. **Critical comprehension processing** is self-initiation of comprehension processes that transform words that are understood literally from characters and events to one's own mental images and life.

Expert reading requires the coordination of many strategic processes while reading a single sentence (Bransford & Schwartz, 1998; Kintsch, 1994). A comprehension process unlocks syntactical clues and identifies relationships among words in phrases and clauses. Among the most effective is to teach children to **think to the end.** When children overlook a clue or connection, and they do not know how to proceed in a sentence, they can be taught to say to themselves, "think to the end." By doing so, they can continue to hold the things they do not understand at bay until they accumulate more blocks of meaning and a complete structure.

This method of thinking is different from telling children to reread or telling them to say blank and move on because both of these instructions are asking students to merely use a skill, which is to perform or not to perform a mental task. However, when teachers ask children to think to the end of a sentence or paragraph children must continue their strategic thinking processes as they add new meanings. As a result, their comprehension processing continues until redundancies in an author's writing style can compensate for the overlooked relationship in a prior sentence. To assist this process, you can teach students to use signal words to make semantic links. Examples of signal words that can be taught as exemplars appear in Figure 4.1. These words, when introduced to students in the categories that appear in this figure, have proven to increase students' abilities to relate the meaning of one sentence to the meaning of the next sentence in the order that the author intended (Block & Mangieri, 1994).

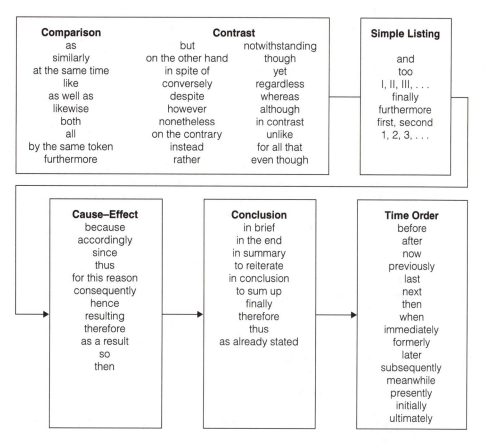

Comparison	Contrast		Simple Listing
as	but	notwithstanding	
similarly	on the other hand	though	and
at the same time	in spite of	yet	too
like	conversely	regardless	I, II, III, . . .
as well as	despite	whereas	finally
likewise	however	although	furthermore
both	nonetheless	in contrast	first, second
all	on the contrary	unlike	1, 2, 3, . . .
by the same token	instead	for all that	
furthermore	rather	even though	

Cause–Effect	Conclusion	Time Order
because	in brief	before
accordingly	in the end	after
since	in summary	now
thus	to reiterate	previously
for this reason	in conclusion	last
consequently	to sum up	next
hence	finally	then
resulting	therefore	when
therefore	thus	immediately
as a result	as already stated	formerly
so		later
then		subsequently
		meanwhile
		presently
		initially
		ultimately

FIGURE 4.1   Signal Words

Source: Reason to Read, Volume 1 (p. 177) by Dr. Cathy Collins Block and John Mangieri. Copyright © 1995 by Pearson Education, Inc., publishing as Dale Seymour Publications. Used by permission.

Crafting Accurate Understanding at the Paragraph Level

Crafting accurate
understanding
at the paragraph level

Teaching students to paraphrase a paragraph as accurately as possible on the literal level is important for them to retain new knowledge. Learning from that text, however, demands more. It requires, "a good situational model linked with the reader's long term knowledge" (Kintsch, 1994, p. 321). Kintsch has designed a construction integration (CI) model, which suggests that texts should induce students to form appropriate mental literal comprehension images. These images should not be simply text-based representations. They must use active inferencing processing and arouse appropriate prior knowledge (Kintsch, 1998).

The CI model assumes that literal comprehension is guided by a top-down understanding of the arguments in specific sentences. Readers link individual sentences and arguments within sentences to subsequent sentences. In the process, they begin to understand that some arguments overlap and involve more than one sentence. Some propositions can be embedded within single sentences that relate to the larger theme conveyed in a paragraph. All propositions and their links are given initial activation, however, because what students remember most is what is important to them. Usually this will only be one link in the vast possibilities of knowledge connections. This model emphasizes the importance of students' exercising control over the strategic processes they use. By doing so, they develop the ability to become textually bound (accurately interpret author's message) and non–textually bound (apply new ideas that were triggered by a connection made by the reader and that were not written or inferred by the author). Simultaneously, they can be taught to use other literal comprehension processes, such as clue detection from signal words, tilling the text thinking, and paragraph functions.

As students integrate these processes into their everyday practice of reading they will come to add imagination to the images they form. This creative aspect of comprehension is a crucial element in literal interpretation. It assists to move students from naïveté to an understanding of authors' intended messages. Creative process thinking allows readers to explore all possible knowledge links and choose how they can best tie new pieces of knowledge together as they unfold before them (Freire, 1999). One method of building creative thinking processes as students work to comprehend literally was developed by Gibbs (1999). According to Gibbs, students as young as age 7 should be taught to recognize and appreciate figures of speech. "Metaphors, metonymy, irony, and other instances of figurative language fill the pages of great literature and provide us with instruments for establishing imaginative connections between diverse emotions, ideas, and events" (Gibbs, 1999, p. 215).

His research proved that we conceptualize everyday life in metaphors. These schemas help us make sense of incomprehensible experiences. One of the pleasures of reading literally is that in both fiction and nonfiction readers can draw metaphors that relate to their own lives and in doing so increase their active literal comprehension. By drawing metaphors, all readers can somehow speak to themselves, remind themselves of their own struggles, and add meaning to their lives. Students can be taught to do this by suggesting that they ask themselves to pause at the end of a short story or picture book and create a metaphor that relates to their own lives. After three sessions of modeling in three think-alouds, ask older students to pause at the end of single pages of text and create metaphors that relate to their lives. This is a difficult task. But it will help you in accomplishing a second goal—continuous reflective thinking while reading. To reach both of these goals, with the ultimate goal of making literal comprehension enjoyable, you can teach students to:

1. Attend to the author's writing style as they read;
2. Establish a purpose for reading material;
3. Overcome word-calling;

4. Expand their content-specific vocabulary knowledge; and
5. Become aware of ways in which their own background knowledge can interfere with or expand meaning making.

The need for these abilities and methods to increase students' use is described next.

Attending to Authors' Writing Styles

Attending to authors' writing styles

One of the first strategies in tilling a text is to use subheadings and print features (such as the paragraph lengths and amount of white space) to determine the conceptual density of a reading. This strategy enables readers to understand how an author divides the topic into subtopics. To perform this analysis, many readers must learn that dense concepts and writing styles require more intense comprehension processing, and that each writing is built by an author with a specific message.

Becoming Less Reality-Bound

Attending to an author's writing style includes the ability to **become less reality-bound.** It means transferring emotions to literary characters. This strategy can also be called **empathetic reading.** Students can learn how to breathe life, feelings, and human emotions into characters that existed ephemerally only as figments of an author's imagination. Some students have difficulty understanding characters because these students are more reality-bound than internally guided (Culp, 1985; Hunt & Vipond, 1985)—in other words, they find it difficult to become personally involved in the story.

Their inability to connect emotionally with characters can also be compounded by a tendency not to select texts that have characters they would want to know—partly because they have not been taught to till the text—and thus they spend more time reading *boring* books and not knowing how to select really good books. In addition, many of these students fail to understand characters' motives because most authors leave these to inference, another strategy that students must engage simultaneously with empathetic reading. Another barrier is that these students rarely stick with a book long enough to truly get to know the characters. To remove this barrier, Comprehension Process Lesson 4 (p. 100) was created. This lesson teaches students the five steps to help them think along with authors as soon as they begin to read.

This lesson teaches students to identify how authors (1) make sentence-to-sentence connections, (2) link paragraphs, (3) create summaries, (4) maintain a consistent depth in their writing, and (5) connect their themes to life and other texts. When students learn this CPA lesson, they can develop an understanding of the depth of writing and author styles that they most enjoy. Without this lesson, students are less likely to vary their reading rates throughout a selection in order to savor certain sentences. Hence, they do not become captivated by the characters (Nell, 1988), and comprehension difficulties increase.

Establishing a Purpose

Establishing a purpose

Another important CPA lesson involves teaching students how to establish their own purposes for reading. To this end, the most important action you can take is not to give students the purpose for reading but to teach them to set their own purposes. When you establish readers' purposes too often, they will not learn to do so themselves—it often takes repeated trials before they trust themselves enough to decide on their own what is important to comprehend. To help them assume such ownership, remind them of the thought processes (listed earlier) that you modeled and instructed. Ask them to scan the text to discern which parts capture their mind and attention. In the process, you can also remind them to be alert to which sections are likely to require more intense concentration for them. Then, ask them to read only the first two pages of the text and then stop. Ask them to look away from the printed page and set their own purposes for this reading. When they do, they will enjoy reading more, and the list in Comprehension Process Lesson 4 (p. 100) can be used repeatedly until the process becomes automatic for all students in your class.

The increased pleasure that arises from using the process of setting one's own purpose is founded on three pillars. First, when students set a purpose after having read two pages, they are less likely to be disappointed that the author did not answer a question they posed. The purpose for reading on will be in line with the author's train of thought. Second, if teachers ask students to set a purpose without reading the first two or so pages, they are likely to set a purpose that they think their teachers want them to set; they have to sacrifice their free choice for the stronger motivator of wanting to please the teacher. Reading for someone else's purpose is less pleasurable than reading for our own goals. Third, if teachers ask students to set a purpose before they have tilled the text reading the first couple of pages first, they force the students to give the most general, lowest-level thinking purpose possible because, if they have to share their purposes orally, they do not want to give a wrong answer before peers. To save face, they give a safe answer and a basic but bland purpose.

Students Trust Their Own Comprehension Processes

Teachers can better understand why self-trust is so difficult for readers who have not been taught CPA lessons when they consider how their attention to print differs from that of readers who are more internally guided. When confusion arises, such students should not focus intently on individual words and letters. Such intense concentration on decoding has repeatedly disappointed them in the past—so they do not really trust themselves to overcome comprehension confusions. When they stop to "sound out" a word and are unable to, they lose meaning and most students merely lift their eyes from the page or press on by pretending to read. Such students will profit from learning to **trust their own tilling** of text. Their processing will illuminate larger meaning-making units. In the process, students come to believe that they are capable of independently guiding themselves away from confusion. With this belief, many students' motivation and drive to guide their own comprehension processes surge. Stress-free reading often results because students have learned how to better allocate their attention to obtain accurate, literal comprehension.

Overcoming Word-Calling

Word-calling is defined as reading every word accurately but not comprehending the meaning. "Word-callers" emerge early, often in first or second grade, partly because CPA lessons were not taught. By third grade, readers are challenged by content that contains words for which they cannot merely guess meanings by using common sense and personal past experiences (Chall, 1998). Also, because they have not been taught the textual differences between expository and narrative text, many content-area readings are too conceptually dense for them to comprehend. Third, because such readers tend to read infrequently, they need the literal comprehension processes presented in this chapter more than avid readers. Less self-selected leisure reading also does not add to their first-hand experiential-knowledge base.

As Adams (1990) and Graves, Cooke, and Laberge (1983) demonstrated, readers who preview a text make better inferences about the material read than those who do not. This previewing strategy assists these readers in relating new vocabulary to overarching concepts. Further, unless these readers learn metacognitive strategies (presented in Chapter 7 of this book), most will resist stopping to reread when they misread or misunderstand (Allington, 2001; Baker & Brown, 1984). Others become so obsessed with reading for accuracy (word-calling) that they literally *forget* to comprehend (Dymock, 1993; Goodman, 1973).

Exposure to predictable or below-grade-level books alone will not eliminate word-calling. These books reinforce readers' ideas that reading should always be predictable from personal experiences and that all words are to be memorized. Therefore, although such books are appropriate in the decoding portion of instruction, they should not be relied on to build comprehension abilities. As a matter of fact, for some readers beyond the second grade, predictable-pattern books reduce comprehension (Roller, 1994). However, when students activate their schemas, they can decode new words and expand their vocabulary. The use of the Sail Away to the Land of Comprehension and Decoding game and the Jeopardy! comprehension game (see Figures 4.2 and 4.3) help students overcome word-calling. They do so because they emphasize the connections among words within sentences.

Directions: Have students play this game with a partner after they have read different books. Each student can use the book to help him or her answer the questions. This game focuses on both comprehension and decoding. For every question answered correctly without the book, the child gets two points; if the book is used, one point is received. The child moves through the entire game board, completing each question. Students complete the scorecard to see who wins with the most points. The spaces on the board that contain only sailboats can be used to add questions for any individual lessons being taught. For example, if you were learning about nouns, every time a player landed on a sailboat she or he would have to say a noun.

Sail Away to the Land of Comprehension and Decoding

5 Sound out three words from your spelling list slowly and give their meanings.

6 What problem did your character have? Why did he or she have this problem?

7 How did the character solve the problem?

The Land of Comprehension and Decoding

3 Write a paragraph that uses at least five of your spelling words.

8 Write three words in parts, if they are made of more than one syllable. This will help you learn the meaning of long words.

12 How did this story make you feel?

14 Put the main character in our class. Write a paragraph long story about what might happen.

9 What was your favorite part of the book? Why?

4 What clue did the sentence give you for a word you didn't know?

11 Spell three words from your list outloud, without looking. This will help you picture words in your mind.

10 Does your list of words contain any rhyming words? If not, write a rhyming word for three words on your list.

3 Where did the story take place? Why is it important that it took place there?

2 Write 10 words you found that you might have trouble spelling.

1 Who was the main character in your book? What kind of character was he or she?

START

FIGURE 4.2 Sail Away to the Land of Comprehension and Decoding

Source: Developed by Christine Cullen, elementary education major with reading specialization, Texas Christian University, Fort Worth, Texas. Used by permission.

Scorecard

• Circle the number of points received for each question

Sailboat 1

Sailboat 2

Player's name: _____   Player's name: _____

	Looked at the book	Answered without the book
Question 1	1	2
2	1	2
3	1	2
4	1	2
5	1	2
6	1	2
7	1	2
8	1	2
9	1	2
10	1	2
11	1	2
12	1	2
13	1	2
14	1	2
Total	☐ +	☐ =

	Looked at the book	Answered without the book
Question 1	1	2
2	1	2
3	1	2
4	1	2
5	1	2
6	1	2
7	1	2
8	1	2
9	1	2
10	1	2
11	1	2
12	1	2
13	1	2
14	1	2
Total	☐ +	☐ =

FIGURE 4.2   Continued

Expanding Content Specific Vocabulary

Expanding content specific vocabulary

Dear Mrs. J.,

I think my vocabulary is growing. I read much faster now. I feel my eyes move across each line. I'm not afraid of trying any book in the library. Also, sometimes when I talk, I hear myself use words I've never used before. Even my parents noticed [that] I speak differently.

Love,
Marie (Stiles, 1991, p. 31)

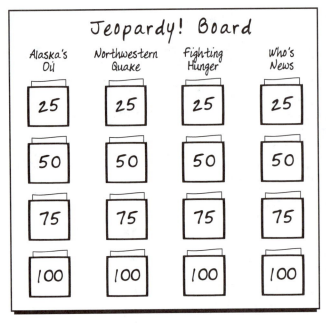

Create a Jeopardy! board using library pockets, index cards, and velcro. Write questions on index cards and the values of the questions on index cards and place them in the same pocket. If a student gets the question correct, the student receives the index card with the value of the question on it. The student with the most points wins. The student is allowed to use the book or magazines to look up an answer only one time. It serves as a "lifeline" for the questions that are difficult.

FIGURE 4.3 Jeopardy! Comprehension Game

Source: Developed by Cherie Canady. Used by permission.

Appropriate vocabulary instruction increases students' comprehension abilities (Nagy & Herman, 1987). Students learn more new words through directed vocabulary instruction than when left alone to learn new terms in independent reading (Carver, 1994, 1995; Nagy & Herman, 1987). Without instruction, it would take most readers about 12 years of reading 2,000 words daily, and learning the meanings of at least seven new vocabulary words each day, to reach the level of reading vocabulary that fluent readers possess by fourth grade. Thus, without the activities in this chapter, many readers may never develop the vocabulary needed to fully appreciate and enjoy reading materials at and above fifth grade readability (Nagy & Herman, 1987). Optimal vocabulary instruction includes only those words central to the theme and purpose of specific reading selections (Beck, McKeown, Hamilton, & Kucan, 1997). Such instruction should occur in the context of sentences that are relevant to both the text and the students (Nagy & Herman, 1987). Moreover, when words are taught thoroughly so that readers recognize relationships between new terms, they can more frequently supply their own meanings for them.

Lessons should identify words that readers want to learn and think are important (Adams, 1990). Instruction should also include postreading activities in which readers can return to new terms as they read to add connotations they create (Beck, McKeown, Hamilton, & Kucan, 1997). Another guiding principle is that "word mastery is a matter of degree" (Dymock, 1993, p. 93). Instruction that calls for deep application of words in multiple contexts when they are introduced is more durable, creates more affinity for reading (Mezynski, 1983; Stahl & Fairbanks, 1986), and increases the enjoyment of students' writing experiences (Duin & Graves, 1987). McKenna, Robinson, & Miller (1993) describe multiple lessons that can be used to build vocabulary in their book entitled *Teaching through Text*.

Once readers cultivate a method of vocabulary development they prefer, they frequently can guide their literal comprehension successfully. Metaphors provide a rich venue in which such instruction can occur. In addition to the lessons that follow, Kirby has written several books entitled *Mind Matters* (1994) that provide additional practice in processing metaphors.

Literal Comprehension Lesson 1: It's Kind of Like. . . . Students can learn how to ask themselves the following questions to learn new words:

What is it kind of like?

When would I use it in my life?

What is it a part of?

What function does it normally perform? (Is it a naming, painting, or doing word?)

When you say "It's kind of like _____" to introduce new words prior to reading, you encourage students to volunteer answers to each of these questions, in a group session, to develop their automatic reference to context clues when they read silently. Through this sharing of peers' ideas, students apply new words to their lives.

Instead of Building Background, Teach Students How to Let Background Build

Instead of building background, teach students how to let background build

You can teach students how to build background rather than teachers building their background for them. Students can be taught how to construct connections in paragraphs as described previously. In many classrooms today, curricula do not develop students' abilities to recognize the frameworks on which genres are built (National Reading Panel, 1999). When students recognize these frameworks, they can practice more than one type of thinking about genre as they read. Students must be taught how to use these frameworks. As Durkin (1981) discovered, past curriculum has not provided such instruction. The strategies presented in this chapter must be included more frequently in teachers' manuals of basal readers. Furthermore, research by Wiley and Voss (1999) indicates that even good teacher preparation programs are merely telling educators what comprehension is rather than teaching them how to teach comprehension processes for specific texts.

Students learn how to let comprehension build as they move across any part of a curriculum by employing a forward-looking stance as they read. Students can learn that curriculum functions as a bridge. Each new section they read serves as a bridge connecting what they already know with what the authors want them to understand. Curriculum must challenge students to use their background knowledge as a means of moving them across the bridge. As they read, students accompany the author across the bridge, while students' thinking processes occur. Curriculum itself provides the support across a strong bridge. This support enables the author's and student's thinking to reach a new level of knowledge. Because the author's and student's thinking is so similar, the new knowledge created will be more encompassing because the student would have met with fewer misunderstandings and omissions in the process. If students make interactive links between paragraphs during the reading process, the author and student will dialogue mentally as they travel across the curriculum.

In addition, when students use three levels of meaning making, as curriculum unfolds and interacts with their ability to attach relevant pieces of information to recent and long-standing strands of background knowledge, fewer important facts are discarded. In the process, when a misunderstanding occurs students stop, reverse, and jump back to where they expected to receive a particular type of information. The first step involves teaching students how to estimate the location of new information. Second, pupils must be taught how to make a lattice of interactive thoughts to search ahead for new knowledge in their reading (Taylor, Graves, & van de Broek, 2000). Unfortunately, when these processes are not demonstrated and practiced in rich curriculum, less able readers tend not to notice markers along curricula bridges. Instead, they opt to go to their lives to fill gaps in their reading comprehension. Their dialogue with the author ends. Oftentimes, they will even "get out of the car" (book) and leave the car stranded halfway across the bridge, guessing from their own experiences alone what the ending will be.

The more automatically appropriate prior knowledge can be elicited while reading, the more comprehension increases. Many readers are unable to continuously elicit these knowledge sources because

- Their out-of-school, culturally driven experiences are too disparate from school texts;
- Text is not clearly written so that it moves distinctly from point to point;
- Vocabulary introduced prior to reading does not relate to the central idea of the book (e.g., teachers cannot introduce *all* the words that might cause trouble); or
- Metacognition is not engaged so that word recognition errors are left uncorrected (Palinscar & Brown, 1984).

Equally important, such readers may need to be taught how to recognize when their prior knowledge contains naïve or incorrect information. In the process, they must learn how to reconcile successfully new and conflicting information. Without this instruction, some students will either ignore new vocabulary because they believe they already have the needed information, or, when a conflict in information occurs, they stop thinking about what they are reading. Equally damaging, today's proficient readers are learning to flexibly adjust their search strategies to fit only their own, prior-to-interacting-with-a-particular-curriculum goal of retrieving only information that is most salient and applying it to their lives in a decontextualized, and less valid form. Many students have not been taught how to think about experiences they have had with a specific topic in conjunction with, and not separate from, the author's theme. As Beck, Omanson, and McKeown (1982) demonstrated, it is not background knowledge in general but knowledge about important story ideas in particular that influence comprehension.

Method 1.   To help students discern naïve background knowledge you can

1. Demonstrate how they can probe their beliefs prior to reading;
2. Model how you know when your background experiences are inadequate to "read between the lines" in a book;
3. Encourage students to place themselves in the story; or
4. Identify the questions they want to ask while they read.

Method 2.   To build background knowledge, you can use a reading log to help students activate their schemas and to ask what they are thinking as they read. For example, if students can identify what background knowledge they are applying at a particular point in a text, they can better understand whether that knowledge is adequate for reflecting about the material and remembering more of what they read. Similarly, once they learn to make predictions as they read, they can determine whether initial predictions were accurate. If they were, they know their background knowledge is interacting with the author's.

Method 3.   Teach students to integrate two processes together as they build background knowledge and set their own purposes for reading. In a study by Hansen and Pearson (1983), fourth-grade strong and weak readers were taught to participate in a prereading discussion designed to teach them how to (1) generate expectations about what the story characters might do based on their own experiences in similar situations and (2) continually make inferences about the story. Such integration required background knowledge to be tied specifically to textual ideas. This technique lead to improved comprehension by young and poor readers on a variety of measures, including the comprehension of new, uninstructed stories about similar curriculum. More importantly, trained but less able readers' performances were indistinguishable from the performance of strong readers who were merely given instructions about what to comprehend, as is often done in building students' background activities in basal readers.

Block (2001b) and Blanton, Wood, and Moorman (1990) have demonstrated the benefits of teaching students to integrate the setting of their own purposes with building background knowledge. Even before expert readers begin the first sentence of a text, they have thought about how to approach that curriculum to attain a rich reading experience, based on achieving their own goals, within the context of the author's theme, purpose, and writing style. To teach how to set a purpose, you can sit beside them as they practice it. Ask them to describe what they thought as they were beginning to make meaning in a specific genre. When you allow them to have at least five days of experience with a particular curriculum or author study, they can diagram that author's writing structure or the story grammar of that specific genre.

They can also use an author's study chart paper in group settings to accomplish the same objective. Doing so increases the probability that they will make all future curriculum simultaneously context free and context bound efferently (responding to information to gain cognitive knowledge) and affectively (having an emotional, value-laden response to a curriculum). Dowhower (1999) also demonstrated that it is important for students to talk about how they had done this. When such lessons occur, students increase their abilities to think about two processes in relationship to each other. You will notice their automaticity in their written think-alouds, as they complete the comprehension process approach lesson in Figure 4.4. Soon students can complete the comprehension process approach lesson each time they read, and they will be able to read many different genre structures.

Rowler (1990) argued that when children are taught that the last word they read could be background knowledge for the next word, they are better able to comprehend a text. This instruction proved to be more powerful than building students' background using traditional means, such as teaching new vocabulary words and discussing the topic to be read. To illustrate, when children were taught to think about all they knew about

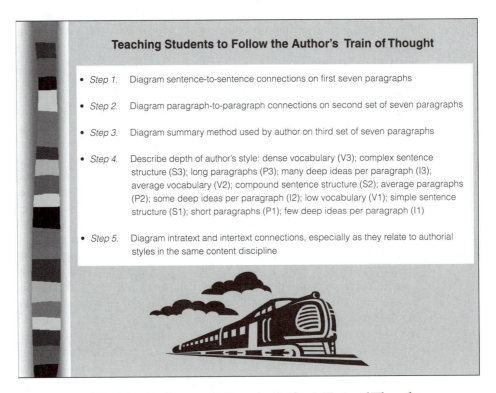

Teaching Students to Follow the Author's Train of Thought

- *Step 1.*   Diagram sentence-to-sentence connections on first seven paragraphs

- *Step 2.*   Diagram paragraph-to-paragraph connections on second set of seven paragraphs

- *Step 3.*   Diagram summary method used by author on third set of seven paragraphs

- *Step 4.*   Describe depth of author's style: dense vocabulary (V3); complex sentence structure (S3); long paragraphs (P3); many deep ideas per paragraph (I3); average vocabulary (V2); compound sentence structure (S2); average paragraphs (P2); some deep ideas per paragraph (I2); low vocabulary (V1); simple sentence structure (S1); short paragraphs (P1); few deep ideas per paragraph (I1)

- *Step 5.*   Diagram intratext and intertext connections, especially as they relate to authorial styles in the same content discipline

FIGURE 4.4   Teaching Students to Follow the Author's Train of Thought

the Revolutionary War, they did not increase their comprehension as much as when they were taught to think about what the last sentence they read might have to do with the next sentence that was about to unfold (Beck et al., 1991). The inability to use immediate background knowledge in a particular selection of curriculum is at least as important as alerting children to the necessity of making a context-bound global image in their mind for full comprehension.

Another deficit of building background knowledge through traditional methods is that teachers tend to impose their own structure and thinking processes on students. Teachers' organizational processes may be disadvantageous. The criteria that teachers use to judge relevance may not be the same ones that students prefer. Students cannot use the salient information that is most important and they become confused because they cannot use the preferred method of making connections between sentences. As a result, they become disinterested and unmotivated and they do not enjoy the reading process. Alternatively, students who can create their own organization for the material to be read can conduct their own dialogue with the author as they progress through a text. They are aware of the barriers, supports, and symbols in the material to process information appropriately. When students work together, they get the benefit of a full group of students having a collective body of prior experiences to interrelate that far exceeds any individual's, which can be a very positive experience in small group work.

In summary, we can no longer help students build background knowledge merely by giving instruction about how we want them to build it; students can let background knowledge build by using curriculum as a bridge. As they move from their bank of background knowledge to specific sentences, the curriculum bridge begins to build. Students must think of material they have just read in a single sentence as new background knowledge. These are connected to the next sentences and the next paragraphs. Teachers must teach how to construct a mental image that is context bound and context free. It is not as important for us to build students' existing knowledge as for them to become aware of their prior knowledge and how to use that information with unfolding curriculum and comprehension processes interactively.

Instead of Finding the Main Idea, Teach Students How Main Ideas Find Them

Instead of finding the main idea, teach students how main ideas find them

Research demonstrates that students cannot identify main ideas easily, particularly if they are not stated directly. For this reason, instructions in curricula significantly influence how children select the most important points in a reading (Pearson & Fielding, 1991). Children should no longer be taught how to find a main idea but rather they should be taught the steps that enable authors' main ideas to emerge in students' mental images. Such teaching would be easier if every curricular paragraph contained a directly stated main idea, and a synthesizing, global idea appeared at every reading's end. Because texts are incomplete, main ideas usually emerge when readers fill gaps and link knowledge in an ongoing comprehension process (Kintsch, 1998).

Without effective curricular instructions, readers only deduce a series of unrelated, knowledge-derived thoughts (chains of single sentences that are connected only when teachers provide a structure through questions posed following a reading).

In addition, if a reader has limited relevant background knowledge, or does not understand a particular word, the main ideas taken from any paragraph will likely be only the literal meanings in the single words that came before the unknown word (Block & Pressley, 2002). At the other extreme, if the reader has extensive background knowledge, but the curriculum is poorly written or disorganized, this student's background experiences will dominate the mental images retained from the text. The following methods enable students to unite background knowledge with text-driven ideas as they read so that comprehension and retention increase.

Teach students to think about two processes at once so main ideas become apparent. The most innovative findings from most recent research suggest that for students to begin to find main ideas easily and repeatedly they must be taught how to use two comprehension processes in conjunction as they read (Greene, Thapar, & Westerman, 1998; Haberlandt & Graesser, 1985). By attending to two different aspects from which ideas flow, children are more likely to retain the central focus of a paragraph (e.g., attending to the author's sea of thought and sequence words).

To illustrate, first you would demonstrate how to make two different predictions as to what the next sentence would be. Later, you would vary and intensify the task by asking what the next idea or action in the next paragraph would be. Tell them that thinking of two possibilities enables readers to create a thought anchor (the nucleus of a main idea or thought to which the mind first references when thinking back on material read previously). As they read on, students attend to details that most easily attach to this thought anchor. These details begin to develop the format of the discourse that the author is building to move his or her thought process along in that particular genre. As students become aware of the relationship between the author's relevant details and thought anchors, their abilities to make predictions of the next sequence of details or events is likely to improve. Their abilities to find main ideas will improve as well.

This instructional session does not rely on artificial teaching aids, such as a worksheet where students list who, what, where, and when to eliminate details or an outline where they list one, two, three, four, which are not usually available when children are outside of the classroom. Students begin to *truly* find main ideas through this lesson.

To review, readers should not be taught separate skills as in the past such as circling the main idea sentence on a worksheet, underlining a topic word, or locating "who did what, to whom, when, and where." Instead, they should be taught thinking processes. Comprehension processes (1) involve intentional and deliberate strategic decisions, (2) involve flexible and interrelated thinking, (3) employ reasoning, and (4) involve metacognition (Dole, Duffy, Roehler, & Pearson, 1991). **Metacognition** refers to two types of thought processes: (1) being aware of what one is thinking and why a person is thinking about it during a reading, and (2) controlling one's own reading so that disruptions in comprehension are overcome through internally guided, self-guided decisions during reading (Baker & Brown, 1984; Jacobs & Paris, 1987).

Several studies have shown that less able readers have no knowledge of how to consciously organize metacognitions while reading. They do not know how to eliminate interruptions in meaning making (Block, 1993; Johnson, 1985; Palincsar & Brown 1984). Whereas expert readers use the following processes without being instructed to do so (Collins, 1991; Johnston & Winograd, 1985), unless you teach comprehension processes to less able readers, they often infer that simply putting the meanings of individual words together is the ultimate outcome of reading. Moreover, many will have great difficulty integrating efferent and aesthetical thoughts (Block, 1993; Borkowski, Carr, Rellinger, & Pressley, 1990; Scardamalia & Bereiter, 1987; Alexander,1992; Wood, 2002).

Students will learn these strategies faster if they are presented through direct instruction, using graphic and descriptive illustrations (thinking guides), and if you explain why a strategy is useful and describe the types of reading situations where they will be most effective (Block & Mangieri, 1996; Schunk & Rice, 1991).

Literal Comprehension Lesson 2: Explaining.   When readers are asked to explain their metacognitive thinking process, comprehension is enhanced (Block, 1993; Block & Mangieri, 1995/1996; King, 1994; Pressley et al., 1989). This occurs because in the description, details in the thinking processes become salient. Important details in the text are relived as well. You can assist students' detail recognition by telling them that the purpose of details is to identify who, what, where, when, how, and why, relative to reasons, actions, and ideas. You should not, however, ask students to locate specific details because this is a skill and not an authentic reading process. Instead, ask readers to point out details they found important, interesting, effective, suspenseful, creative, or humorous as they describe what they were thinking as they read. Then, if students desire, they can analyze the differences that exist between details that they did and did not remember. Also, students can discuss what characterizes the most effective way to use details for explanations. Students can then practice giving effective explanations that incorporate the following principles:

- Explanations do not simply tell what something is or describe it; they tell the *how* and *why* about it.
- Explanations should be in students' own words—not simply a repetition of something heard and memorized.
- When teachers explain something, it is often helpful to use information that is already known to make the explanation clearer, comparing the new information to something students already know.

Literal Comprehension Lesson 3: Summarizing.   When readers learn to make mental and written summaries of their readings, retention increases by 14 percent, on the average (Block & Mangieri, 1996; Stein & Kirby, 1992). Summaries become our record keepers of thoughts, which enhances the application of reading to life. An effective activity to establish the summarization strategy is to use the **KWL plus strategy sheet** (Know-Want-Learn) shown in Table 4.1. In the two left columns of the KWL plus strategy sheet (Ogle, 1986), students list what they know prior to reading and what they want to find out. In the third column, they put what they learned or still want to learn after they have read. As shown in Table 4.1 (which a group of fourth-grade readers completed

TABLE 4.1   KWL Strategy Sheet*

What We Know	What We Want to Find Out	What We Learned or Still Need to Learn
1. Volcanoes erupt. 2. Lava comes out. 3. Mount St. Helens is in Washington state. 4. Lava is molten rock.	1. Why it erupted? 2. Will it erupt again? 3. Was anyone killed? 4. What do animals do when a volcano erupts?	1. Differences between igneous, metamorphic, and sedimentary rocks and soil. 2. Shifting in continental plates causes eruptions. 3. It has erupted only once in 150 years (about). 4. 57 people died. 5. Animals fled or were killed by lava, heat, or "stone winds." 6. It took a long time for animals and plants to grow back but some, like insects, moss, fungi, and woodpeckers, came back soon.

Categories of Information We Expect to Use in Our Report and Future Reading:

A. Description of how volcanoes erupt
B. How people and animals die
C. How terrains change after a volcano
D. Types of animals that came back first
E. Plants that came back first
F. How we can avoid losses of lives of people, plants, and animals in the future
G. Predict how long it will take before Mount St. Helens is back to top form

Summary of What We Learned:

Volcano taught us why Mount St. Helens erupted, what happened when it did, and how it is healing itself with the help of nature, man, animals, and plants.

---

*Completed by a group of fourth-grade students before and after reading *Volcano: the Eruption and Healing of Mount St. Helens.*

Source: Adapted from Ogle, Donna M. (1986, February). K-W-L: A teaching model that develops active reading of expository text. *The Reading Teacher, 39*(6), 564–570. Reprinted with permission of the International Reading Association.

before and after reading the Newbery Honor Medal book *Volcano: The Eruption and Healing of Mount St. Helens)*, this strategy increased students' active thinking while they read, as demonstrated by the summary at the bottom of the table.

Next, you can also teach readers to write summaries about their reading using the comprehension process approach lesson shown in Figure 4.5. This example was created by second graders as they read the first three pages of *The Velveteen Rabbit.*

1. **Delete duplication.** ⋯⋯⋯⋯⋯⋯⋯⋯⋯⋯⋯⋯⋯⋯⋯⋯

- *Example:* There was a rabbit and in the beginning he was really splendid. He was fat and bunchy as a rabbit should be.

- *Summary:* The splendid rabbit was fat and bunchy.

2. **Combine ideas with the same subject.** ⋯⋯⋯⋯⋯⋯⋯

- *Example:* He had a brown coat with white spots. He had thread whiskers and his ears were lined with pink satin. His spots made him stand out among plain red stockings.

- *Summary:* His brown coat, white spots, and pink-lined ears made him stand out among the plain red stockings.

3. **Restate in fewer words.** ⋯⋯⋯⋯⋯⋯⋯⋯⋯⋯⋯⋯⋯⋯

- *Example:* There were other things in the stocking: nuts and oranges, and a toy engine, and chocolate almonds, a mouse and candy canes; but the rabbit was the best of all.

- *Summary:* The stocking was filled with Christmas treats, but the rabbit was the best gift.

4. **Use summary words.** ⋯⋯⋯⋯⋯⋯⋯⋯⋯⋯⋯⋯⋯⋯⋯

- *Example:* Summary words include *almost all, in conclusion, in brief, the main point, on the whole, ultimately, to sum up.*

5. **Remove details that are not about the main subject.** ⋯⋯⋯⋯⋯

- *Example:* On Christmas morning when he sat wedged in the top of the boy's stocking with a sprig of holly between his paws, the velveteen rabbit looked charming.

- *Summary:* The velveteen rabbit looked charming.

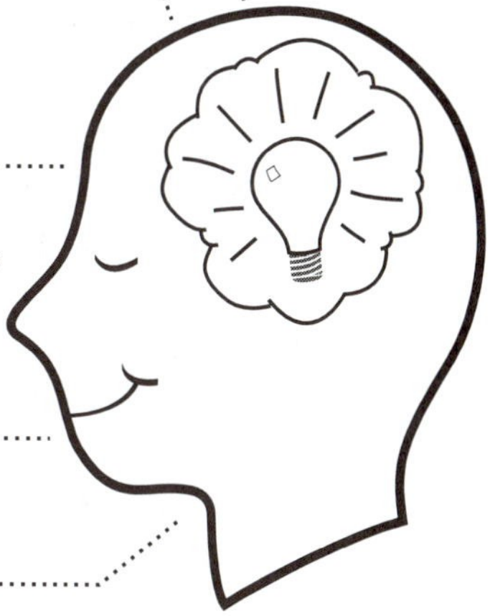

FIGURE 4.5   Comprehension Process Approach Thinking Guide for Summarizing

Source: Reason to Read, Volume 2 (p. 138) by Cathy Collins Block and John Mangieri. Copyright © 1995 by Pearson Education, Inc., publishing as Dale Seymour Publications. Used by permission.

These two lessons are so valuable because in writing their summaries, students are reviewing material read and learning to shift main ideas to the forefront: two processes many readers need to improve their literal comprehension.

Literal Comprehension Lesson 4: Reciprocal Teaching.   **Reciprocal teaching** is a procedure that assists readers in integrating the strategies of asking questions, summarizing, clarifying, and predicting (Palinscar & Brown, 1984). In this activity, students become the teachers and report their metacognitive thinking to peers. As each student completes a turn at teaching, he or she selects the next teacher by asking, "Who will be the next teacher?" Through this control, readers' self-esteem increases as they choose to help others and share when they are ready.

A reciprocal teaching activity begins when you (and subsequently each student who becomes the teacher) initiate a discussion about the next section of a text to be read and ask questions about its content. The group discusses the questions, raises additional ones, and resolves disagreements by reading the text. Next, the discussion leader summarizes to identify the gist of what was read, clarifies words and ideas that others misunderstood, and predicts upcoming content. After others share their predictions, the leader asks a peer to lead the discussion of the next section of text, as illustrated in this scenario:

> *Mrs. Mackey:*   (reading the following text) The pipefish changes its color and movements to blend with its surroundings. For example, a pipefish that lives among green plants changes its color to a shade of green to match the plants.
>
> *Clare:*   (the student teacher is leading the discussion): One question that I had about this paragraph is, what is special about the way that the pipefish looks?
>
> *Keith:*   (clarifying) Do you mean the way that it is green?
>
> *Andy:*   (elaborating) It's not just that it's green; it's that it's the same color as the plants around it, all around it.
>
> *Clare:*   (resuming) Yes. That's it. My summary is that this part tells how the pipefish looks and that it looks like what is around it. My prediction is that the next part will be about its enemies and how it protects itself and who these enemies are.
>
> *Monty:*   (adding to Clare's summary) They also talked about how the pipefish moves.
>
> *Keith:*   (rejoining) It sways back and forth.
>
> *Andy:*   (adding) Along with the other plants.
>
> *Mrs. Mackey:*   OK! Let's see if Clare's predictions come true. Who will be the teacher? (Hiebert, 1991, p. 125)

Reciprocal teaching models competent use of comprehension and metacognition processes. It also supports students' efforts to explain text; pushes for deeper understanding, reflection, and metacognition; consciously releases more control of comprehension to students; and increases students' abilities to lead discussions in groups.

Literal Comprehension Lesson 5 "You Be the Counselor."   This lesson builds metacognition. It enables readers to walk in another person's shoes and to think as that person thinks. The purpose of **"you be the counselor"** is to assist readers in understanding the reasons behind literary characters' actions; to separate facts from opinions and assumptions; and to question these facts, assumptions, and beliefs as they read. In this lesson, you ask students to assume that a fictional character came to them for advice. Students being the counselors helps them connect their thoughts to the story in several ways. First, students must place themselves in the story and identify with the main character's emotions, motives, and actions. Second, students must discern how their opinions, emotions, and responses to the events in the story will likely differ from the main character's. Last, most will imagine a future event upon which their advice and projections rest. The more frequently students practice these metacognitions through repeated participation in this activity, the more rapidly these strategies become a part of their automatic comprehension processes.

Using Comprehension Processes Synergistically

Internally guided comprehenders are more flexible in their thinking processes than weak readers. They are more likely to activate a variety of processes when texts become difficult (Kletzien, 1991). The following activities increase these readers' abilities to use comprehension processes interrelatedly. Weaker comprehenders prosper by repeating these activities frequently.

Literal Comprehension Lesson 6: Tape Recording Improvements. Tape recording can be used as an assessment before and after using the activities in this chapter. It consists of asking students to select books they would like to read and tape recording their readings for 1 minute. At the end of this time, students reveal what they thought about their reading and the content of the book. Tape record these answers immediately following the reading so that levels of each student's comprehension, understanding, and strategic reading are documented. Next, you can ask each student to return to his or her seat and count the total number of words he or she read as well as the average number of words per page in the book that the student selected. Then, students write this information (along with the counter numbers on the tape in which their reading can be found) in their portfolio or on a record form to be kept until the end of the year. Last, before calling the next student to perform the tape recorded reading, fast forward the tape recorder for three times the number of counter spaces each student's readings and answers used. In this way, you have blank spaces between each student's readings so that at the end of the school year, posttest readings can be recorded on the tape immediately following the student's first reading.

After you have taught all the lessons in this chapter, you can reimplement this lesson, allowing students to choose any book they would like to read. Ask them to describe what they were thinking as they read and what they think about the content of the book, just as before. When each student has finished, ask him or her to again count total number of words read as well as the average number of words per page of the book selected. Then, you and the student can assess growth in readability of books chosen and number of miscues in oral readings on pre- and post readings by rewinding the tape and listening to both readings back to back. Most students want to hear both the pretest and posttest recordings, but some want to listen to the posttest only.

Literal Comprehension Lesson 7: Literal Understanding of an Entire Text. When students are able to grasp an author's sea of thought, the main purpose of the author's writing, they must take the whole body of knowledge that they have gleaned throughout the entire text into account. Students have text-based information that is directly expressed by the author literally, but it must be organized and structured in such a way that it contains two features. First, according to Kintsch (2000), students must follow the local structure or the microstructure that the author has used to put single words, sentences, and paragraphs together. Second, they must develop a global structure or the microstructure. This is the structure of how rapidly the author unfolds events and facts that lay in the central theme. When students are able to construct this text-based knowledge, the extraction of literal information from a text develops more easily. In the CI model, this takes the form of interrelated networks of proposition. Thus, the comprehension process of transforming words into literal meaning involves a certain amount of inferential reflective activity at the same time.

These reflections can be as simple as determining the reference for a single pronoun, so that the student identifies a word that is not stated, or recognizing synonyms in order to fill in glaring gaps that the author intended so that their work on the global structure is complete. Also, students have to bridge large inferences between paragraphs as time lapses occur. The result will be a globally and locally well-structured representation of the text so that it can be processed in memory and retained. In general, researchers have found that people remember information that they have actively generated better than information that has been presented to them, and they are better able to put such knowledge to use in novel situations (Kintsch, 1998) for a summary of this information.

Recent research indicates that one of the most important reasons students fail to determine a literal understanding from a text is that they are unable to form a coherent text mentally and link it to their prereading knowledge base (Kintsch, 1998). In one study, 340 students were asked why they were unable to comprehend. Findings indicate students wanted teachers to (1) explain comprehension processes more, (2) tell them more about the books they are about to read, (3) sound out words and letters and explain what individual words were until they could understand them unaided, (4) explain directions until they could completely understand them, and (5) let them read information at home after they had read them at school (Block, 2001a).

Nonfiction requires special types of instruction. The first step that must be taken is to match the after-reading comprehension measure with the instructions given to students about what they were to focus on while reading. For example, if, prior to reading, a student is told to summarize a text, to build a schematic representation of the text, or to categorize ideas by level of importance in the text, comprehension will improve most relative to that outcome (Ambruster, 1991; Pearson & Fielding, 1991).

Students who are knowledgeable about and able to follow the text structure and the author's sea of knowledge can recall text more easily than those who are not (Mackey, 1998; Richgels, Mackey, Lomax, & Shepard, 1997). More good than poor readers are able to do this with instruction (Taylor, 1980). Story structure has been noted both to increase literal comprehension of specific stories and to transfer it to other texts (Pearson & Fielding, 1994). Several problems have emerged that limit children's ability to make connections and to comprehend literally from the beginning to the end of a single book or chapter. Doane, McNamara, and Kintsch (2000) discovered that readers get help from abstract statements that can help them interpret literal comprehension of sentences that followed. Unfortunately, such statements are less worthwhile for students who are less able readers. So that as far as can be demonstrated less expert readers need events and prompts that tell the order in which events occur.

When such prompts are given, students are able to retain information they have learned on a literal level. Researchers also have discovered that when information is so vague that students cannot comprehend they tend to make substitutions. There is a rise in substitution errors because better readers tend to be able to guess or carry on the message even if they are at the frustration level of comprehending. These substitutions serve an important function for less able readers because they have not been successful and cannot invest more knowledge to make these conceptual jumps in inferencing from their own preknowledge or from the knowledge that they are able to gain from the author. For those reasons it is important to allow students to learn how to actively process their own path of generating information and fill in gaps.

When they lack a local as well as a global coherence of text, it is important to allow them to stimulate their own active processing. When they do, recall of text and of the literal propositions, single sentences, paragraphs, and full bodies of text improves (McNamara & Kintsch, 2000). It is important to note, however, that the ability to do so involves students' ability to sort out single facts and to make inferences to leap over conceptual gaps so that they can generate their own mental picture and macrostructure of the text they are processing. Thus, rather than using a full coherent text read to them where we fill in all of the inferential gaps, many students learn better when they have to provide the coherence itself both at the local and global level. That is, in the future when students are having difficulty with text, it will be important to teach them to stimulate their own ability to leap over coherence gaps and to develop their own bridges in the text, to provide their own comprehension processes, and to form a macrostructure that makes sense to them. When students become active processors during reading they are making the text conceptually coherent themselves and they are going to build a macrostructure just like expert readers do. This macrostructure will enable them to understand the local level knowledge better at the sentence and paragraph level.

Literal Comprehension Lesson 8: Teaching Intertextual Literal Understanding. Once students develop the interest and ability to understand single books, often their interest increases. It is important for students to learn how to use the literal understanding they gain from sentences, paragraphs, and whole texts and to transfer it to a domain of knowledge (i.e., understanding life cycles) in which they can gain more expertise. The depth of a student's domain knowledge is a discriminate factor in determining whether someone becomes a good literal comprehender (Kintsch, 1998). Readers with a high level of domain knowledge can take literal content from one text to another. They can understand new texts better and retain more information than peers who do not possess such a high level of domain knowledge.

Three factors determine how much literal information is remembered. First, students who gain a successful coherence of an author's message in one text about a topic will retain significantly more information from subsequent texts on the same topic. Second, if a first text was well organized and had strong stylistic features that frequently occur in writing from that specific discipline, student retention will increase when they read another text about that domain of knowledge (Block, in press). Third, if the readability of a text is appropriate, students will comprehend more.

If multiple texts are used in a thematic study, students need to be taught how to read across texts. This is a difficult comprehension process. Students must answer a question using one source and compare that answer to the same question in another text. As a first step, students mimic this comparative thinking process in future readings of early chapters in books. The second step is to teach students how to develop a critical approach to reading a second book on the same topic. They must learn to disregard incomplete prior knowledge and substitute more complete understandings. They must gather information, synthesize, and evaluate more often when they read a second and third text on the same topic because they will have a richer knowledge base of support with which to begin. As a result, they can selectively combine facts and move beyond merely trying to grasp all knowledge on a page in a quest to obtain a critical mass of information on a subject.

Chi, Slotta, and deLeeuw (1994) noticed that novices have more difficulty in acquiring abstract than concrete facts from multiple texts. They also cannot synthesize knowledge unless they have been taught how to disregard incomplete or inaccurate interpretations from prior readings and substitute newer, more accurate, integrated thoughts. Finally, they must learn how to keep the new inflow of information in a temporary state until they can synthesize it into a stable, coherent schema. Incoming data from a second text will not yet have been verified to determine whether the new knowledge is better than the knowledge they currently hold. This three-stage, interrelated comprehension processing for intertextual understandings can be developed by teaching knowledge structures.

Knowledge structures are knowledge schemas that go beyond an understanding of an author's or a discipline's preferred writing style relative to syntax and semantic links. Knowledge structures involve the generation of thinking processes to resolve difficulties or changes in content direction in a text's content and answer questions that arise in a reader's mind as a reading unfolds. One way to expand knowledge structures involves asking students to perform think-alouds of what they processed from texts at the end of two pages of a reading. A second way is to teach students to engage their sequencing processes with the goal of placing temporary knowledge units into clumps that can easily be stored in short-term memory until it can be verified. You can assist students by teaching them that at the same time that they are making these clumps, they must sustain their quest to reach their own purpose-setting goal. Doing so increases the energy that they are investing in their comprehension processes, which will result in making rapid links between new information and the author's sea of thought, former content knowledge structures from prior readings, and genre syntactic and semantic clues.

Wiley and Voss (1999) developed a third method of making intertextual knowledge structures stronger. They demonstrated that giving three choices of what students want to improve in comprehension ability, combined with multiple sources, makes for a learning context that promotes highly constructive activity on the part of the learner. They also proved that merely giving more facts to weaker comprehenders does not make their comprehension better. Merely giving them a book to read that contains more facts than the last book they read will not ensure that they are understanding the text or that they are able to apply their domain knowledge to the new text. In addition, if the amount of knowledge they are given is not as in-depth, they will not put forth the effort to become active processors. This is the argument posed by those who disagree with using easy texts to increase comprehension ability (Doane, McNamara, Kintsch, Polson, & Clawson, 1992).

Similarly, teachers cannot simply list the events in a story as a recall task or present the task in sequential order from a fictional text and tell a novice the order in which events in the story will occur. By telling the main events in advance, teachers inadvertently decrease the amount of energy that students have to use to make causal links themselves, and limit the amount of practice they have in developing knowledge structures that they build to create more coherent domain knowledge bases independently. To move away from this "telling," the length of the directions to be given must be determined. If students are overtaxed because of the amount of information they are asked to process, working memory freezes, and substitution miscues increase. Teachers should also be available to answer students' questions when reading silently or in Strand 2 lessons.

Literal Comprehension Lesson 9: Asking Questions to Increase Literal Comprehension.   As discussed in Chapter 3, it is important to teach students to ask themselves questions about content as they read. Graesser, Lang, & Roberts (1991) discovered that good literal questions give answers that can be found in the text. Because literal knowledge occurs in phrases, or arcs of meaning units, it is important to teach children to ask questions that can be answered within the next arc of incoming text. To teach students to ask such questions, you can demonstrate through modeling the types of questions that you ask yourself when you read. For example, you could introduce the book, written in poetry format, entitled *The Whales* by Cynthia Rylant. In the first page of that book the author describes the blackness of the Black Sea and wonders what the whales are thinking today. You could then stop reading, and tell children that the most important question that you could ask to link the next piece of information on this page would be one that would leap one arc in front of the last thought that the author had. You could even draw this arc:

Black, black sea ⌒ whales thinking

And say to the students

I am asking myself: "What are the whales thinking?"

Then, you could turn the page and demonstrate that Cynthia Rylant, like most authors, will tie the next sentence to the former one by answering the question that the former statement implied. Thus, for instance, when you turn to the next page of Rylant's book, it will state the answer to the question you posed: the whales are thinking about friends, family, and supper. You can tell students that the author will not often go beyond one arc of information away. That is, Rylant's next statement did not describe the color of the skin of whales or begin to describe dolphins as her next sentence.

You can continue in this way for a few pages and then gradually ask students to state the questions that the last sentence on one page raised in their minds before you turn to the next page in a book. You can continue in this way until you determine that students are ready to independently practice posing questions to complete the arc of information between knowledge structures. Then, you ask students to write their questions prior to turning each new page in books that students select to read. Students are to write whether the author answered their questions. If they did not, students write why the author did not. When students stop reading long enough to ask themselves questions to complete arcs of information, they increase the number of mental images about the literal information contained in a text (Keene & Zimmerman, 1997). Questions you can teach students to ask were introduced in Chapter 1, and shown in Table 1.3 (p. 19).

Literal Comprehension Lesson 10: Teaching Students to Ask Questions of Themselves While They Read.   To help students ask questions to complete arcs of information, you can select from the following activities. Each one enables students to practice this comprehension process until it becomes automatic. You can have students choose to read a historical nonfiction or fiction book of which you have multiple copies, and to form small reading response groups in which all group members read the same book. In these discussions, they share their end-of-page questions (described previously). They teach each other why some of the questions that they wrote were not arc questions. Then, students analyze the benefits of asking questions as they read. Alternatively, students could choose to write a book in which each subsequent sentence completed an arc of information. Then, they could ask peers to read it and write the questions that individual pages raised in their minds as they read to test the effectiveness of students' understanding of information arcs. Stipulate that each drama must include five questions from Table 1.3 in the plot. Students could stage a panel discussion in which they act as famous historical figures who respond to questions from their classmates.

In social studies classes, you can invite students to practice asking questions about content topics in small group discussions. They can also explore a current political event and write questions that might clarify the issues involved in the event. In addition, you can have students

- Write a question–answer book about a historical period, and then quiz peers who have studied the same period.
- With a partner, create the front page of a newspaper that reflects a time period of their choice.
- Write and illustrate a picture book for younger students about a specific period in history. Read this book to younger children and ask them whether they have any questions about the events described in the book, or they can teach these schoolmates how to ask information arc questions when they read.
- Keep a diary or write letters in the voice of a famous historical figure.

In Summary

By teaching students the lessons in this chapter, they can learn how to build a coherent macrostructure using the microstructure of the author. You can use the 10 lessons to teach students the thought processes that authors use in a text to recognize arcs of information, to retain literal concepts, and to build intertextuality. In the next chapter, you will learn how to improve students' inference abilities. In the recent past many people believed inferencing was a more difficult skill to be learned after literal comprehension. It is now understood that inferencing also helps children gain a rich literal understanding. Thus, inferencing should be taught in conjunction with instruction that builds students' retention of literal meanings.

REFLECTING ON WHAT YOU HAVE LEARNED

1. In one paragraph write a concise description of your understanding of teaching children literal comprehension. Describe your instruction and assessment plans for teaching children to literally comprehend. This description will help you communicate to students, parents, and colleagues how you are helping students who have difficulty comprehending literally.

2. What is the advice that you will give to fellow educators concerning the first steps that should be taken relative to the information in this chapter? What can we do to assist students in being able to comprehend and understand more accurately?

3. Teach a lesson from this chapter. Compare it to one that you experienced as a child. How did the lesson from this chapter increase students' literal comprehension in a more effective manner than lessons that you experienced when you were in school?

4. *Your Professional Journal: Reflection Journal.* In your journal, define literal comprehension. Describe the new pieces of research that will increase effectiveness in teaching literal comprehension.

5. *Field Applications and Observations.* The five-finger method is used when children read. They learn to put down one finger for each word on a page that they do not know. If the student has all five fingers down before the end of the page the text is likely to be too difficult for him or her to determine an accurate literal understanding. Similarly, if a readability level of a selection of children's literature is unknown, you can follow a basic formula to determine the level of difficulty. Usually, in a kindergarten text, one full sentence does not appear on each page. By first grade, there is one full sentence per page on average. By the second grade there are usually two sentences per page; third grade, one paragraph; fourth grade, two paragraphs; fifth grade, three paragraphs; and by the sixth grade there are usually four paragraphs per page. You can teach this formula to students to increase the quality of their literal comprehension of books that they select to read. With this in mind, survey books that are in your classroom library, or a classroom library in an elementary or middle school that you observe. Recognizing that a minimum of 100 books should be present in classroom libraries, are there 20 books that are two grade levels of readability level below, 20 one grade level below, 20 on grade level, 20 one grade level above, and 20 two grade levels above the class grade level? Why is this distribution recommended?

6. *Multicultural Application.* Read a chapter from a book in which the main character comes from a culture other than your own. Demonstrate how the cultural knowledge base in that book affected the number of knowledge structures and arcs of information

questions that you had to generate. Teach students that readers outside of the cultural group represented in the content will likely read the book more slowly and they will take longer to generate arc of information questions, fill gaps in coherence, and make intertextual connections. Ask students what the lesson and out-of-culture reading experience taught them relative to the patience that they will have with peers who read out-of-culture books in the future.

7. *Key Terms Exercise.* Following is a list of concepts introduced in this chapter. If you have learned the meaning of a term, place a checkmark in the blank that precedes that term. If you are not sure of a term's definition increase your retention by reviewing the definition of the term. If you have learned 10 of these terms on your first reading of this chapter you have constructed many meanings that are important for your career.

_____ skill (p. 74)

_____ strategies (p. 74)

_____ critical comprehension processing (p. 74)

_____ thinking to the end (p. 74)

_____ becoming less reality-bound (p. 77)

_____ Empathetic reading (p. 77)

_____ trusting their own tillings (p. 79)

_____ word calling (p. 79)

_____ metacognition (p. 88)

_____ KWL-plus (p. 89)

_____ reciprocal teaching (p. 91)

_____ you be the counselor (p. 92)

_____ tape recording improvements (p. 93)

_____ knowledge structure (p. 96)

8. *Comprehension Process Lesson 4: Teaching Students the Comprehension Process of Analyzing Character Traits.* Comprehension Process Lesson 4 describes seven strategies that students can learn to analyze memorable literary characters. This lesson has been demonstrated to increase students' abilities to identify with characters as they read. It also enhances writers' skills in creating vivid personalities in their compositions.

COMPREHENSION PROCESS LESSON 4
Analyzing Character Traits

Directions: Teach each of the following seven strategies on separate days. Then ask students to place this thinking guide beside a book as they read. Students are to write the page number at which they thought about one or more of these strategies as they read. Last, students are to either (1) write a sentence that the author could have added that would make a character more memorable, or (2) describe how using this thinking guide improved their comprehension. Making students aware of the following character traits alerts them to these qualities in every book that they read. These can be taught through direct instruction, minilessons, or through the creation of student-generated semantic maps.

Pay attention to the qualities exhibited in characters' voices:
1. What the character talks about
2. Qualities of the voice; kind or stern, for example

    3. State of being, such as strong personality or indefinite in phraseology
    4. Depth of vocabulary

Be aware of the stories about character that are revealed through the plot:
    1. Flashback of conversations
    2. Projections of hopes or fears about the future
    3. Whom they associate with
    4. Choices and actions

Make use of what has been revealed about the character in terms of theme:
    1. Main characters appear frequently in the story
    2. Position they take relative to the theme
    3. How rapidly they adjust to changes in the theme

Notice the physical characteristics:
    1. Gender
    2. Age
    3. Race
    4. Body type and carriage
    5. Strength
    6. Health
    7. Movements
    8. Speech
    9. Dress
  10. Sibling rank in family

Make note of the mental characteristics:
    1. Native intelligence
    2. Thinking habits
    3. Education
    4. Originality

Focus on the personal characteristics:
    1. Basic attitudes: likes, dislikes toward life, toward other characters
    2. Ways of meeting a crisis, conflict, or change in environment
    3. Capacity for deep feeling
    4. Stability
    5. Self-control
    6. Temperament

Interpret the social interactions:
    1. Profession; daily routine
    2. Nationality
    3. Religion
    4. Social class
    5. Economic status

5

Developing Inferential, Predictive, and Interpretive Comprehension

While Jennifer works alone, Mr. Armstrong teaches students to create inferences and predictions. Other students shown have already learned to till their texts and comprehend books of their own choosing.

DEVELOPING INFERENTIAL, PREDICTIVE, AND INTERPRETIVE COMPREHENSION

Theories relative to inferencing, predicting, and interpreting

Why inferencing, predicting, and interpreting are so difficult for children

Teaching inference using hypothesis testing

Teaching inferencing using the structure of a text's writing style

Teaching an author's macrostructures

Jennifer, a vibrant third-grade student, listened intently as Mr. Armstrong taught the inferencing lesson in this chapter's comprehension process lesson. She loved poems and worked hard for 3 days to improve her inferencing abilities so she could understand poems better. It was about 2:30 on a Friday afternoon when she grew tired and sleepy. She was supposed to be reading silently while Mr. Armstrong moved about the room conducting a Strand 2 "stop and ask" lesson. He was assessing students' independent inferencing abilities. Jennifer's eyes grew heavy, so she stopped reading and laid her head on her desk.

She must have just fallen asleep. She felt a slight nudge on her shoulder. As she looked up, she was staring directly at Mr. Armstrong's inquisitive face. Before he could speak, Jennifer implored: "Mr. Armstrong you don't need to be upset because I was resting my eyes. I know how to inference perfectly, and I can prove it. You didn't say a word to me, but I could read the words all over your face. I infer that you are wondering why I'm so tired and stopped reading." ∎

Chapter Overview

Research during the past 20 years has increased our understanding of inference (Fisher, Schumaker, & Desheler, 2002; Kintsch, 1993). Among the illuminating findings is that the ability to inference, predict, or interpret is not a single process. Rather, inferences are various branches of thoughts that unite to create meaning from text and readers' thoughts (Baker, 2001; Kintsch, 1998; Omanson, Warren, & Trabasso, 1978).

Recently, inference, predicting, and interpreting have been added to high-stakes criterion-referenced literacy tests. The reasons commonly cited for such a significant increase in inference-based assessment questions follow. First, such questions allow for intense thinking about stories. More children are coming to school today without having had opportunities to think deeply about texts that were read aloud to them by adults. Second, in the past 10 years it has been shown that inference questions enable students to process and integrate text-based ideas into their own background knowledge significantly more rapidly than literal queries (Hanson, 1980; Pearson & Fielding, 1996). Prediction questions, in particular, encourage readers to stay actively engaged because they are continuously connecting upcoming story events to their personal experiences (Hansen 1980; Hansen & Pearson, 1983). In fact, Schmitt (1988) discovered that prediction was the most frequently reported behavior of students who had been taught to use inference thinking.

Unfortunately, research has not been conducted to analyze students' abilities to predict and interpret text in multiple ways. This is a new direction for teachers to focus future instruction. As educators, we must learn how to assist learners to predict and interpret text to gain increased perspective as to the "one human family" reality that exists in our world today (Britton & Graesser, 1996; Kintsch 1998).

The purpose of this chapter is to (1) report research relative to how inferential understanding can be developed, and (2) describe new methods that assist students to inference effectively.

By the end of this chapter you will be able to answer the following questions:

1. How can inferencing, predictive thinking, and interpretation be taught as hypothesis testing?
2. How can inferencing, predicting, and interpreting be taught as knowledge structures?

3. How can inferencing, predicting, and interpreting be developed through instruction about macrostructures?

Theories Relative to Inferencing, Predicting, and Interpreting

Theories relative to inferencing, predicting, and interpreting

Inferencing is one of the most complex and unique human cognitive activities (Taylor, Graves, & van den Broek, 2000). During inferencing, a successful comprehender connects previous experiences, persons, events, and objects "that she encounters so that the text appears to be a coherent whole rather than a random list of facts and events. Frequently, the relations in a text are implicit and therefore must be inferred. If all goes well, the result of inferential processing is a mental representation of a text that is relatively stable and can be accessed at a later point in time to answer questions and retell the story" (p. 165). **Inferencing** can be defined as the ability to engage six mental processes, which are:

1. Understand and assemble multilevel text representations;
2. Understand the construction of a coherent representation;
3. Understand a complex dynamical system of symbols;
4. Engage long and short-term memories interactively;
5. Predict and interpret;
6. Construct coherent representation within the bottleneck of a limited-capacity working memory (Britton & Grasser, 1996).

Inferencing combines these comprehension processes to judge, conclude, and reason from literal content. **Predicting** is an inference in which readers deduce the next event, action, or idea. **Interpreting** is an inference in which readers apply literal information to their lives. Weaver and Kintsch (1991) analyzed more than 100 textbooks and found that as many as 12 to 15 inferences may be ignited in every sentence in the paragraphs of these books. This textbook content density demands that inferencing becomes a cornerstone in readers' comprehension abilities before high levels of understanding are possible.

One of the most thorough studies on inferencing was conducted by Haenggi, Kintsch, and Gernsbacher (1995). They discovered that before students can draw an inference, they must (1) place facts into categorical arrangements, (2) direct these categories toward a goal, and (3) maintain an awareness of the major focus of an author's writing goals. In this study, although weaker readers who had not been trained in the lessons in this chapter could image, they could not inference. They had to be taught how to engage the many processes previously mentioned first. When they did so, they became aware of the arcs of inferred information that authors depend on readers to make. These inferred leaps of thought occurred between single words and sentences.

This finding also explains why weaker readers must be taught to think about what a text means to them as they are making literal sense of printed words. To develop this ability, students need more than simply to be asked an inference question after they have read a selection (Cornoldi & Oakhill, 1998). If the lessons in this chapter are not taught students may have difficulty because they cannot identify and interpret an author's cohesive devices, such as his or her use of pronouns and connectors. Another reason for inferencing difficulties is because of a poorly developed concept of story grammar headers. Some students do not appreciate that stories consist of a series of connected, related events. They fail to realize that these events have an overarching main idea, message, or theme (Yuill & Oakhill, 1991).

Because less skilled comprehenders have demonstrated that they are poor at selecting the main idea of literally presented material, even when stories are presented aloud or in pictures, additional support is needed before they can integrate facts. Specifically, only 29 percent of less skilled readers (and 25 percent of less able comprehenders told to listen to important events in the story) were able to say how they could recall character names and answer inferential questions in the future (Yuill & Oakhill, 1991). These results demonstrate that inferencing is necessary to process literal information, and that literal and inferential comprehension instruction can achieve best results if they occur in the same lesson.

Other studies have clearly proven that before such abilities occur, students must be led to a fourth step through an explicit but personally contextualized instructional lesson. This step teaches students how to deduce authors' intended relationships between facts and themes (Fitzgerald & Spiegel, 1983). Such lessons should provide training on (1) identifying various aspects of a story and its structure, and (2) how to inference by making categories of single facts (Kintsch, 1998; Long, 1994).

Why Inferencing, Predicting, and Interpreting Are So Difficult for Children

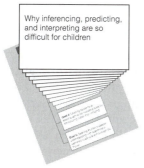

Why inferencing, predicting, and interpreting are so difficult for children

There are many reasons why students have difficulty inferring about and interpreting text (Piaget, 1963; Singer & Ritchot, 1996). One reason is that many readers believe too strongly in a personally constructed, nontextually based interpretation that is inconsistent with the facts presented in a text. In this situation, readers simply overlook facts and cause/effect patterns that would more closely align their thoughts with the author's. By sidestepping clues in subsequent paragraphs, such readers continue to sustain personal interpretations, which if held strongly, will cause them to blatantly reject specifically printed evidence that contradicts their interpretations.

Second, studies have proven that students must dispel their own desires to move material in a certain direction when their interpretation of facts in a book is inconsistent with the author's train of thought (Otero & Kintsch, 1992). A third reason is that students have not been taught how to comprehend a broad range of rhetorical structures by having been taught how to write a particular pattern that an author uses in a text (Chambliss, 1993; Kintsch, 1991). When readers can recognize macropropositions, generalizations, and themes, independent inferencing can engage. By practicing and mastering signal clues, readers can learn how to infer an author's links between propositions within sentences and connections between sentences and paragraphs.

Next, students' inference abilities have been demonstrated to improve when they are taught to reread, and to pause and reflect. Pressley and colleagues (1995) examined one method of doing this. Students who had trouble inferencing and predicting, but who were taught to talk about their comprehension processes, remembered more about the information from the text than did a control group. Discussions of comprehension processes, as occurs in CPA groups, are powerful because they enable students to close **gaps in coherence.** When coherence gaps are closed, students do not stray too far from an author's specific, intended **arcs of information** (links between propositions made by the text's macrostructure). Moreover, discussion enhances their ability to (1) express their reliance on their own knowledge and belief systems; and (2) explain difficulties that they are having as they try to inference, interpret, and predict. There are eight roadblocks that should be addressed in CPA discussion groups concerning inferencing (Pressley, 1999). Students must discuss how they

1. Recognized the link between two ideas (Colizar, 1993);
2. Searched for important ideas (Guthrie, Cox, Knowles, Buehl, Mazzoni, & Fasulo, 2000);
3. Made transitions between two sentences by using the bank of rich content that they have read as their thought anchors; and predicted the author's natural inclinations using the author's writing style, real-world cause-and-effect chains that are likely to be represented in the next sentence's meaning, and their personal prior knowledge (Block, & Johnson, 2002);
4. Recognized that their personal filters could interfere with proper inferencing;
5. Deleted insignificant details (Gambrel & Koskinen, 2001);
6. Were not seduced by irrelevant details;
7. Generalized familiar to unfamiliar domains of knowledge (Block, 2001b; Pressley et al., 1993); and
8. Identified gaps in their background knowledge.

In another study, without comprehension instruction, fourth graders could not recognize authors' arguments (Kintsch & Otera, 1992). Instead, when asked to pick out an author's argument, untrained pupils stated main ideas, subtopics, or simply elaborated on details that they had read. This occurred because a component of the inferencing process is knowledge elaboration. This elaboration occurs when a reader connects one node of information to the next. Whenever students make irrelevant links from a text to other books or prior personal experiences, elaborations can go awry. Moreover, while reading if students weigh too heavily on a piece of information that is not in the text or a distortion of facts, readers can develop a bias that has not been indicated by the author (Kintsch & Otera, 1992).

Another problem that interferes with inferencing occurs when students do not know how to make **slot-filling inferences** (Leu & Kinzer, 1995). A slot-filling inference is a specific type of interpretation that occurs when a reader uses background knowledge to add meaning to a text. Poor readers are unable to make connections because they do not have a strong enough familiar bank of knowledge on which to connect new information that they read. To correct this problem, researchers are developing new lessons for inferencing instruction (Kintsch, 1998). Researchers have discovered that good readers automatically infer from a fictional body of knowledge while reading because they construct inferences as they go. This thinking process is similar to a peak performance in other kinds of physical or cognitive activity. When readers are at peak performance, they create valid inferences and macrostructures of the subject being read. In addition, they pose questions and recognize questions that authors expect them to ask.

Nonfiction texts demand additional skills. Students must anticipate how a content discipline will unfold. To do so, the rhetorical structure of the discipline must already be a part of that student's knowledge, and information retrieved from long-term memory must be easily added to newly constructed facts from a book. Thus, inferencing nonfiction requires more links to memory than fiction. By contrast, fiction requires more keeping track of location and movement of actors, which is easier to visualize, so that imagery can play a larger role in inferencing from fictional text than is possible in nonfiction reading. As a result, inferencing from stories is often easier than inferencing from nonfiction text (Block, 2001; Keene & Zimmerman, 1997; Kintsch, 1998).

There are many types of inferencing. Those most commonly accepted by researchers include: drawing conclusions, making reasonable predictions, testing and revising predictions, discerning cause-and-effect relationships, linking new ideas to background knowledge, adjusting one's interpretations continuously during reading, making critical judgments, remembering and applying what is read, discriminating and analyzing texts and biases, and reflecting.

Teaching Inference Using Hypothesis Testing

Teaching inference using hypothesis testing

One of the new approaches to inference instruction involves teaching students to infer as if they are testing hypotheses. Good readers have many ways of forming sophisticated hypotheses (Carr, 1998; Fredriekson, 1981; Stanovich, 1986). They do so, by finding the correct answer to their hypotheses in the material being read rather than guessing or using only one salient word or detail (Brown, 2002; Mackey, 1998). Students who are unable to infer also lack the ability to create a model of "where the author is going," or the sea of thought the author is creating. As a result they can not use an author's sea of thought to set hypotheses, seek answers to their own queries as they read, or make inferences.

By contrast, students who make good inferences are able to express meaning, refer to individual facts, state the author's style, interpret figures of speech, identify the macrostructures upon which arguments are built, and unite all this information together to infer (van Dijk & Kintsch, 1983). Another aspect that distinguishes valid from shallow inferences is the degree of certainty developed by the reader by using multiple facts. Whenever students do not spend enough time acquiring information before inferences are made, the chances are that resultant interpretations and predictions will not be accurate (Fisher, Schumaker, & Deshler, 2002). Thus, to learn how to inference by creating hypotheses as they read students must be taught how to increase the amount of time that they spend collecting and reflecting on details, main ideas, themes, and the author's sea of thought while they read. The following methods have been demonstrated to increase students' abilities in these areas.

Inference Lesson l: Writing Hypotheses.   Ask students to make hypotheses as they read and to write them down. For weaker comprehenders, content for this lesson should be well structured and coherent so that the hypotheses that authors' are depending upon readers to make are easier for students to recognize (Fisher & Trabasco, 2001; Kintsch & van Dijk, 1978). This lesson is similar to the literal comprehension one in Chapter 4 in which students write the questions that they asked themselves while they read to connect sentences (arcs of information) together. The difference between the two lessons is that in this one you place self-adhesive notes on the pages of a text at points in which an author encourages readers to infer, predict, or interpret. Then, you instruct students to stop wherever they come to such a note paper and write a hypothesis about the inference that they think the author is expecting. When students take time to write this educated guess, it increases the time that the mind spends in synthesizing facts. When this lesson is repeated often, students become more comfortable with the experience of inferring and reflecting as they read.

Inference Lesson 2: Diagramming the Inference Process.   The purpose of diagramming is to demonstrate how students make hypotheses that become valid inferences, predictions, and interpretations. In Chapter 4, you taught students to draw an arc to denote the arc of information chains between single sentences. In this lesson, you teach students the three-part thought process involved in making inferences that are depicted in the comprehension process lesson at the end of this chapter.

This lesson begins by performing an expanded explanation of the inference process as you explain the three columns on the thinking guide. This modeling is based on inferences that students are likely to have already made in their lives. For example, you might say

> If your mother, father, grandmother, or grandfather told you to take your umbrella to school, your brain would automatically think of rain, although no one has said that word. This is an *inference, a comprehension* process you use to make meaning, called *inferring*, and you can do this when you read and listen.

To infer, you think about what the author wrote. [At this point you will have folded the thinking guide on page 116 to show only the first section.] For example, read the first stanza of a poem and ask students to write down the thoughts they had about that first verse. Then, you describe how the thinking process of inferring continues in their minds by suggesting they think about prior knowledge they have about similar experiences that have occurred in their lives. [At this point you make this process visible by unfolding the thinking guide and displaying the second section of the thinking guide sheet. You refold and reopen this second section as you tell them that their minds process in a similarly linear fashion as this when they infer as they read.] You then write your thoughts in the second column on this sheet that you had relative to the first stanza of the poem that came from prior similar experiences in your life. Then, ask them to record their thoughts on the second column of the thinking guides. Then show the last column on the thinking guide and explain that when they combine the information in the first two columns they can generate a hypothesis that is likely to be what the author wanted them to infer.

Next, distribute a second inferencing thinking guide to each student. Ask them to fold it along the two vertical lines as indicated. Then you will ask them to read the following sentence that you will have written on a chalkboard, chart pad, or overhead acetate: "Nibbsie came running, with the stick in his mouth." Have students write that sentence on the thinking guide in the first column. Then, ask students to unfold to the second section on their page. Then you state, "As you read, your mind added a few things based on what you know. You came up with an entirely new thought as you read that sentence. Write what your mind added, based on what you know about names like 'Nibbsie' and about living things that run with sticks in their mouths." Ask students to write their thoughts in the middle section of the inferencing process thinking guide. Then, ask the students to unfold the third section; tell them that this action is similar to what their minds do each time they infer as they read. It is moving from the words read, to adding things that they already have stored in their brains, and combining these two thoughts together to generate a hypothesis about an author's implied meanings. Have students write their hypothesis in the third section.

Discuss with students what they have learned about the inferencing process. Review that the author did not tell readers that Nibbsie was a dog. They knew that Nibbsie was a dog because the author gave clues so readers could infer that it was a dog. Tell students that as they read, they should look for clues and use more than one clue to generate hypotheses about what an author means. When they do so, they are inferring. Have the students practice. [Use the power of three at this point in the lesson. Show one picture and ask students to unfold their thinking process guide as they write their three steps in inferencing. Then, show a second and then a third picture.] Continue by reading three poems, having students write their three steps in the inferencing process on their thinking guides for each photo and each poem. They will write after each verse. Last, ask students to read silently, and write the three steps to the inferencing process, in the same manner, as they read a text selection of their choice.

Teaching Inferencing Using the Structure of a Text's Writing Style

Teaching inferencing using
the structure of a text's
writing style

Another method of increasing children's inferencing ability has been labeled the **spreading activation approach** (Britton & Graesser, 1996). Spreading activation is a process in which concepts from one body of knowledge are spread to related concepts, which causes the related concepts to become more activated in the brain. This spread of activation continues as long as readers continuously think about the material being read. Three types of "spreading" can occur and can be taught. The first involves making strong application of knowledge to students' lives. The second involves making positive emotional responses to information. The third involves identifying when negative inhibitory connections occur between two ideas.

When students are challenged to read material that is of interest to them and have choices in what to read, each concept read could activate a strong influence on understanding for prior and forthcoming information (Fisher, Schumaker, & Deshler, 2002). This spreading of knowledge occurs more rapidly in areas of interest because students are more motivated to read harder material. And as a result, they can more instantly connect numerous concepts to the author's overarching goals as they read. When students already judge a text to be important, the relationships between knowledge structures and the literal comprehension arcs of information do not have to be constructed. Because less energy has to be invested in literal comprehension, students can pay greater attention to inferring, predicting, and interpreting.

Inference Lesson 3: Explaining the Reasons Behind Inferences (Block, 1995).   Figure 5.1 contains an example of one reader's explanation of his predictions. It can serve as a model for your students. Students can be taught to explain how they made the inferences they did by describing how specific traits of literary characters were combined to infer whether a character was a hero or villain. You can also describe how students can infer characters' traits by noting details about relationships they form with other characters. Books that students enjoy discussing and reading to practice inferring include: *The Great Gilly Hopkins; Sarah, Plain and Tall; The Eighteenth Emerging; Goodbye, Chicken Little; Julie of the Wolves; One-Eyed Cat; Sea Glass;* and *The Summer of the Swans.*

Inference Lesson 4: Using Photographs and Cartoons to Teach Inferencing.   You can ask readers to make inferences from pictures. Less able readers who were taught to infer an artist's message from photographs rather than having to make an inference based on text demonstrated that they could infer as well as expert readers do (Beal, 1996; Holmes, 1987). Similarly, if you remove the dialogue from the last two sections of a cartoon and ask readers to write their inferences on them, many less able readers can learn to infer with less difficulty than if they had to read from text. Ask students to write what they inferred would make sense in the last two cartoon captions. After these are read aloud, ask students to explain their inferring process.

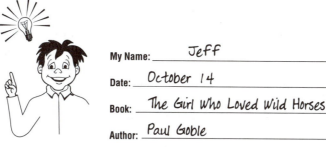

My Name: _____ Jeff _____

Date: _____ October 14 _____

Book: _____ The Girl Who Loved Wild Horses _____

Author: _____ Paul Goble _____

My Prediction	Why Did I Make That Prediction?
I think the book is about a girl who loves horses.	Because pictures of horses look dreamlike.
I predict she gets a horse.	Because on the picture on back of the book she is on a horse.
I predict she's really a princess.	There is a "Princess" word in here.
I think I am going to like it.	The sentences are like music playing.

FIGURE 5.1   Sample of a Reader's Explanation of Predictions

Teaching an Author's Macrostructures

Teaching an author's macrostructures

One of the most long-standing bodies of research about inferencing includes information about the role that reader-friendly and reader-unfriendly texts play in the process (Beck, McKeown, Hamilton, & Kucan, 1997; Beck & Dole, 1994). Reader-friendly texts are well organized, contain familiar content, and have well-marked macrostructures. Recently, it has been established that when children have to read texts that are inconsiderate, it is very difficult for them to make inferences (Britton & Graesser, 1996). For this reason, the following lessons have been developed to assist students when they have to read such text.

Inference Lesson 5: Paraphrasing.   Considerate text is coherent and contains supports for comprehension that were presented in Chapter 4. We must teach children not to contribute to inconsiderate texts in kind, but rather in kindness. In other words, whenever children are reading a text in which it seems particularly difficult to make connections between individual sentences, we must teach them how to do so by extending kindness to the author (Beck, McKeown, Hamilton, & Kucan,

1997). Kindness can be shown by allowing students to paraphrase what they would anticipate the author could have used to make a connection between sentences. This same instructional direction could be given to assist students to make probable connections between paragraphs. After students have created four paraphrases alone they should be able to identify that author's macrostructure and writing style, which they can follow throughout the remainder of the text.

Inference Lesson 6: Teaching Inferencing with a First-Person Narrative.   This lesson begins by providing students with a first-person story in which the narrator is identified only as "I." Students must infer who "I" is. You can divide the story into paragraphs and have readers use the first paragraph as their first inferring clue. Then, you can discuss their ideas and what they thought as they read to come up with these ideas. Continue to discuss subsequent inferences in this manner, one paragraph at a time, until the correct narrator is identified, and individual readers explain the inferences that they used to inference. In a similar exercise, you can lay pages with separate paragraphs (each with clues as to the narrator's identity) on a table and ask readers to select the first one only. Students read subsequent paragraphs, working at their own pace, and thinking about the information they read until they are sure they have inferred the correct first-person narrator. When they are ready to predict the identity of the narrator, you ask them to whisper it in your ear. You can record the amount of time it took each student to make a particular inference. Allow them to change their minds if they wish and to choose whether to read on or reread previous paragraphs after their first inference. When all students have inferred at least once, ask the first few who accurately identified the narrator to explain the inference process they used.

After students have practiced their inferring skills for a week, you can reinitiate this activity by presenting a second set of paragraphs on the table for students to read in the same manner. When they have identified the correct narrator, record their times again so they can realize the improvements they have made in inferring. Table 5.1 contains a story that can be used in this lesson.

Inference Lesson 7: Think-Alouds to Model How to Identify Gaps in Knowledge That Limit Inferencing.   As students present a retelling, gaps in macrostructure knowledge that they retained from a reading will become clear. As Galda (1998) discovered, "It is easier to continue crafting a story alone when the reading is about people, especially people that have experiences that are similar to us. When there are big differences between the experiences and ourselves or the decoding demand is too large, the characters and events in the story push readers out of the book"(p. 123). Therefore, instead of pushing a culture onto a student we must mentor students into understanding divergent ideas and unfamiliar words and text. This mentoring process can occur through think-alouds that you perform to model for students how to fill gaps in knowledge with text-bound inferring. The buddy retelling evaluation form, presented in Chapter 3, is an excellent teaching aid for this lesson. It keeps students engaged because it breaks the predicting, inferencing, and interpreting processes into steps that pairs can discuss.

TABLE 5.1 Sample Story for Identifying and Inferring

Clue 1

Lunch made me sleepy, so I curled up to take a nap. With sleep came a wonderful dream. I was stretched out on a lovely green lawn with the sun warming my body. Birds were singing gaily overhead, and little yellow daffodils peeked out through the grass. I reached out to touch one—and suddenly there was no sun.

A heavy shadow had shut out the light. Something grabbed me and I cried out, fighting to get free. It was no use; I was traveling through space. This was no dream. It was real. I had been captured, and there was nothing I could do about it.

Clue 2

Soon I felt something solid at my feet. I could move, but it was hard to stand. My legs felt limber. Where was I?

Cautiously, I stepped forward. OUCH! I bumped into the wall and went in the other direction, but every time there was a wall. Four walls and no door. I'm in a cell!

All of a sudden there was a blast of cold air above. I looked up but could see nothing. Where was the air coming from? Suddenly I knew: there was no roof on my cell! I had to discover a way out.

Clue 3

Stepping carefully toward the wall, I attempted to reach the opening. I wasn't tall enough, so I sat down again to think. The cell was still rocking. Maybe I could throw myself against one of the walls and tip the cell over. Again and again I rushed at the wall, but I finally gave up, defeated.

Sitting down, I tried to gather the energy for one more try. If that didn't work—Wait, the movement stopped!

A minute later I heard an earthshaking bang as I felt a different motion. My cell was moving up and down, not back and forth. I couldn't keep my balance. I said to myself I'd conquer whatever it was. I'd be ready. In an instant there was a horrible crunch, and the wall nearest me was ripped away. Beyond the opening I could see a dazzling light.

Clue 4

"Now's your chance," I told myself, cautiously crawling to the opening. At first, I saw nothing but a shiny wood floor. Then I saw *them!*

Feet! Giant feet! They seemed about to surround me, so I quickly retreated. I could be ground to smithereens out there! Of course, that's what they were planning—that's why they made it easy for me to escape! Well, I'd fool them; I wouldn't move.

Clue 5

No, I couldn't stay. I had to try to get out.

Once again I crept to the opening, but the feet were still there. Then I noticed something else. Near two of the feet, four round posts rose from the floor. The posts were topped by a thick, low roof. I could easily squeeze under it, but those giant feet couldn't.

I took a deep breath and moved quickly. Racing out of my cell, I skidded under the thick roof. I made it! My legs felt like rubber again, but I was safe for the moment.

(continued)

TABLE 5.1   Continued

Clue 6

What would happen next? I wondered. I didn't have long to wait, however, for I heard voices high above the roof.

   "Oh, Donald, she's afraid of us!"

   "Well, naturally," came the reply. "That must have been a very frightening trip for such a little _____."

Inference Lesson 8: Continuous Checks.   In the continuous checks method, on a sheet of paper, students write a series of checks to denote how many sentences an author takes to reach a concluding thought or goal.

In Summary

Seven CPA lessons and Comprehension Process Lesson 5 in this chapter can be used to develop students' inferencing, interpreting, and predicting abilities. To make valid inferences readers must (1) fill gaps in textual coherence, (2) complete arcs in literal information, (3) engage domain knowledge, and (4) activate the spreading process. This chapter described several lessons that have been demonstrated to increase students' inferencing abilities. These were: (1) Writing Hypotheses, (2) Diagramming the Inference Process, (3) Explaining the Reasons Behind Inferences, (4) Using Photographs and Cartoons to Teach Inferencing, (5) Paraphrasing, (6) Teaching Inferencing with a First-Person Narrative, (7) Think-Alouds that Model How to Identify Gaps in Knowledge Which Limit Inferencing, and (8) Continuous Checks. Once students become proficient inferencers, teachers can focus more instructional time on developing students' imagery abilities. Methods of doing so are presented in Chapter 6.

REFLECTING ON WHAT YOU HAVE LEARNED

1. How could you fit these lessons into your current reading program, especially in programs and organizational plans such as Success for All, block schedules, integrated approaches, and departmental settings?

2. What is the advice that you will give to fellow educators concerning the first steps that should be taken relative to teaching inferencing?

3. *Your Professional Journal: Making Contextual Decisions.* In one paragraph write a concise description of how to teach inferential comprehension. Describe your instruction and assessment plans. This description will help you communicate to students, parents, and colleagues how you are helping students overcome any difficulties they may be having in inferential comprehension.

4. *Field Applications and Observations.* Implement one of the lessons from this chapter. Evaluate its effectiveness and describe to colleagues how you determined its level of success.

5. *Multicultural Application.* Which of the basic approaches to teaching inferencing would be most appropriate for students from minority cultures? Answer and then check your response. (The first approach should be to teach English-language learners more background knowledge to profit from the hypothesis generation and knowledge structure lessons.)

6. *Key Term Exercise.* Following is a list of concepts introduced in this chapter. If you have learned the meaning of a term, place a checkmark in the blank that precedes that term. If you are not sure of a term's definition, increase your retention by reviewing the definition of the term. If you have learned five of these terms on your first reading of this chapter, you have constructed many meanings that are important for your career.

_____ inferencing (p. 104)

_____ predicting (p. 104)

_____ interpreting (p. 104)

_____ gaps in coherence (p. 106)

_____ arcs of information (p. 106)

_____ slot filling inferences (p. 107)

_____ spreading activation process (p. 110)

7. *Comprehension Process Lesson 5: Teaching Students the Comprehension Process of Generating Inferences Rapidly and Continuously.* Comprehension Process Lesson 5 contains the directions and the thinking guide that enable students to practice inferencing. The lesson contains several steps you can take when you meet with students in one-to-one settings or in groups.

COMPREHENSION PROCESS LESSON 5

Teaching Students to Generate Inferences Rapidly and Continuously

Jumping from Accurate Information to Valid Conclusions
Teaching students to generate inferences quickly is as fun and simple as a frog jump. First, divide students into groups of fours. Each student needs paper and a pencil. Designate one student as the timekeeper. This student will be given a kitchen timer and will be responsible for setting the time and alerting the group when it is time to jump.

Say to the students, "Today we will be learning how to inference quickly. Remember, when we make an inference we are using information from the text as well as our background knowledge to infer or predict what will happen next. It is important that we learn to do this quickly so that it can be done easily while we read."

Instruct the class that at your signal, they will have 5 minutes to write a story about a frog. The students may take the story in any direction that they wish, as long as a frog is included. When the timer sounds at 5 minutes, each student will jump to the right and sit down at a neighbor's desk.

Using the neighbor's story, the students must infer and write what happens next on the trifolded thinking guide. It is important that the students only use background knowledge,

(continued)

COMPREHENSION PROCESS LESSON 5   **Continued**

Thinking Guide

Drawing Inferences

Name _____   Date _____

What is said or read + **What you Know** = **What is meant**

Fold

Fold

1. Look for clues when you read!

2. Use more than one clue.

3. Put the clues together with what you already know to draw an inference.

as well as the characters, events, and setting that are included. This way, the students will practice inferring correctly. At your signal, they will begin to write again.

Every moment the timer sounds and the students jump, their writing time will be progressively shorter from 5 minutes to 4 minutes to 3 minutes to 2 minutes. By shortening the amount of time given, students will learn to generate inferences quickly.

When the timer sounds for the last jump, instruct students to complete the story by inferring the ending. Remind them that although they only have 2 minutes to do so, they can only infer using background knowledge and information given in the text.

COMPREHENSION PROCESS LESSON 5   Continued

At the sound of the timer, students return to their own desks. They will be given a few minutes to read what their classmates wrote. Then, you will distribute the frog pattern. Each child will copy his or her story on the frog pattern and then title and decorate it. The frogs can be displayed on a bulletin board complete with lily pads and water. By concluding in this manner, the story becomes a published work and not simply an activity. The integration of art with writing makes learning fun and a process they want to repeat.

Source: Created by Samantha Randklev, education major with reading emphasis candidate, Texas Christian University, Fort Worth, Texas. Used by permission. Figure from Reason to Read, Volume 3 (p. 132) by Cathy Collins Block and John Mangieri. Copyright © 1995 by Pearson Education, Inc., publishing as Dale Seymour Publications. Used by permission.

Imagery: Looking Within and Up and Away without Moving Too Far from the Text

Reid and Douglas so look forward to Strand 2 lessons. It is easy to see why. Both fall quickly under literacy's spell through the vivid mental images that they have been taught to create. Mr. Walters used the imagery lessons in Chapter 6 to do so.

IMAGERY: LOOKING WITHIN AND UP AND AWAY WITHOUT MOVING TOO FAR FROM THE TEXT

- Research concerning imagery
- Teaching imagery by deepening domain knowledge structures
- Teaching imagery by inducing and invoking images
- Teaching imagery using poetry and art

Mr. Walters was aware that less able readers struggle to blend literal and inferential comprehension into visual images. To build their skill, he taught his students to (1) look up and away, (2) write similes, (3) paint mental pictures, (4) translate audio books into print, and (5) write with vivid words and phrases. These Strand 1 CPA lessons were rewarded when his least able reader, at the end of a discovery discussion burst into a glowing, bright smile and beamed, "Thanks to you, Mr. Walters, I read really, really good now! The words just hop off of the page and pop into my head. I can't stop the pictures they make no matter what I do." Soon after that, Susanna began reading chapter books at a fifth-grade readability level. ■

Chapter Overview

Imaging is defined as learning how to paint pictures in one's mind while reading. Doing so increases retention. Before mental images can emerge, readers must first have an accurate literal understanding of details and sense an author's purpose. They must also recognize the arcs of literal information that flow from one paragraph to the next, and predict information that will unfold in upcoming sentences. They must understand an author's writing style so that the next arc of unknown information can be inferred to complete a mental picture. Although some students learn how to **image** when they are young, for others this ability is difficult. Without instruction, many struggling readers create significantly fewer mental representations than their more able peers (Gambrell & Koskinen, 2001; Sadoski, 1985; Sadoski & Paivio, 1994).

Today's students have a vast store of vivid images from real-world events they view through the media of television, e-commerce, and the Internet. They also have continuous access to rapid-paced images that convey information through music videos and advertisements. As a result, their minds have adapted to absorb rapid-paced images in microseconds, even when these scenes appear in a dense, highly stimulating, thematically linked visual array (Block, 2001c; Van Dijk, 1980). To teach students how to use these same mental processes to create accurate images from print, we as educators must capitalize on the mental agility that today's students' real-world experiences have created. We can also implement the lessons in this chapter.

By the end of this chapter, you will be able to answer the following questions:

1. What findings from imagery research can improve the effectiveness of instruction?
2. How can the quality of comprehension instruction be improved so that less able readers become more proactive imagers?
3. How can students be taught to add their imagination to information while they read so that imagery becomes a natural process that instantly increases students' comprehension?
4. How can teachers assist students to evoke more vivid images, so that they receive maximum benefits from imagery processing?

Research Concerning Imagery

The easiest image to create from text is a depiction of an explicitly stated spatial relationship (Haenggi, Kintsch, & Gernsbacher, 1995). When a story describes the actions of a main character moving through a building, many students can picture every arc of information between sentences because each one describes an object or event that readers have experienced in their lives. Thus, when a literary character climbs from a house's basement to its top floor, the objects on each floor can become vivid and memorable images for a reader. These mental pictures can also be easily stored in long-term memory. Constructing them, students retain more facts because numerous details are almost effortlessly inserted into the almost automatically imaged scene the brain constructs because it is designed to complete images, patterns, and **gestalts** (Britton & Graesser, 1996).

A second condition that makes it easier for students to image is when a text contains vivid verbs and explicit, specific nouns. For instance, it is easier to picture the word screamed than the word said; and fourth-grade and fifth-grade students who were taught to picture the outlines for each of the United States as they memorized the capitals of those states remembered significantly more capital cities than a comparable group who were given an equal amount of time to learn without being taught how to image each state's outline (Levin, Barry, Miller, and Bartel, 1982).

Another factor that increases readers' ease and effectiveness in building imagery is when they are taught how to recognize when they misunderstand a sentence in a text (Baker, 2001; Baker & Anderson, 1982; Ruffman, 2000). Such instruction can occur as early as 4 years of age (Perfetti, Marron, & Foltz, 1999; Piaget & Inhelder, 1971). However, when such instruction is not provided, even many adults have difficulty imaging when decoding demands or idea density in a text are too complex (Sadoski & Paivio, 1994). The readability level of a text and the size of a student's own imagination also contribute to a reader's ability to image. The instructional lessons in this chapter are designed to overcome these difficulties and enhance readers' abilities to ignite their creative thinking during their imagery processing of text (Levin, 1991; Perfetti, Marron, & Foltz, 1999).

Three theories of **creativity** thinking explain how mental imagery works (Gowan, 1980). The first declares that images arise from a fusion of closely related, divergent thinking processes, which, when united, disperse vivid mental pictures. A comprehensive list of these divergent thinking processes appears in the structures of intellect model created by Gilford (1978). This theory identified more than 100 separate processes that readers can elicit to create diverse images.

A second theory is based on the 30-year research program of Maslow (e.g., 1968). His body of data suggest that imagery is the *culmination* of a *complete integration* of all details read in a text and the removal of barriers between readers' literal and inferential text processing. According to this theoretical perspective, images will not occur until students' own interpretation of text has been processed. The third theory is similar to the previous one. It adds one factor (Terman, 1961) to Maslow's propositions. Terman's model claims that it is a reader's ability (as opposed to the author's skill in writing) that is the supreme authority in making images.

When students were taught these theories, they eliminated more mental blocks to their own imagery-making abilities (see Block & Pressley, 2002; Block, Gambrell, & Pressley, 2003 for descriptions of these studies). This growth occurred because students no longer thought stereotypically or allowed authorities to dominate their own creative thinking as they read.

External conditions also contribute to imagery formation (Torrance, 1981; Torrance & Sisk, 2001). First, readers need freedom to form random, often unrelated, insights from text. Second, students must associate facts that, on the surface, appear to be unrelated. This condition explains why students remember items on a list better when each listing is associated with an unrelated object in a room (e.g., subjects remember to buy milk as the first item on their grocery list by creating a mental image of a milk carton being placed on the entry table in the hall of their home because the entry table is the first piece of furniture that the person sees on entering the home [Beyer, 1986]. Third, a large body of evidence, indicating that readers' degrees of extroversion on the Myers-Briggs Personality Scale (Myers & Briggs, 2001) as well as their maturity level enhance imagery abilities.

Imagery behaviors can be learned (Block, 1993; Block & Mangieri, 1996) and teachers ranked imagery as one of the most important comprehension processes that should be taught to less able readers (Block & Mangieri, 2003; Block, Oakar, & Hurt, 2002; Cazden, 1991).

Regardless of the theory of imagery to which one subscribes, images cannot emerge, unless (1) readers know they are free to reach deep into their creative thinking, (2) blocks to students' literal comprehension are eliminated through Strand 1 lessons, and (3) teachers are available when an inability to image occurs.

For some, the imagery lessons in this chapter will be the first instruction they will have ever received. These lessons are also likely to enable many readers to become so immersed in the reading experience itself, and in creating images evoked by the language process, that for the first time their minds will no longer be consumed merely in decoding language (Fleckenstein, 1991). Moreover, because imaging evokes a reader's personal emotions, it is the best strategy to increase a student's positive, aesthetic responses to text. The following excerpt describes this power in the words from Reid, the boy pictured in the photo that opened this chapter. He said at the end of Imagery Lesson 1,

> As I read, the scenery came back as it was all supposed to be, and emotions started pouring in. When I got to the part about turning around, I lost the fact that I was reading and I started reliving the whole thing in my mind. Right when I read the word "mom" I could picture my own mother. A feeling of warmth gushed over me. What power a single word has when I picture it in my mind!

The most important first step in any imagery lessons is to ensure that students have information about the subject about which they are to read. A second step is to teach imagery through concrete words and short instructional sentences. For instance, you can begin an imagery lesson by asking students to raise their hands when they have pictured the words *leaf, red leaf, green leaf,* and so on (Poltrock & Brown, 1984). A third step is to teach children to construct relationships among their prior knowledge, experiences, and literal facts they are reading (Au, 1993; Wittrock & Alesandrini, 1998; Wittrock, 1998). Familiar words in stories can also be used at the early stages of teaching imagery. Such words, in familiar contexts, make the unit to be pictured small enough so that not only single words can be imaged but also the contextual sentence in which they appear.

As a result, students can predict what a next sentence could be and describe the image they created that linked the two sentences together in their minds. Last, each of the imagery lessons that you will read about in the remainder of this chapter can be increased in effectiveness when you teach students to underline main ideas as they read (Chi, Slotta, & DeLeeuw, 1994; Locken, 1981; Pearson, Hansen, & Gordon, 1979). When these four steps are included in imagery instruction students take less time to generate images (Koslyn, Brunn, Cave, & Wallach, 1984; Poltrock & Brown, 1984).

Teaching Imagery by Deepening Domain Knowledge Structures

Teaching imagery by deepening domain knowledge structures

Imagery can be taught by asking students to look within, and then up and away, to reflect periodically on the structure used to build sections of text. Four lessons follow that increase students' schema or domain knowledge structures to teach imagery during comprehension processing.

Imagery Lesson 1: Look Up and Away.   You can model how you image pictorial nouns. Next, ask students to read pictorial nouns and describe the images these words evoked (Miller, 1987). Then, you can ask pupils to turn to a partner and describe each image that these words produced. Last, have each partnered team read an entire paragraph and write one sentence together about how their images changed as they read each successive sentence.

When they feel comfortable and competent in image making, you can instruct students to read silently and stop whenever they have created a vivid mental image that they want to share. Evaluate whether student images contain enough sensory information and use of prior personal experiences to ensure that they have made an emotional connection to the text. If either of these comprehension processes is not present, conduct a mini lesson about how to add these thinking processes to image making and engage two or more periods of silent reading and descriptions of mental images so students can improve their imagery skills. A lesson format, sample curricula, and student examples that can be used in this lesson appear in Comprehension Process Lesson 6 at the end of this chapter. This lesson also illustrates how you can use the power of three instructional method described in Chapter 1 to teach imagery.

Finally, you can teach students to look within, and then up and away from the text when they pause to image. You can explain that doing so may help them because research indicates that people generally look up when they are trying to build images or project to the future (Caine & Caine, 1997). A list of books that teachers have found work well in teaching this lesson appears in Table 6.1.

Imagery Lesson 2: Write Similes.   Another instructional method is to teach students how to write similes to describe the main ideas that they read. For example, Natalie, a first-grade student, wanted to describe how she had arranged all the snowballs in the

**TABLE 6.1   Books with Surprise Endings and Vivid Images
That Build Students' Imagery Abilities**

Young Readers

Clifford and the Grouchy Neighbors by N. Bridwell, 1990, Scholastic

Bert and the Missing Mop Mix-Up by S. Roberts, 1989, Children's Television Workshop

Dr. Desoto by W. Steig, 1983, Scholastic

Frog Medicine by M. Teague, 1991, Scholastic

The Frog Who Drank the Waters of the World by P. Montgomery, 1983, Atheneum

Hugo and the Spacedog by L. Lorenz, 1991, Simon & Schuster

Miss Nelson Has a Field Day by Allard, 1985, Houghton Mifflin

The Mysteries of Harris Burdick by Van Allsberg, 1984, Houghton Mifflin

Oscar Mouse Finds a Home by M. Miller, 1985, Dial

Pleasant Dreams by A. B. Francis, 1983, Holt

The Principal's New Clothes by S. Calmenson, 1989, Scholastic

Snow Lion and other books by D. McPhail, 1989, Dutton

Something Special for Me by V. B. Williams, 1983, Greenwillow

A Toad for Tuesday and other books by R. E. Erickson, Lothrop

The Vanishing Pumpkin by T. de Paola, 1993, Putnam

The Velveteen Rabbit by M. Williams, 1984, Running Press

Who Sank the Boat by P. Allen, 1989, Orchard

Older Readers

Arthur's April Fool by M. Brown, 1983, Little, Brown

The Borrowers by M. Norton, 1974, Caedmon

The Castle of the Red Gorillas by W. Ecke, 1983, Prentice Hall

Christina's Ghost by B. R. Wright, 1987, Scholastic

Coffin on a Case by Eve Blunting (10 and up), 1992, Harper and Collins

Encyclopedia Brown and the Case of the Disgusting Sneakers (7–12) by Donald J. Sobol, 1984, Bantam

A Flight of Angels (9–13) by Geoffrey Trease, 1989, Lerner

Garbage Juice for Breakfast (6–9) by Patricia Reilly Giff, 1989, Bantam

The Hoax and You (8–12) by Marilyn Singer, 1989, Harper

Judge Benjamin: The Superdog Secret by V. McInerney, 1983, Holiday

The Lockkey Kids by S. Terris, 1986, Farrar, Straus & Giroux

My Dog and the Knock Knock Mystery and other books by D. A. Adler, 1985, Holiday

The Mystery of the Smashing Glass by W. Arden, 1984, Random House

Nate the Great and the Halloween Hunt; Nate the Great and the Musical Note; Nate the Great and the Stolen Base; Nate the Great Goes Down in the Dumps (6–9) by Marjorie Weinman Sharmat, 1984, Coward

The Revolt of the Teddy Bears by J. Duffy, 1985, Crown

Tom's Midnight Garden by P. Pearce, 1984, Lippincott

The Twiddle Twins' Haunted House by H. Goldsmith, 1989, Scholastic

The Vandemark Mummy (10 and up) by Cynthia Voigt, 1991, Atheneum

Wake Me at Midnight (8–12) by Barthe DeClements, 1991, Viking

What's That Noise? (3–6) by Mary Roennfeldt, 1985, W. Morrow

Wild Geese by Ellis Dillon (10 and up), 1980, Simon & Schuster

A Wizard of Earthsea and other books by U. K. Le Guin, 1986, Chivers

World Famous Muriel and the Magic Mystery (5–8) by Sue Alexander, 1990, Crowell

story that she wrote. She wanted to communicate the splendor of this final product which had taken her an hour to create. Mrs. Armstrong took this opportunity to teach the entire class imagery lesson 2 on writing similes. A **simile** is a figure of speech likening one thing to another by the use of *like*, *as*, and so on (for example: *tears flowed like* *wine*). Mrs. Armstrong wrote three examples on the chalkboard and performed a think-aloud which illustrated how she creates similes in her mind to help her image:

> This paper is *as light as a feather.*
> My heart is *fluttering like a butterfly.*
> My head is *spinning like a top.*

Next, she asked students to discuss and write as many similes as they could. She described how these figures of speech could help them to image and remember text. As a result, on the next day Natalie wrote: "I formed 25 snowballs. I put them side-by-side in a perfect half circle. It glistened in the sun. It was beautiful." Natalie was not satisfied with this description. She said, "I wanted people to really see it, so I added 'It looked like a huge diamond necklace for a giant princess.'" By using the word *like* and knowing how to use similes to create effective mental images, Natalie left her writing experience with strong feelings of accomplishment and pride. Mrs. Armstrong felt equally fulfilled because she had increased her students' abilities to image.

Imagery Lesson 3: Create Mental Stories before Students Scribe Them.   A third lesson that develops imaging is to ask readers to tell you about events about which they are going to write. The process of orally describing an unfolding event often stimulates images in students' minds. For instance, Cedric, a fifth grader, described the following image when this lesson was implemented. Cedric's teacher asked him to just talk about what he wanted to write before he wrote. Cedric said: "The second time Michael Jordan shot from the foul line he missed the basket. Patrick Ewing jumped up and wrestled it away from everyone else!" Following his oral description, Cedric wrote about this scene, and included even more details from the mental images that his conversation had stimulated.

Imagery Lesson 4: Create Mental Transformations.   Barrows (1985) was the first to suggest that teachers use guided imaging in a gamelike activity. In this lesson, small groups of students assign human traits to an animal or inanimate object. Doing so builds mental agility and has been shown to increase the speed and vividness with which students image. For example, one student might say, "An elephant is riding a bike." Then, a second student explains why that image would be beneficial by adding a second oral sentence for the class to image with (e.g., "That's a good idea because the elephant can get around faster.").

Next, a third student would create another oral sentence that depicts another trait the elephant possesses, such as, "The elephant can talk and he says 'What's for lunch?'." Then, a fourth student explains why this trait is a good idea (e.g.," That's a good idea because the elephant can communicate with people and other elephants as he rides past them on his bike."). The next student then gives another trait to add to the visualization: "He flies kites as he rides his bike."

As this process continues and more ideas are expressed, one student writes all of them on a chart for the class to see. After all students in this small group have contributed, they orally read the chart and compare the images that this lesson created. Last, students write their own paragraphs using a different subject. When each student has finished his or her paragraph a peer reads it and writes about the image that friend's paragraph created.

Teaching Imagery by Inducing and Invoking Images

Teaching imagery by inducing and invoking images

Another method of teaching imagery is to invoke images through beautiful language. These lessons are enjoyable and easy to implement. Ask students to image before, during, and after they read. Research has documented that only a few lessons are necessary for most students to begin to image while they read (Gambrell, 1982; Pressley, 1976).

Imagery Lesson 5: Paint Mental Pictures. Bales and Gambrell (1985) asked fourth and fifth graders to "make pictures in their minds to help them understand" while a control group was instructed to "do whatever you can to help you understand and remember what you are about to read" (p. 136). All students who were told to construct images found more inconsistencies in the material, and 70 percent of these experimental subjects used imagery to retain information compared to only 1 percent of the control group. This lesson also increased experimental subjects' comprehension and retention (Gambrell & Koskinen, 2001). The full description of how to teach students to "paint mental pictures" appears as steps 1 through 3 of Comprehension Process Lesson 6 at the end of this chapter.

Imagery Lesson 6: Translate Audio Tapes into Print. Many students in grades 1 to 6 have significantly increased their abilities to image when they listen to books on tape (Block, in press). In this lesson, students listen to books from five different genres. To teach this lesson, teach Comprehension Process Lesson 6 first. Then, instruct students to image as they listen to a tape of a book. Students are told to stop the tape after 15 minutes and write a description of the next image that is likely to occur in the story. Then, they are to turn the tape back on to find out if their images were correct. Students are to be reading from a print version of the story as they hear the tape and they are not to turn pages ahead of the tape.

Teaching Imagery Using Poetry and Art

Teaching imagery using poetry and art

Poetry and art are a third method of teaching imagery. Both of these venues stimulate visual, audio, kinesthetic, and tactile input systems. Poetry draws the reading into a union of sound and descriptive word play in which the rhythm of our language is added to literal and inferential comprehension processes to increase understanding. This magnetism arises because "poetry becomes new experiences that readers create out of this memory, thoughts, feelings, and by paying attention to the ordered symbols of text" (Elster, 2000, p. 7). In like manner, art involves the use of one's hands to build a new concept or object, which can then be more readily repictured when only the words in a text are used to describe it.

Imagery Lesson 7: Write Poems with Vivid Words and Phrases.   Poem writing begins by reading a few poems filled with descriptive words to students. As you read, do not show pictures. Excellent poets to select are Douglas Florian, Shel Silverstein, Judy Viorst, and Eloise Greenfield, whose works such as "*Insect-opedia,*" and "*Laugh-eteria,*" "*Why I Hate School,*" and "*Honey I Love*" contain vividly described words and images. After reading, you can perform a think-aloud in which you ask students to describe the images or pictures that occurred in their minds. Then, you explain to students that they were able to image because the words selected by the author were very descriptive and guided them to see with their mind's eye. Each time they read, they are to attend to the vivid words authors use because they were chosen with care to establish mental images. As a result, they too can help their readers to image by selecting vivid words and vivid phrases for their compositions.

Next, you can read three different formats, such as haiku, diamante, and free verse. Ask pupils to write one of these types of **format poetry** (poems that follow a distinct rhyming scheme) that you read. Second, lead students to brainstorm subjects and topics for the poems. Some examples that can be shared and valued by younger children appear in Figure 6.1 because they describe simple themes of best friends, pets, favorite foods, toys; or events such as going to theme parks, zoos, and shopping centers. Next, model for students how they can write many descriptive words on the top of the sheet of paper on which they will write their poetry. You can model how you inserted these words into three sample poems that the class creates and displays. Last, ask students to write and share poems that they wrote individually. In the discussion following each reading, peers can describe the images that each poem elicited. Following this lesson, the class can select a poet laureate to write poems to be read at the end of the week, following which a new poet laureate can be chosen.

Imagery Lesson 8: Create Shadow Boxes in Art Classes.   Creating **shadow boxes** (small display created of cut out objects set inside boxes so shadows from objects create added depth to these artistic depictions) begins with all students bringing shoebox lids to school. You can teach students that imagery can be enhanced by color, foreground, middle ground, and background. You can explain these concepts by showing shadow boxes that you created as samples. Students can make shadow boxes about a room in their home, the zoo, a grocery store, a schoolroom, or other three-dimensional spaces in their lives. After students have chosen their topic, they can stencil the background on the lid of the box and then color in the facsimile of the colored visual image in their minds. Students then cut 1-inch square tabs and fold them so that they can be used to glue the middle ground objects to the background and foreground pictures. The final product may look like a sky, clouds, and a field in the background; horses eating in the middle ground; and a fence in the foreground.

Imagery Lesson 9: Write Format Poems and Format Stories.   The format poem and format stories, as shown in Figure 6.2, can be used with any of the prior lessons in

Eggshells

Eggshells
Crumbling, cracking
Wanting to break
The struggle pains one Life

Oh, Recess

I can't wait til recess
So I can swing high
Sway back & forth with my feet
Frolic in the grass.

I can't wait til recess
I want to pedal the fire bike
Hide in the wooden house
Play with my friends

I can't wait til recess
I will twirl on the yellow slide
Hang on the bars
Chase the boys
And be me.

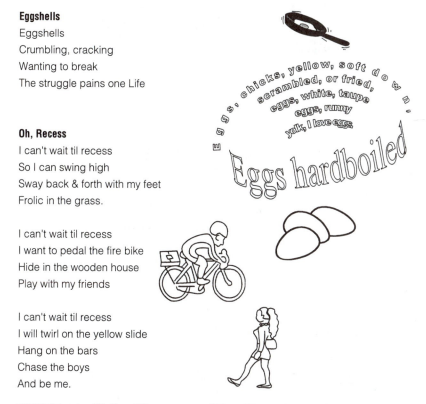

FIGURE 6.1   Haiku, Diamante, and Free Verse Written by Children

Source: Designed by Rachel Escamilla, administrative assistant, Texas Christian University, Fort Worth, Texas.

this chapter. They can be used to create mental images, or to describe mental images that arise in the process of reading or writing. Format poetry and stories stimulate students to image through vivid words and phrases.

In Summary

There are three methods of building students' imagery: (1) deepening students' schema and domain knowledge, (2) invoking images through beautiful language, and (3) using poetry and art. These methods can be presented through nine imagery lessons and Comprehension Process Lesson 6. These activities reinforce vivid words,

Title The litle Puppy

I like Puppy.

Puppy, Are cuot, and Cuouiy.

I drew a picture of A Puppy. and I was

HAPPY.

When I am with MI PUPPY I feel GlAD

and HAPPY

I really like PUPPY.

BY ASHLEY

FIGURE 6.2 Format Story Written by First-Grade Spanish Student
Source: Created by Dionne Adkison. Used by permission.

experiences with imagery, and the power of the rhymes and rhythm in language as meaning-making tools. Using poetry and art can also increase students' imagery during reading and writing because they teach students to visualize story grammar. Figure 6.3 summarizes all imagery lessons. It can be duplicated and used in your lesson plan book to build a complete teaching repertoire so your students have optimal opportunities to master this important comprehension process.

FIGURE 6.3   Summary of Nine Imagery Lessons That Build Students' Abilities to Image

Lesson 1: Look Up and Away.

Ask students to image single words, then sentences, and lastly paragraphs after you have modeled how to "look up and away" from the text to reflect, by saying: "Pay attention to the familiar retrieval clues or signal words as I draw this picture in our minds using only words." (Describe a vivid object feature by feature and then display it.)

Lesson 2: Write Similes.

Ask students to write similes to describe main ideas or themes from books read.

Lesson 3: Create Mental Stories before Students Scribe Them.

Ask students to tell you about events before they write them down.

Lesson 4: Create Mental Transformations.

Assign human traits to an animal or inanimate object.

Lesson 5: Paint Mental Pictures.

Students are taught how to paint mental pictures.

Lesson 6: Translate Audio Tapes into Print.

Ask students to listen to books on tape and write a summary at the end of their most vivid mental image and what the author did to make that image so memorable.

Lesson 7: Write Poems with Vivid Words and Phrases.

Demonstrate how poets create images with words and ask students to write poems like those in Figure 6.1.

Lesson 8: Create Shadow Boxes.

Have students create a foreground, middle ground, and background in shoebox lids with cutouts from construction paper.

Lesson 9: Write Format Poems and Format Stories.

Give students a format to follow in writing a haiku, diamante, or cinquain poem or story. Then they draw an image around their finished product that depicts the writing's theme.

REFLECTING ON WHAT YOU HAVE LEARNED

1. *Your Professional Journal: Learning Log.* In your journal, define imagery. Describe the three approaches that teach imagery. How would you implement the nine lessons in your classroom (e.g., once a month, as a thematic unit, once a week and so on)? After you implement your plan, evaluate how effective it is and record your observations in your journal to keep a record of your experiences. How hard were the lessons to use? How effective were they?

2. *Field Applications and Observations.* What is the advice that you will give to fellow educators concerning the first steps that should be taken to teach students how to image? How can you help students comprehend and understand accurately using imagery?

3. *Multicultural Application.* In one paragraph write a concise description of your understanding of teaching imagery to students. Describe your instruction and assessment plans for teaching imagery. This description will help you communicate to students, parents, and colleagues how you are helping students who have difficulty using imagery.

4. *Key Terms Exercise.* Following is a list of concepts introduced in this chapter. If you have learned the meaning of a term, place a checkmark in the blank that precedes that term. If you are not sure of the term's definition increase your retention by reviewing the definition of the terms. If you have learned three of these terms on your first reading of this chapter, you have constructed many meanings that are important for your career.

_____ image (p. 119)	_____ gestalt (p. 120)
_____ imagery (p. 119)	_____ simile (p. 123)
_____ imaging (p. 119)	_____ format poem (p. 126)
_____ creativity (p. 120)	_____ shadow boxes (p. 126)

5. *Comprehension Process Lesson 6: Teaching Students the Comprehension Process of Imaging as They Read.* The following comprehension lesson demonstrates the step-by-step instructions that you can use to teach students to build mental pictures as they read. The lesson also contains questions that you can ask when you meet with students in one-to-one settings to help them overcome their individual blocks to completing effective images. Students' answers to these questions will help them to become active participants in improving their abilities in making meaning.

COMPREHENSION PROCESS LESSON 6
Structured Mental Imaging Activities

Objective
To promote children's ability to draw mental pictures with words.

Listening and Drawing Forms

Prereading Stage

Step 1: Ask students to close their eyes and imagine a topic, event, or character about which they are to read. Then tell them to open their eyes and draw what they saw in their minds from vivid sentence descriptions that you gave to them orally, which transform objects in some way, such as:
   1. Picture a small red ball.
   2. Place it on top of a green table.

COMPREHENSION PROCESS LESSON 6   Continued

3. Put a white volleyball on its right side.
4. Put an orange basketball on its left side.

Step 2: Have the students share their drawings with at least two other students. Here they can talk about and analyze why they depicted the topic as they did using the words they heard. Ask them to explain the personal experiences and sources of information that helped them in their drawings.

Reading Stage

Step 3: Have students open their textbooks to the appropriate selection or distribute the relevant reading material and have them read the passage with their drawings in mind. The text would describe objects or events that you had presented orally in Step 1 above.

Step 4: Engage in a small group or whole class discussion of the reading and then ask the students to develop a new drawing or change the existing one to correspond to the new information read.

After Reading Stage

Step 5: Have students tell you (and list on a chart) the actions they can take to add imagery to comprehension processes in the future to create more vivid and accurate mental images as they read.

TALKING AND DRAWING FORM

Prereading Stage

Step 1: Close your eyes and think about [a growling dog]. Now, open your eyes and draw what you imaged.

(continued)

COMPREHENSION PROCESS LESSON 6   Continued

Reading Stage

Step 2: Read ["a dog has glasses and reads a book"] and then draw a second picture to show what you learned.

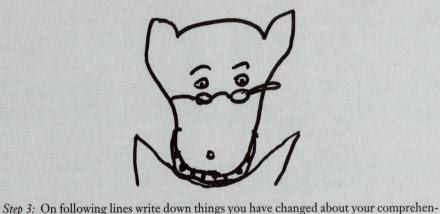

Step 3: On following lines write down things you have changed about your comprehension because you image better now.

_____

_____

_____

_____

_____

_____

_____

Metacognition: Monitoring One's Own Comprehension

Ms. Armstrong knows that teaching, monitoring, and diagnosing students' metacognitive processes takes time. Each week she sets aside 10 minutes to teach one of the lessons in this chapter, individually and in small groups. By mid year, her students are describing their comprehension processes fluidly because of Ms. Armstrong's weekly emphasis.

Ms. Armstrong often asks her students the following questions: "What comprehension processes did you use to learn the meaning in that phrase?" "What did you do when you misunderstood a sentence?" "If you could talk to the author, what would you ask him or her?" "If this story had taken place today, how would it have been different and why?" "If the main character in the book ___ had lived today, what would she have done differently?" "How would the main character in the book you read yesterday have benefited from what you learned

---

METACOGNITION: MONITORING ONE'S OWN COMPREHENSION

Theoretical background

Overview of methods that develop metacognition

Teaching domain 1 of metacognition: Controlling one's thoughts during reading

Teaching domain 2 of metacognition: Developing text sensitivity

Teaching domain 3 of metacognition: Increasing knowledge of one's goals

Catch-up comprehension processes

Evaluating metacognitive domains and catch-up comprehension processes *today about this book's moral?" The classroom conversations that revolve around these questions are rich and increase students' metacognitive comprehension processes.* ■

Chapter Overview

Metacognition can be defined as a reader's awareness of (1) what he or she is thinking about while reading, (2) what thinking processes he or she initiates to overcome literacy challenges, and (3) how a reader selects specific thinking processes to make meaning before, during, and after reading (Brown, 2002). We know that students can learn how to correct misunderstandings in the process of comprehending (Delisle, 1997), and the purpose of this chapter is to describe how this is done. A second goal is to describe new methods of teaching students to achieve personalized, automatic metacognitive thoughts during reading.

National committees concluded that metacognition can be developed through instruction (Baker, 2001; Baker & Zimlin, 1989; Baumann, Jones, & Seifert-Kessell, 1993; Bereiter & Bird, 1985; Block, 1993; Collins, 1991; Miller, 1985; National Reading Panel, 1999; National Research Council, 1998; Payne and Manning, 1992), with the National Reading Panel identifying 20 research studies that documented the impact of instruction on students' metacognitive growth (National Reading Panel, 1999).

This chapter describes the metacognitive research bases that enable students to increase their metacognitive comprehension processes. The lessons in this chapter are designed to prepare students to think metacognitively as they read.

By the end of this chapter, you will be able to answer the following questions:

1. What can teachers do to improve less able comprehenders' metacognitive processes?
2. How can students be taught to initiate effective metacognitive processes when they misunderstand what they read?
3. What methods improve students' abilities to correct their own confusion as they read?

Theoretical Background

Theoretical background

Readers think metacognitively when they (1) consider the implicit meanings in texts, (2) reflect on their own understanding, and (3) use multiple strategies to remove blocks that interrupt comprehension (Block, 2000; Block & Johnson, 2002; Block & Pressley, 2001; Keene & Zimmerman, 1997). Metacognitive lessons are valuable because many students have had few adult mentoring experiences in which elders explained the thinking processes they use when they encounter reading difficulties (Baker, 2001; Block & Mangieri, 1995, 1996; Flavell, 1976).

A second reason that metacognitive instruction is increasing at the elementary school level is that recent research proves that even young children have the ability to evaluate their own comprehension. However, most students will not engage such metacognitions without instruction (Baker, 2001; Block, 1998; Paris, Wasik, & Turner, 1991). There are seven metacognitive processes (Baker, 2001) and four additional ones identified by Block (2002b) described as follows:

1. **Semantic processes.** Checking the meaning of individual words
2. **Syntactic processes.** Attending to the grammatical structure of sentences and phrases
3. **Checking for internal consistency.** Checking that ideas are logically consistent throughout a text
4. **Monitoring external consistencies.** Verifying the facts that are presented in a text with respect to a student's life experiences
5. **Checking propositional cohesiveness.** Checking that there is a cohesive relationship between the proposition in a paragraph and the story or text
6. **Ensuring structural cohesiveness.** Evaluating the thematic compatibility of ideas throughout a text
7. **Evaluating informational completeness.** Verifying that all parts of a text that have been read are understood
8. **Noting the direction of a character's thoughts.** Identifying clues in characters' personalities and interactions with other characters as to the reason an author depicted a character as he or she did
9. **Comparing events read to similar events in their lives.** Applying text to individual students' lives through reflecting and thinking as they read
10. **Fusing semantic and syntactical information.** Contrasting cases and examples during reading will enable students to do unprompted metacognitive thinking
11. **Verifying an internal consistency with the order present in a text.** Teaching students to coherently tie their lives and background knowledge with the information in the text is called metacognitively creating coherence

Researchers have grouped these eleven metacognitive abilities into three instructional categories (see e.g., Cornoldi, Debeni, & Pazzaglia, 1998): (1) lessons that develop students' competencies in controlling their on-task thinking while reading, (2) lessons that increase pupils' sensitivities to textual changes as they read, and (3) lessons that enable readers to retain and relate the metacognition of prior textual facts as they process new text. According to Brown, Collins, and Duguid (1989), much of these mental tasks becomes artificial when we try to teach metacognition as a skill. Therefore, lessons in this chapter do not separate the eleven abilities; they do not teach students only to do the first, and then the second, and so on until all eleven have been taught. Instead, the methods described in the next section of this chapter models how to initiate several metacognitions in rapid succession when a reader becomes confused.

In her recent work, Baker (2001) found that adults could engage three processes simultaneously when given explicit instruction to check for propositional, structural, and informational completeness. When researchers taught young students to do so, both strong and weak comprehenders benefited equally from the instruction. Moreover, these researchers found that metacognition could be developed even if literal (Block & Johnson, 2002) comprehension and decoding proficiencies were below grade level (Baker, 2001; Block, 2000; Dyson, 2001).

When students truly become effective metacognitivists, they construct personalized "benchmarks" in a text which serve to connect the textual events to their lives (Trimble, 1994). This "pausing to reflect and apply" is the ultimate goal of the lessons in this chapter. It is positive evidence that students have guided their own minds to comprehend. For example, a student may mumble to herself, "Hmm, that's the way Grandma spells her name" or "He is a pitcher, just like my brother." The more personal benchmarks students create as they read, the more new textual structures and knowledge will be related to their lives. Moreover, without the abilities to make such links, many students will not approach new texts with a strong sense of self-efficacy.

Overview of Methods That Develop Metacognition

Metacognition is (1) crucial to the development of the application level of comprehension; (2) learning how to learn, a highly advanced metacognitive ability, with an enduring affect on student achievement; and (3) able to enhance readers' motivation and positive attitudes toward reading (Chipman & Segal, 1985; Cullinan, 1999; Presseisen, 1987; Smey-Richman, 1988). Researchers have also discovered that even young children can describe and learn to monitor their own comprehension effectively when they talk about and hear their peers' descriptions of how they think while they read (Baker, 1984a; Block, Gambrell, & Pressley, 2002, Glaubman & Ofir, 1997).

As early as age 5, students can initiate metacognition, and such energy positively increases their motivational drive, interest, and reading pleasure (Borkowski, Carr, Rellinger, & Pressley, 1990; Hacker, 1998; Paris & Winograd, 1990). This research is supported by the theoretical work of Vygotsky (1978). His work demonstrated that children begin to mimic other people's thinking when an expert initially assists them in taking responsibility for regulating the metacognitive processes that they use. Next, such readers begin to see that planning before one reads is necessary, and that there is much one should ponder during reading. Other researchers emphasize the importance of instruction that involves discussion and collaboration among peers (see Block, Gambrell, & Pressley, 2002; Block & Pressley, 2002). Therefore, the lessons in this chapter encourage teachers to perform oral renditions of their thinking. These think-alouds support children's ability to fill gaps and identify the explicit steps in their own metacognitive processes (Baker, 2001; Brown & Campione, 1998).

Teaching Domain 1 of Metacognition: Controlling One's Thoughts during Reading

Teaching domain 1 of metacognition: Controlling one's thoughts during reading

Because so many benefits result from increased metacognition, two lessons to increase the first categories of metacognitive abilities follow. These lessons assist students to focus their thinking on key ideas while reading.

Metacognitive Development Lesson 1: Teaching Semantic and Syntactic Processes.   To introduce metacognitive reading processes, you can model what you do to overcome comprehension difficulties. You can make an overhead transparency of a story. Then, you can distribute a handout, which describes the eleven metacognitive processes (or only two processes for younger students) identified earlier in this chapter. After teaching how each process works, you can read a sentence orally and perform a think-aloud about how you use two (at first) or more during subsequent lessons of these metacognitive processes consecutively to enrich your comprehension of each sentence. For example, if you projected a paragraph on an overhead, you could describe your metacognitive thinking to your class using a think-aloud that is similar to those printed in the bracketed sections of the example that follows: Projected sentence is "The night sky was dark and a wolf howled." [Boys and girls, when I read this sentence I think that the author is trying to make readers feel scared, because the words dark night sky and a wolf howled were chosen to remind us of times in our lives when we were scared by these two events occurring together.]

Then, you can ask students to describe what they think their minds are doing while they read. List descriptions on a chart about what they are thinking. When more than 670 children were asked, "When you are reading alone and you understand what you're reading, what do you think your mind is doing?" many metacognitive processes were cited (Block & Mangieri, 2003). Representative answers (from children from kindergarten to grade 5) follow:

1. Josh (kindergarten): "My mind is reading to me." (p. 17)
2. Kasandra (first grader): "My mind is drawing pictures for me." (p. 28)
3. Mesong (second grader): "It is doing what Amelia Bedelia is doing." (p. 39)
4. Trisha (third grader): "My mind is wandering around in the story to see what it is about." (p. 60)
5. Kevin (fourth grader): "It is thinking and having a certain feeling, part of it is relaxing and the other part is reading." (p. 91)
6. Maryann (fifth grader): "My mind is in pained attention." (p. 112)

As students' ideas are expressed, write them on a chart. After all students in this lesson have contributed, they orally read the chart and compare the thoughts that this reading created in their minds. You can end the lesson by asking students what new metacognitive process they would like you to model in a future lesson. For instance, if they asked you to model "what to think when they come to a word we don't know," you could model a metacognitive process similar to the following:

> When I come to a word I do not know, I think to myself about what I should do, which is a metacognition. I first look at the length of the word and its letter pattern to deter-mine if I should use phonic generalizations, sight word memories, or structural analysis to learn the word. While I'm making this decision, I move my eyes back to the first part of the sentence and reread the other words so I can put their meanings with the sound of the first letter in the word that I don't know. If I still do not know the word, I read to the end of the paragraph, and by that time I have made the decision whether I know the word, will ask someone for the meaning, look it up in a dictionary, or read on to gain more context clues. Now, try to use this metacognitive process to figure out this word [pointing to a word in a book a student(s) has selected to read].

Metacognitive Development Lesson 2: Teaching Students to Check for Internal Consistency.   Getting readers to talk about their metacognition helps them learn to do so on their own, but may require repeated prompts, as illustrated in this exchange:

> *Teacher:*   Jimmy, can you tell us one of the things we talked about that can help us figure out a new word?
>
> *Jimmy:*   First letter.
>
> *Teacher:*   I'm not sure I understand what you mean. Could you give me some more words that will help us understand how the first letter can help figure out a new word in reading?
>
> *Jimmy:*   Look at the first letter.
>
> *Teacher:*   How would looking at the first letter help us figure out a new word in reading?
>
> *Jimmy:*   Look at the first letter and think about what sound it makes. Then try to think of a word that starts with that letter and makes sense in the sentence.
>
> *Teacher:*   Good Jimmy. Now you've given enough words for us to understand how the first letter helps us figure out a new word. (Euler & Hellekson, 1993, p. 7)

Next, teach students to filter distracting thoughts from their minds as they read. This lesson also teaches them how to generate their own as they read. Factors as gen-eral as age, gender, social class, the desire to collectively communicate, and ability to interpret influence a child's use of positive metacognitive filters (Dyson, 2001).

Thus, this **metacognitive filtering lesson** enables you to teach children how to (1) control their own points of view, and (2) reflect momentarily, to make sense as they read. When students decide what is relevant, their unofficial personal worldview can help overcome any comprehension difficulties, and the organizational structure they devise can be used to overcome metacognitive challenges. You perform a think-aloud to describe what you think as you read. Then, you can ask students to stop at the end of each page for five consecutive pages. At the end of each page, ask students to describe what they were thinking as they read that page.

As students talk, write their comments in the first column of a two-column chart. Use the first column to describe positive, meaning-building metacognitive processes. List statements students make about what they misunderstood on that page in the second column. Write the metacognitive filtering process that can be used to eliminate these confusions in parentheses after and in a different color marker from all other words on the chart. Following is an example from a third grade lesson in which students stopped at the end of reading *Volcano* (Lauber, 1985).

Positive Metacognitive Processes

1. "When I read: 'For many years the volcano slept,' I thought that volcanoes were part of the earth like people, and I related this volcano to myself and how good it feels to sleep late on Saturdays. Thinking about this book in my mind, like this, made it very interesting and I wanted to keep on reading."

Metacognitive Processes to Be Improved

1. "I stopped thinking when I came to a word I didn't know." (Think to the end)
2. And so on.

In summary, most children (by age 10) can intertwine three different strands of metacognitive comprehension processes as they read. Lessons 1 and 2 can be used to develop students' depth of self-initiated metacognition.

Teaching Domain 2 of Metacognition: Developing Text Sensitivity

Teaching domain 2 of metacognition: Developing text sensitivity

Once students can focus their minds on what they are reading, you can teach the lessons which develop the second domain of metacognitive comprehension processes—the ability to detect salient and subtle author clues as they read. Lessons aimed at developing students' abilities to identify writing style and comprehend the author's thought follow. As you will discover, each instructional sequence increases students' abilities to use more than one metacognitive process interactively.

Metacognitive Development Lesson 3: Developing Students' Abilities to Follow an Author's Story Map (Developing a Sensitivity to Internal Consistencies). Among the most effective methods of teaching students to monitor their thinking during reading is to develop their abilities to create a **gestalt** (a cognitive process that places single pieces of information into categories so that a completed sense of understanding can be attained) of an author's writing style. This lesson is designed to teach students that each text has a structure, scope, and sequence that the writer uses to communicate. For example, some authors begin paragraphs by stating a main idea, and adding subsequent sentences to give details. If students are taught to use their internal consistency metacognitive process, they could read the first sentence in the first paragraph of new texts with the dual purpose of obtaining meaning from the words and deducing the author's writing style (e.g., Is this author going to write main ideas first and then delineate details, or is the author going to instead write several detail sentences and build toward a main idea?). When students use this metacognitive process they tend to discover an author's inferential arcs of information sooner. You can teach the internal consistency metacognitive process by using the thinking process guide in Figure 7.1. It provides more information to teach students how to identify an author's sequence of sentences within a paragraph.

Metacognitive Development Lesson 4: Teaching Structural Cohesiveness by Developing Students' Recognition of Authors' Writing Styles.   This lesson also uses Figure 7.1. In part 1, students can be taught the four patterns that authors and speakers use to communicate ideas depicted in this figure. In parts 2 through 4, they can use these patterns to follow speakers' and authors' ideas and to comprehend more when they read.

To introduce this lesson, you can ask students to define patterns. You can help them understand that patterns in writing and speaking create a definite direction,

FIGURE 7.1   Sample Thinking Guide to Teach the Internal Consistency Metacognitive Comprehension Process

Demonstrate how to think about the meaning in a paragraph as well as the way in which an author has ordered his or her ideas within that paragraph. You can do so by demonstrating that most authors place the main idea as the first or the last sentence in a paragraph. Similarly, in remaining sentences, most authors will use one type of detail more frequently than others. For instance, Patricia Lauber, in her award-winning expository text *Volcano: The Eruption of Mount St. Helens*, relies almost exclusively on "what" details in each paragraph. The internal consistency map that she created (see below) to write paragraphs in this book can be taught to students. Lauber followed the same internal consistency map in each paragraph, and when students become aware of it, they can predict what type of information will appear in upcoming sentences in this (and all) book(s) before they read each subsequent statement. The internal consistency map for *Volcano*'s paragraph is as follows:

First Sentence: Describes main idea.

Second Sentence: "What" detail is reported, a new vocabulary term is included, boldfaced, and defined.

Third Sentence: Second "what" detail about the main idea is written.

Fourth Sentence: Third "what" detail about the main idea is written.

Fifth Sentence: "Cause" or "effect" of these details is reported.

Thinking guides such as this one, which describe the internal consistency map that each author uses, can be created and taught to students right before they read each book.

grouping, or organization that assists listeners and readers to predict upcoming details. Then, you can explain that in this lesson students will learn to recognize patterns that people use to organize their thoughts so others can appropriately comprehend what they read and hear. Just as scientists classify species of animals according to common characteristics and patterns of behavior, authors organize their thoughts into recognizable writing patterns so readers can predict where main ideas and details will appear. When students recognize patterns people use, they can more easily understand and remember the ideas being communicated. For example, tell students that they will remember more when they read mathematics and history textbooks if they recognize that mathematicians order elements according to their ranking in increasing or decreasing numerical order; historians order temporally or sequentially in time; and some people organize their conversations by placing the most important ideas first. Explain to students they will know they have identified a pattern when they can use this pattern to predict an upcoming event, categorize new information, and remember ideas because of an awareness of the sequence within that pattern.

At this point, you may wish to outline an easily recognizable pattern on the chalkboard. For example, the circular pattern of the seasons of the year may be illustrated by writing the names of the four seasons within a circle and connecting them with arrows. Ask students to discuss how the visual representation of the pattern helps them to understand and remember it.

Next, you can ask students to share the titles of their favorite books and list them on the chalkboard. Tell students you will ask them to describe how the author patterned his or her thoughts to make that book so enjoyable, but first have students listen to three of Chapter 1's opening paragraphs from *Call It Courage*. As you read, ask students to identify how the author, Armstrong Sperry, patterns his ideas. Where does he place his main idea? Does he order ideas by placing events sequentially or thematically?

Discuss patterns students identified in Armstrong Sperry's writing style. Then return to the list of students' favorites. Ask if they can identify the types of patterns they enjoy in these books and have them write their answers next to each title. You may want to provide examples before students think about their responses. For instance, the author clearly moved from event 1 to event 2; the author always stated the main idea in the first sentence of each paragraph; or the author gave lots of details about topics.

Distribute one pattern at a time from the thinking process guides shown in Figures 7.2 and 7.3. Ask students to look at each illustrated pattern while you explain it. For four days, you can re-explain, and have students practice recognizing each of these author writing patterns using the information that follows.

1. *The **main ideas followed by details writing pattern*** explains a topic, concept, or theme by stating the main ideas (represented by circled ideas), and elaborating on them with details (represented by lines that emanate from each circled main idea). This pattern is used by many people and can be recognized because main concepts are repeated often and emphasized. Ask students to return to four of the paragraphs from *Call It Courage* and create a diagram that demonstrates the method Armstrong Sperry used to create internal consistence in his writing style. A sample answer is shown in Figure 7.2.

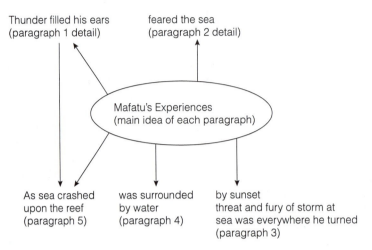

FIGURE 7.2   Example from *Call It Courage* of Writing Style That Presents Main Ideas First Followed by Details

2. *The **problem to solution writing pattern*** (see Figure 7.3) occurs frequently in life. In literature a problem is presented and usually three (or more) attempts to solve this problem occur before the climax (defining turn in events) and solution occur. To teach this pattern, you can conduct a strand 1 lesson in which you read *Princess Smarty Pants* and display Figure 7.3 on the overhead projector. You can explain how you used your metacognitive comprehension process of attending to the author's problem-solving story map to sequence important actions. Next, you can return to the list of books on the chalkboard and ask students to identify which authors followed this pattern in their writings. As a class, students can diagram the events in that book on a problem-solution pattern, similar to that on the thinking guide example in Figure 7.3.

3. *The "telling both sides" and **similarity/difference writing pattern*** defines how things are and are not alike. People who think this way often say "on the other hand," "sort of . . . but," and "consider this." When talking to someone who thinks this way or when reading a book that has this pattern, it is easier for students to keep track of the ideas by visualizing the similarity/difference pattern while listening or reading. To teach this pattern, ask students if they know anyone who uses this pattern to organize his or her ideas or if any of the authors in the list on the chalkboard uses this pattern. If students recognize this pattern in either acquaintances or literary figures, have them list a few of the statements that typify these people's speech or writing styles. If students cannot recognize this pattern, return to your example from *Call It Courage* and pretend you are Tavana Nui, Mafatu's father, and use the similarities/difference pattern to write statements that Tavana Nui might say about how his son is brave in other ways than going out to sea. List these statements in two columns. The left-hand column is labeled "Statements That Show Similarities Between Ideas in Sentences"; the right-hand column is labeled "Statements That Show Differences Between Ideas in Sentences." Once three are listed on both sides, teach how authors that use this pattern tend to give one

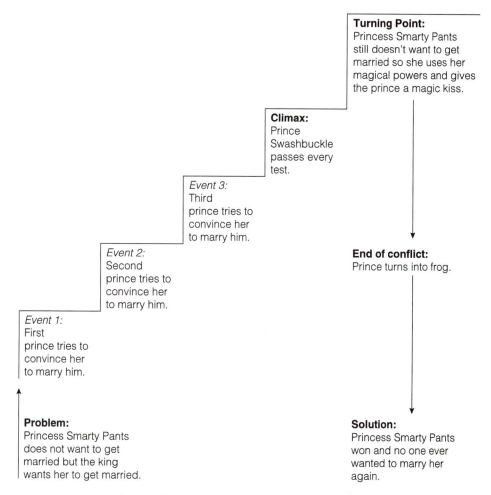

FIGURE 7.3 **Example from *Princess Smarty Pants* of Author's Writing Style That Follows the Problem-to-Solution Story Pattern**

to three points of similarity and follow these with one to three points that contrast with the prior statements. Lastly, ask students to read independently from a text that follows this pattern in a "stop and ask" Strand 2 lesson so you can check each of their columns as they create them, correcting errors immediately.

4. *The "telling things in order" or **sequential writing pattern** uses time to link thoughts and events. For example, historians and authors who write how-to guides and cookbooks follow a sequence pattern. Sequence patterns are often easy to recognize because books and people who use it frequently use sequence words such as "first," "then," "next," "after," and "finally." To teach this writing pattern, you can explain, perform a think-aloud, and use a section from a sequentially patterned book to demonstrate each of the metacognitions you used to follow the author's train of thought. Next, tell students that most directions that they will read throughout the rest of their lives will use this sequential writing pattern. Knowing this can increase their ability to follow instructions. Ask students to return to the list of books on the chalkboard and identify any books that use the sequence pattern. If students cannot identify any books that use this pattern, either show a page from a workbook that has directions or demonstrate the pattern orally by giving directions to a location in the school without telling students what the final destination is. Before you begin the directions, explain that because they know that directions follow a sequential pattern, students can listen for key sequence words to improve their comprehension. After you give the directions, ask students to tell what destination the directions describe and how using their metacognitive comprehension processes of sequence patterning helped them remember the directions better.

On another day you can help students practice using all four patterns whenever they think throughout their personal lives. Ask them to suggest games, natural phenomena, or everyday events that follow these authorial writing patterns.

You may wish to point out that the thinking process guides illustrate only a few frequently occurring thought patterns. Students may recognize other patterns as they complete the activities in this lesson. Encourage them to create and diagram these new patterns. Next, students can continue reading the first chapter of *Call It Courage* or select another textbook chapter to read. Ask students to identify a pattern or patterns from the thinking process guides that this author followed to organize his or her ideas in that book. Last, have students work in small reading response groups, as they complete one of the following activities:

- Read a chapter from a textbook.
- Read a chapter from a nonfiction book.
- Identify the order in which you present ideas from another content area during a class period later in the day and share why they chose the pattern that they did.

Metacognitive Developmental Lesson 5: Teaching Students to Use Propositional Cohesiveness and Sequence Words When Confused.   Tell students that an important metacognitive comprehension process that they can use when they do not understand something is to look for sequence words; these words describe how details are combined. Explain to students that when they are reading (or listening to) new information, they should ask themselves whether the author is using words such as *before*, *next*, *then* . . . or *first*, *second*, *third*. . . . Add that such words indicate that these words mean that the author (or speaker) wants you to add new ideas together and that doing so can reduce misunderstandings. Share the following example and ask students to listen and tell you what the example is explaining. The example comes from *The World's First Baseball Game* (Holmes, 1981): "First, he wound yarn around a cork. Then he cut a piece of leather into four sections, which were shaped like the peeling of a quartered orange. [He put these pieces side by side to completely cover the cork center.] Finally, he stitched the pieces over the ball of yarn" (p. 6). Now ask students what the author was describing (i.e., making baseballs). Add that by listening to the sequence pattern of *first*, *then*, and *finally* students were better able to comprehend the new material and that you want them to use this strategy any time they read or listen.

Next, ask students to suggest books that they have read in the past and not comprehended. List these on the board and identify if any prior incident of "not knowing something" could have been eliminated had this comprehension process of checking for sequence words been used.

Metacognitive Development Lesson 6: Teaching Students to Use Main Ideas to Build Structural Cohesiveness. You can explain that looking for the way authors connect paragraphs together is another metacognitive process that eliminates misunderstandings when listening or reading. Tell students that if the first few sentences a person says or writes are more general statements, it is likely that the next sentences will be more specific, and vice versa. Demonstrate how knowing this can help them as they read or listen by having them read from a book silently as you read it aloud. Stop to perform a think-aloud to tell students how this particular author tied paragraphs together. Then demonstrate that by thinking about *how* specific a sentence is, students can predict how specific the following sentence is likely to be. For instance, if any sentence has an idea that is broad it usually means that the next sentence will be a specific explanation or an example that explains the previous sentence. However, if they read an idea that is very specific, the next sentence is likely to introduce a new point or summarize previous points.

Now ask students to listen as you read an example from the book *North American Indians* by Marie and Douglas Gorsline (1977): "The pioneers had to take many things along the way" (p. 2). Pause and ask students to predict whether the next sentence is likely to be more specific or more general than this first one (i.e., the first sentence does not describe what kinds of things or how many things the pioneers took with them, so the next sentence is likely to provide more specific information).

The next sentences read: "Barrels of food were piled in the wagon. . . . A large trunk held wool shirts and trousers for the men and wool and linen dresses for the women . . . " (p. 2). Ask students if they were correct in predicting and better understand how to use the metacomprehension process of finding how authors tie paragraphs and sentences together to predict how sentences are connected. Then ask them to list books read recently and identify any in which their knowledge could have been improved if they had used this metacomprehension process.

Metacognitive Development Lesson 7: Teaching Students to Look for the Frequency with Which an Idea Is Repeated. You can explain that looking for the frequency with which an idea is expressed can help students in locating the most important information in a book or conversation. For example, ideas that are repeated frequently in a textbook are likely to be the most important pieces of information. Then, you can follow the same set of instructional steps in metacognitive development lesson 6 to develop the metacomprehension ability of noting idea frequency.

Metacognitive Development Lesson 8: Teaching Students to Note the Direction of a Character's Thoughts. You can explain that noting the purpose of people's and characters' thoughts is a metacomprehension process students can use to identify the direction authors and speakers take. You can demonstrate that by asking themselves: "Is a literary person trying to inform readers (by presenting new information), entertain, or persuade?" Share that simply by identifying an author's, literary character's, or speaker's purpose comprehension can improve. As an example of identifying purpose, you could read a portion of a textbook from the middle of a chapter without revealing the title or the topic. Ask students if the characters are trying to inform, entertain, or persuade. Tell pupils that knowing the characters' purposes makes it easier to predict what the main ideas of future paragraphs will be.

Metacognitive Development Lesson 9: Teaching Students to Compare What Is Read to Similar Events in Their Lives.   You can explain that comparing literary events to ones that occur in students' own lives is another metacognitive strategy they should use when they do not understand something. At this point, you may want to read an excerpt from *The Magic School Bus inside the Human Body* by Joanna Cole, a book that uses the familiarity of the classroom to explain how human bodies function. You can ask students to refer to the list on the board of books they have read recently and identify any situations in which students could have compared what was happening in something they read to their own life experiences to improve their comprehension.

Last, select any book you are presently reading to the class or read a selection from their anthologies. As you read each paragraph, stop at a difficult sentence and model what you want students to do if a misunderstanding occurs. You can demonstrate how, at times, when they are reading and are tempted to say, "I don't know," they are to say, "I'm not sure, but I think it is like . . . because I used the metacognitive process of _____ to make the information clearer." Model using think-alouds and the processes taught in lessons to date in this chapter until you have finished two pages of the book. You can close this section of the lesson by asking students to review their metacognitive processes and identifying which one they use most frequently; list these on the board. Tell students that these processes seem to be the ones that they can use frequently to overcome misunderstandings for the rest of their lives.

Teaching Domain 3 of Metacognition: Increasing Knowledge of One's Goals

Teaching domain 3 of metacognition: Increasing knowledge of one's goals

The ability to keep one's purpose and goals in mind throughout the reading of a text disciplines one's mind and channels metacognitive energy. Another major finding concerning the power of teaching this third domain of metacognition is that there is a striking difference between age-dominated developmental abilities. When students are asked to generate questions, for instance, about a particular issue about which they want to read, younger students and those who are less mature tend to focus on individual incidents or items rather than on the theme. More expert readers or older readers draw diagrams in their mind of the total theme before they seek answers concerning single events (Vye, Schwartz, Bransford, Barron, & Zech, 1998).

The third important component in goal maintenance is to build students' desires to set goals (Vye et al., 1998). As the work of Marzana (2001) demonstrated, learning increases significantly during the first three lessons in which one attempts to use a new metacognitive process. If the method does not change a student's learning style, the amount learned as well as the desire to learn decreases so significantly that repetition of that method results in successively less learning. Thus, whenever a third repetition of any comprehension method in this book is taught, students should exhibit evidence that they are learning by this approach or a different lesson should then be taught. To develop this ability, you can provide students with a checklist of comprehension processes to review before they read. Then, after reading a selection, ask them to place a checkmark in the blanks that precede each comprehension process that they used. Table 7.1 is useful for this purpose; it lists some of the comprehension processes that have been described in this book. Among the first studies demonstrating the close connection between students' control of their own purposes and thoughts, metacognition and transfer occurred as early as 1901 (Thorndike & Woodworth, 1901). When students improved their metacognition while they read, reflections after reading increased qualitatively (Lin et al., 1995; Pressley & Afflerbach, 1995).

Metacognitive Development Lesson 10: Teaching Students to Use Semantic and Syntactical Information by Contrasting Cases and Examples during Reading. Simply having experiences with a set of different examples or contrasting cases (as described in Chapter 4) will not necessarily enable students to do unprompted metacognitive thinking (Broudy, 1989; Vye et al., 1998). Students must be shown how to analyze two contrastive cases or sets of information. This can be done by having students read variant versions of the same book, fairy tale, or theme. This lesson builds metacognition

TABLE 7.1   Student Self-Assessment of Metacognitive Strategies

_____ 1. Tilled the text.
_____ 2. Identified author's writing pattern as
     _____ a. Concept pattern;
     _____ b. Problem solution pattern;
     _____ c. Similarities/differences pattern; or
     _____ d. Sequence pattern.
_____ 3. Looked for the author's sequencing patterns with words such as First, Then, or Next.
_____ 4. Determined whether the main idea was clear or reread if it was unclear.
_____ 5. Looked for frequency of ideas and if the same idea was repeated in different ways.
_____ 6. Noted the direction of the author's or characters' thinking.
_____ 7. Compared what I read to similar events in personal experiences.
_____ 8. Contrasted the text in my mind as I read.
_____ 9. Organized the text in my mind as I read.
_____ 10. Found the inferences that the author wanted me to make.

by presenting variant perspectives. As students reason through the differences between opposing positions and viewpoints, their minds draw on the metacognitive processes taught in metacognitive development lessons 1–9. To begin, have students read two texts that present slightly variant perspectives on the same theme or topic. Because these texts are read consecutively, students' abilities to notice similarities and differences are strengthened. As each difference is noted, ask students to describe and list the values and details that each involves.

Another reason that contrastive thinking is effective is because it increases children's sensitivity to an author's point of view. As a result, students learn how to contrast purposes in their mind as they read. They no longer cling to either the author as the authority or to their own purpose conceived before reading to determine an author's intent in writing a text. Uniting an author's intended purpose with their own "setting purpose process" increases students' active monitoring of their current levels of understanding, and is an excellent example of well-developed metacognition (Schwartz & Bransford, 2001; Vye et al., 1998).

Metacognitive Development Lesson 11: Teaching Students to Check for Internal Consistency by Organizing Their Background Knowledge with the Order in Which Information Is Presented in a Text.   Students must be taught how to coherently tie their view of the world to an author's; simply recognizing that these two viewpoints are different is not enough to build reflective metacognition after reading. This thinking process is called **metacognitively creating coherence.** When students compare their lives to similar literary characters or events, their metacognitive thoughts lead them to collaborate effectively with an author, and a strong bond between author and reader develops. In turn, enjoyment of reading increases.

In summary, eleven metacognitive development lessons have been described. Before students can learn how to initiate these metacomprehension processes, they must know how to clarify meaning when they become confused. They must also know how to surmise. This is a different ability than merely knowing the order of the main ideas. Finally, they must know how to reengage motivation, adjust their own ability to assert more effort at certain points during a reading than at others.

To teach these self-initiating processes, teachers must communicate respect for students' goals, agendas, and perspectives. They can do this by having children set their own goals. Students need time to contemplate their own metacognitive comprehension progress and to assess how much energy they are asserting toward understanding a text.

Catch-Up Comprehension Processes

Many instructional programs for less able readers center on review and practice of separate skills, which reduces motivation and comprehension (Santa & Hoien, 1999). Because of this reality, most poor comprehenders do not catch up with their peers. This achievement gap increases as students age (Stanovich, 1986). In addition today's classes contain greater academic diversity than ever before (Allington, 1996). Typically, in a class of 26 children, (1) eight students have vast weaknesses in comprehension processes (Mangieri

& Block, 1994); (2) three have a limited knowledge of English (Carnegie Foundation, 1995; Moll, 1997); (3) three have been raised in poverty (Children's Defense Fund, 1992); (4) seven have been diagnosed as being at risk or having learning disabilities, mild mental challenges, emotional challenges, attention deficit hyperactivity disorder, attention deficit disorder or dyslexia (Council of Exceptional Children, 1997); (5) two take medication for hyperactivity or stress-related disorders (American Medical Association, 1996); (6) four have no or limited reading materials in their homes (American Library Association, 1996); and (7) five have *not* been taught by caregivers to value and appreciate the mental energy that is necessary to gain meaning or pleasure from reading.

Moreover, many students who are not good comprehenders today exert little or no effort to improve. Schools are not addressing their cognitive needs. A strong meta-comprehension program is vital for these students.

New methods must be created for students who are unable to select appropriate books for independent silent reading (Shoemaker & Deshler, 1992), visualize what is read (Shoemaker & Deshler, 1992), ask themselves questions to monitor their understanding (Clark, Deshler, Shoemaker, Alley, & Warner 1984), or summarize what they read (Shoemaker & Deshler, 1992).

Research indicates that the following methods improve less able readers' comprehension capabilities. These methods present abstract concepts in concrete ways, teach the organizational structure of an author's writing style, make relationships among bits of information explicit, and distinguish between important and less important information. The needs for such lessons are increasing because today's textbooks are growing denser and contain more information that is written at a level that is above students' instructional and independent reading levels than ever before (Fisher, Schumaker, & Deshler, 2002). The lessons described next will build upon the early works in the "key word program" by Ashton-Warner (1966), literacy charts (McKay, Thompson, & Schabuh, 1970), dictation (Clay, 1979), and process reading and writing (Block & Johnson, 2002). Through them, less able readers can begin to also satisfy their need to set and reach their own comprehension goals independently.

In addition, many whole class activities can be modified to meet these students' special comprehension needs. First, when you read aloud, readers who are less skilled will profit by simultaneously reading the text silently. Second, you can engage students in paired reading activities. When less able students are paired with others, the principles described in Chapter 3 are enacted daily. Third, when you end discovery discussions you can ask less skilled readers to read orally and perform a think-aloud about a difficult comprehension process. These activities and lessons in this section of this chapter have the following effective qualities in common: (1) they demonstrate the complexity of effective comprehension processing; (2) they teach comprehension in a challenging context, using different methods than students may have experienced previously; and (3) they embrace the age-appropriate developmental qualities described on pages 150–151.

Catch-Up Comprehension Process Lesson 1: Multisensory Additions. By grade 2, instruction for weak comprehenders will increase its effectiveness if it contains a multisensory component. Students who struggle to comprehend must quickly rise above their present levels or they may fall so far behind their peers that they give up and cease to exert themselves. Each lesson described up to this point in this book can be retaught with multisensory elements. These new additions will elicit a kinesthetic and tactile dimension that enables students to become more engrossed and immersed in pleasurable comprehension than is possible through only reading print. For example, instead of teaching weak comprehenders sequence signal words only with books you can bring in model cars, trains, and other crafts. Weaker comprehenders can touch and see the effects of words like "next," "third," and "finally" as they use these directions to make a model of their choice.

Catch-Up Comprehension Process Lesson 2: Fluency Lessons.   Fluency lessons should be conducted weekly for weak comprehenders. For 15 minutes on one day a week, students should practice reading 200 words more fluently. To begin this lesson, you read a page orally with fluent and appropriate phrasing. As you read, weak comprehenders read along silently listening to your rendition. Second, you and the student read the text orally together using the same pace and appropriate phrasing. Third, the student reads it to you and then pairs with a classmate and practices reading the text with his or her partner. Fourth, ask this student to "perform" the text for an interested audience, usually a group of peers in the class that have not yet read that text (Optiz & Rasinski, 1999).

Catch-Up Comprehension Process Lesson 3: Create Age-Appropriate Adaptations.   By grade 3, instruction for less able comprehenders must focus more on identifying the best bridge that individual students can use to cross major gaps between their and the majority of their peers' comprehension abilities. Because the importance of overcoming each comprehension deficit is so urgent, by third grade and above, instruction for weaker comprehenders must become more personalized. Teachers can do so by finding the right individual mixture, tempo, and context for each child's catch-up lesson instruction.

By grade 4, weak comprehenders also need instruction in *new, highly dense,* metacognitive processes. This is true because by age 10 if children have not yet learned to comprehend through the methods in their basic programs, they are less likely to do so no matter how creative the lessons are (Block, Oakar, & Hurt, 2002). Moreover, less able fourth-grade comprehenders also tend to develop low self-concepts and a lack of self-confidence, and as a result, they restrain their efforts. Their textbooks have become so adult-like that these students need help approaching them and teachers have less time to support them. For 10 year olds, teachers must first help these students trust that they can learn to comprehend well. The students' trust will be directly proportionate to the degree to which teachers have given them new ideas and ways to think better when they come to comprehension challenges that previously seemed insurmountable. By age 10, they will have spent at least half of their lives trying to catch up and comprehend. If they have not succeeded in the first half of their lives as readers, they need teachers to convince them that the efforts they exert now will be worthwhile.

By grades 5 through 8, catch-up comprehension lessons must be concerned not only with building fluency but also with assisting students to overcome self-deprecation. At the same time, educators must introduce highly effective methods of stimulating interest in, motivation for, and confidence in their own comprehension abilities. In the process, through novel and sophisticated instruction, a program should release (little by little) the responsibility of overcoming literacy difficulties to these students individually (Block, 2001b; Elbaum, Vaughn, Hughes, & Moody, 1999).

For many years, a common practice among elementary school teachers was to divide students into small, same-ability groups for comprehension instruction. During the 1970s and 1980s, this prevailing practice "began to draw criticism on the grounds that ability grouping lowers self-esteem and motivation among students with reading problems, restricts friendship choices, and often widens the gap between high and low achievers" (Elbaum, Vaughn, Hughes, & Moody, 1999, p. 372). This criticism led more teachers to turn to cross-age tutoring groups. Such formats help classroom teachers accommodate the multiplicity of different reading levels of students who have trouble comprehending. Research from impoverished but successful schools indicates that such tutoring also enables every child to receive instruction every day. After these tutoring sessions, students should spend time in small group instructional settings where they describe what was learned and misunderstood during these tutoring sessions. When these two-pronged methods end with home applications for parents to implement each evening, comprehension catch-up process lessons can be reinforced continuously (Hiebert, 1999).

Evaluating Metacognitive Domains and Catch-Up Comprehension Processes

Evaluating metacognitive domains and catch-up comprehension processes

There are several methods of assessing students' metacomprehension processes. The first is to determine the amount of skill that readers have in controlling their thinking while they read. Students can be asked about this information directly or they can perform think-alouds as they read (Pressley & Afflerback, 1995). Second, students can also be asked to complete interviews (or written questionnaires) concerning the comprehension processes they use when reading. When such questionnaires are used, it is important not to draw the students' attention too narrowly to the names or features of the processes themselves but rather to the necessity of describing exact types of thinking they do as they read.

Anecdotal records, observations, and student self-assessments are other methods by which teachers can document students' metacognition (Baker & Cerro, 2001). The following interview questions are recommended: What do you do when you come to a paragraph you do not understand? When you come across part of a sentence that is confusing, what do you do? What do you do when your mind wanders so you can bring yourself back to comprehending? What authorial writing patterns do you like and why?

A third evaluation technique is to ask children to describe confusions that arose as they read. When children report that they have found something that does not make sense, teachers can assume that they are monitoring the text through their metacognitive abilities (Paris, 1991). Moreover, if you tape record students tutoring each other, what they teach each other can be used to assess the metacognitive processes that students use when they read. Lastly, students can be taught to use a portfolio to check their own progress and monitor their own understanding using the checklists in Chapter 10.

Each of these evaluations has limitations (Baumann et al., 1993). Verbal reports can be tainted because students can merely tell you what they think you want to hear (Pressley & Afflerback, 1995). Open-ended interviews are often difficult and time consuming to score. For this reason, multiple-choice questionnaires have been developed such as the Index of Reading Awareness (Paris, 1986, 1991), the Metacognitive Strategy Index (Schmitt, 1990), the Metacognitive Reading Awareness Form (Mihohic, 1994), the Reading Strategy Form (Preia-Raldeanne, 1997), and the Index of Science Reading Abilities (Craigs & MacGuire, 1998). Observations can supplement verbal recall because they can provide evidence of what students are actually doing rather than what students say they are doing. Observation checklists to use for such observations are available in additional resources (Block, 2001b; Block & Mangieri, 1995/1996; Rhodes, 1993; and Rhodes & Shanklin, 1993).

In Summary

Every basic reading series published in the past 5 years considered lessons and activities that foster metacognition (Pressley et al., 1994; Schmitt & Hopkins, 1993). Teachers' manuals provide information about how to teach some metacognitive processes, but educators request additional assistance in developing children's abilities to (1) control their thoughts during reading, (2) use context clues to interpret text, (3) establish their own goals, and (4) initiate metacomprehension processes to overcome confusion. Instructional adaptations must be made for weaker comprehenders in the form of catch-up comprehension process lessons.

Many teachers monitor students' silent reading and perform think-alouds that advance students' thinking during reading (Block & Pressley, 2002). Others find such think-alouds difficult to create or produce think-alouds that model literal comprehension processes only. Few teachers are able to describe accurately their own metacognitive thinking. For this reason, it is important to increase teachers' metacognitive awareness of their own reading processes (Edwards, 1999). As this is occurring more broadly in teacher education programs across the United States and Canada, more professionals are using the more personalized and individualized instructional lessons and assessments presented in this chapter for weak as well as stronger comprehenders (Thomas, Barksdale-Ladd, 2000).

REFLECTING ON WHAT YOU HAVE LEARNED

1. In your opinion, what is the most important metacognitive lesson in this chapter that we must address in a more focused manner at a grade level that you teach (or will teach)? Describe the instructional methods and books that you would use to teach this lesson.

2. Describe the three domains of metacognition as well as one method of teaching each domain and one method of assessing what you teach.

3. Summarize the key points that you have learned thus far in the text. Make a graphic to depict your thought processes. How could this review method be adapted and used as an activity to increase your students' retention?

4. *Your Professional Journal: Diaries.* In your journal, describe a professional difficulty you face. Journal for 12 days on what you do to overcome this challenge. The resultant diary can be used as a model for weak comprehenders. If you share your diary and discuss the benefits you received from this process, they may begin their own diary to document what they are doing to overcome reading problems.

5. *Making Professional Decisions.* In one paragraph, describe a new research design that you believe should be undertaken to increase students' abilities to think metacognitively. In this design, describe the comprehension process to be researched and the method to be used in the research.

6. *Field Applications and Observations.* Describe the most effective method of teaching and assessing metacognition in an elementary or middle school classroom that you have observed or led. Analyze which domain of metacognition the lesson was designed to develop. Be prepared to defend your answer.

7. *Multicultural Application.* Devise a think-aloud for a student who is having difficulties in one of the three metacognitive domains because English is not his or her first language. Deliver your think-aloud, hold a discovery discussion, and evaluate the effects. How can you use the results of these actions to plan the next lesson that you will administer for that student? Be prepared to discuss your results with colleagues.

8. *Key Terms Exercise.* Following is a list of concepts introduced in this chapter. If you have learned the meaning of a term, place a checkmark in the blank that precedes that term. If you are not sure of a term's definition, increase your retention by reviewing your definition of the term. If you have learned 8 of these terms on your first reading of this chapter, you have constructed many meanings that are important for your career.

_____ metacognition (p. 134)

_____ semantic processes (p. 135)

_____ syntactic processes (p. 135)

_____ checking for internal consistency (p. 135)

_____ monitoring external consistencies (p. 135)

_____ checking the propositional cohesiveness (p. 135)

_____ ensuring structural cohesiveness (p. 135)

_____ evaluating informational completeness (p. 135)

_____ metacognitive filtering (p. 138)

_____ gestalt (p. 139)

_____ main ideas followed by details writing pattern (p. 141)

9. *Comprehension Process Lesson 7: Template for Developing Students' Metacognition—Teaching Students the Process of Asking Oneself Questions As One Reads.* This comprehension lesson demonstrates how students can integrate all the metacognitive processes that they have learned in this chapter. This lesson can be taught before students read silently. Remind students to use these comprehension processes when they read silently in the future.

COMPREHENSION PROCESS LESSON 7
Teaching Students the Process of Tilling the Text

Reading should be a fun and exciting experience for everyone. To help you to enjoy and get the most out of what you read, follow the steps on this sheet to develop the ability to ask yourself questions as you read. These questions will increase your metacognitive processes.

Before You Read
1. Pick a place.
   Where in the world do I want to go to read?
   What type of environment do I need?

2. Scan the book.
   What do I expect to learn about?
   What do I want to learn?
   What do I expect to feel?
   What is my purpose for reading?

While You Read
1. Get involved.
   Where do I want to go from here?
   How does this book make me feel?
   Have I ever experienced anything like what I am reading about?
   Would I have done the same thing if I were the character/author?

2. Reread and question.
   Am I understanding what I am reading?
   What is not clear to me?
   Why did that happen the way it did?
   What do I need to go back over?
   What things do I need to ask about?

COMPREHENSION PROCESS LESSON 7   **Continued**

After You Read
1. Reflect and evaluate.
   What pieces are still missing in this puzzle?
   Have I fulfilled my reading purpose?
   What questions do I still not have answers to?
   Did things happen the way I would have expected them to?

2. Seek others and share.
   Who can help me better understand what I have read?
   Who might help to answer my questions?
   Who would also enjoy hearing about what I have read?

3. Read more.
   What will be the next books/topics I can check off my list?
   What other books should I read next?
   What will be the purpose of my next reading?

CHAPTER 8

Comprehension Instruction Is Not Generic—It's Genre Specific

Roberto and Andy learned to sequence story grammar through story frames. Now, they want to demonstrate to their class how to do it by using the pocket chart. They will present this method of sequencing story parts to their class, and challenge them to predict the upcoming sentence strip by describing the comprehension processes that they used to identify it.

COMPREHENSION INSTRUCTION IS NOT GENERIC— IT'S GENRE SPECIFIC

- Why comprehension instruction is genre specific

- Teaching genre-specific comprehension processes

- Teaching children to appreciate nonfiction

- Teaching the history and social science genres

- Teaching the math genre

- Teaching the scientific genre

- Teaching the fine arts genre

Andy is a student in Ms. Ellison's second-grade social studies and mathematics classes in Mishawasha (Indiana) Public Schools. He rides the early bus, lives on a rural farm, and loves to read. On his trips to and from school, he becomes engrossed in reading a wide varity of genres and current event magazines. In September, he asked Ms. Ellison if he could become the class librarian. Each week he makes a list of books and topics that the class would like Ms. Ellison to add to their library. Ms. Ellison uses the instructional guidelines in this chapter so that Andy and his classmates can comprehend authorial writing patterns that characterize trade books and current events literature in social studies and mathematical genres. By making him the class librarian, she capitalized on Andy's preference for reading expository books. ■

Chapter Overview

This chapter focuses on methods of teaching comprehension in content areas. In the following pages, you can learn research that describes the special features of nonfiction text. Immediately following these discussions, four methods are presented that have been shown to increase students' comprehension of mathematical, scientific, social studies, and fine arts genres. By the end of this chapter you will be able to answer the following questions:

1. What makes the comprehension of nonfiction text different from fiction text?
2. How can teachers increase students' ability to comprehend expository text?
3. Which methods increase students' comprehension of historical, mathematical, scientific, and fine arts content areas?

Why Comprehension Instruction Is Genre Specific

Why comprehension instruction is genre specific

For the purpose of this chapter, **informational, expository, and non-fiction texts** will be defined as texts or technologically-based contexts that contain many (or all) of the following features:

- The ability to communicate information about the natural or social world;
- Textual context based on facts as opposed to fictional creations about a topic;
- Use of the timeless verb tense of "is";
- Use of generic nouns more than proper nouns;
- Introduction of technical vocabulary words;
- Classification of definite concepts;
- Adherence predominately to comparative, contrastive, problem-solution, or cause-effect textual organizational patterns;
- Repetition of a topical theme; and
- Inclusion of graphic images, such as diagrams, tables, maps, graphs, and figures (Christie, 1987; Duke & Kays, 1998).

When these comprehension features of expository text are taught, literal, inferential, and applied comprehension increase because the inferential gaps that nonfiction writers leave to readers' meaning making processes can be bridged more accurately because students elicit their logic and knowledge of such features rather than merely insert their own background experiences (Iser, 1978). Because most readers have fewer background experiences with informational topics than the authors, relying only on their own prior knowledge base to overcome nonfiction obstacles will have limited success.

Another reason that expository comprehension processes must be taught is that informational texts do not end in the traditional fictional, "happy ever after" form. As Maduram (2000) stated, "When children are able to identify, use and discuss the features of non-fictional text, even after they've used a fictional work such as a movie of *Beauty and the Beast*, the images that they discuss become propaganda free" (p. 244). Television and fiction novels often "sell" stories through sensational details. Alternatively, using the lessons in this chapter, children can learn how to present arguments objectively as they practice comprehending by using the thinking processes employed by scientists, mathematicians, historians, and artists as they created their texts.

Moreover, when students create mental images from nonfiction text, the resultant pictures are mental representations of realities in their world. These representations resemble a network, with nodes that depict individual text elements and connections that focus on meaningful relationships. While many children come to school already having an internal representation of the concept of story, and are thus able to comprehend and retell basic story elements quite easily, the same is not true for nonfiction text. Most students must be taught to read many texts that characterize each domain of knowledge before the "organizational system can be developed and metacognitive processes mapped onto them" (Taylor, Graves, & van den Broek, 2000, p. 192). Instruction that is genre specific provides such a road map. The more experiences students have with nonfiction text, the better their nonfiction genre-specific road markers will become (Ambruster, 1991; Block, 1993; Meyer, 1975; Taylor & Beach, 1984). Unfortunately, in prior years, most kindergarten to grade 3 students were not taught genre-specific comprehension (Duke, 2000). An objective of this chapter is to assist you to fill this instructional void.

As early as grade 3, most children have developed a positive or negative attitude toward expository texts. Most pupils have also deduced, incorrectly, that comprehending is a generic process. They approach every book with the same set of before reading expectations, during reading metacognitions, and after reading meaning making actions. Thus, it is important to teach students the truth: Comprehension processes are not generic. Students must learn to recognize and remove comprehension obstacles that are genre specific. When students learn to use different types of thoughts with different genres, their comprehension abilities increase and they rate themselves as more competent readers (Block & Johnson, 2002; Smolkin, 2002).

Teaching Genre-Specific Comprehension Processes

Many students choose nonfictional text without teacher prompting. Informational books provide them with detailed vocabulary and suggest that children can depend on natural laws and natural phenomena in the world. Such texts also satisfy pupils' innate curiosities and present vivid facts about topics of personal interest. Moreover,

Teaching genre-specific comprehension processes

when teachers of students as young as 5 years of age read nonfiction books aloud, children's problem-solving abilities improved (Duke & Kays, 1998).

It is important to teach *how* to comprehend nonfiction books, however, in order to enhance other readers' self-efficacy and the value they place on learning to read a broad range of expository texts. When we do, we can ignite a positive cycle of effects. Students who read expository text with ease and pleasure augment their self-efficacy and enjoy reading a wider variety of genres. This increased pleasure will motivate them to choose books from a wider spectrum of interest areas. This, in and of itself, helps children grow as readers because they develop higher-level thinking processes, and they learn how to think specifically. By contrast, students who do not read as well have fewer experiences of success, most often because they have not had adequate exposure to diverse genres. This void in experiences not only reduces their opportunities to learn how to comprehend genre-specific text but also reduces their experiences practicing genre-specific reading comprehension processes, which in turn significantly decreases their self-efficacy and their abilities to make meaning from expository texts (Lysaker, 1997).

Genre-specific comprehension instruction is important for another reason. When students enter the work force, the majority of their reading will involve expository text. Moreover, more than 60 percent of the passages that students read on standardized state or national reading comprehension tests are expository, genre-specific texts (Alverman & Mosie, 1991). For these reasons, it is becoming increasingly important that we help students acquire the skills to obtain knowledge and pleasure from reading nonfiction.

The majority of students today recall narrative text sequentially, because fictional story grammar follows a sequential pattern, and this pattern is well established as a schema in their minds (Kintsch, 1998; Nelson, 1978, 1996). Settings, characters, events, sequences, and problem/climax/solution chains act as retrieval and retention aids (Noordman & Vonk, 1998; Trabasso & Bouchard, 2000). Such causal relationships are also imprinted more quickly than the additive text structures found in nonfiction expository texts (Haberlandt & Graesser, 1985).

Recent research also suggests that students from as young as 3 years of age can learn how to comprehend informational text (Hapgood, Palincsar, & Magnusson, 2000; Moss, 1989; Pappas, 1991, 1993). One reason that students are developing such skill is that teachers are describing how fiction and nonfiction texts share similar features (e.g., temporal order, hierarchies of ideas within single paragraphs, analogous and metaphorical references, figures of speech, as well as details and main ideas that revolve around a central theme). The differences between narrative and expository texts is that the latter usually contain more difficult concept loads, a lack of repetition of ideas, complex ideas, and content-specific vocabulary.

In the past, too often, teachers were asked to present expository text with methods that were similar to those used to teach narratives (e.g., begin on page 1 and read continuously, at the same speed and with one continuous purpose, to the end). Nonfiction comprehension instruction must develop students' understanding of the distinct structures that frame the writing styles in each genre and content area. For example, pictures, tables, figures, graphs, diagrams, maps, cartoons, and photographs communicate different information if they appear in historical, scientific, or artistic texts. Such books also have specific parts, such as tables of content, glossaries, and indexes that are not available in other fiction and nonfiction texts. Psychologists agree that these natural language features exist because they represent different methods of thinking and writing that characterize each discipline of knowledge (Weaver & Kintsch, 1996).

Even the most sophisticated set of comprehension processes used to make meaning from fiction texts may not be sufficient for expository texts. Understanding nonfiction content requires: (1) the ability to recognize textual features that are used to convey meaning in a content area (such as cross-sections superimposed on photographs of trees to show the growth band rings in scientific textbooks); (2) the ability to create a coherent mental representation of many facts in a paragraph (such as the procedure for computing carbon dating that appears in anthropology texts); and (3) the ability to understand the chain of logic and deliberate thinking that characterizes mathematicians and historians. When these comprehension processes (and others noted later in this chapter) are taught, students can infer arcs of information that were not explicitly stated.

Teaching Children to Appreciate Nonfiction

Teaching children to
appreciate nonfiction

The first step in this instructional process is to develop lessons that motivate students to explore a broad base of genres. As one of Andy's classmates realized after learning the lessons in this chapter, "I now know how to learn the words and get ideas in lots of books. I can take lots of ideas and deal with them. I'm having a good experience reading for the very first time, in all subjects, and that has made a big difference in my life and grades."

It is also important that children learn how to respond emotionally as well as cognitively to nonfiction text. One of the traits of high-quality expository text is that a book's contents are so reader friendly that students want to pause and reflect on what they are learning while they read. For children to truly enjoy reading nonfiction, texts must be so well written that the stark contrasts between themselves and elements found in high-quality fiction enable children to increase their motivation to read both types of genre. Students can learn how to comprehend nonfiction when they are taught to "scamper and scan until I choose to stop and savor." This is a style of reading whereby students are taught that it is acceptable to quickly skim over some pages in a nonfiction text when the content is already known by them. Then, when a section of a text becomes interesting or contains new information, students can stop for extra time to ponder and learn.

By teaching students these two reading speeds, they can establish a pace for reading nonfiction that is distinctive from the mental ebb and flow patterns created as they effectively comprehend fiction. Specifically, when students learn that they can control their own nonfiction reading speed they appreciate this genre more. For example, they appreciate that expository texts do not demand a thorough careful attention to setting, plot, characterization, climaxes, and resolutions to be comprehend as do fictional texts.

When students choose which part they want to read first, they engage metacognition (which is a very satisfying, self-esteem building, thinking activity, especially for less able readers). They begin to think

- "Which problem about _____ do I want to think about?"
- "Where would I like to start really reading in depth?"
- "What question do I want this book to answer?"

Students should also be able to set their own purpose for reading after reading the first two pages. When students stop reading the first two pages and set their own purpose for nonfiction, this comprehension process aids understanding more than trying to establish a purpose by merely looking at the cover of the book. Students can assess an author's writing style and topics in a book to help them reach the same main ideas as the author. The inferences and the length of arcs of information used by a specific author can be recognized. Further, readers can identify an author's placement of special textual features, such as titles, headings, boldfaced print, italics, bullets, and labels. These special effects signal that an author's important information (e.g., "*Readers* [I italicized this so you would pay attention. What is coming up is going to be very important; so read carefully.]"). You can also teach students that proficient adult readers automatically attend to these clues. By being alert to them, when they appear, students can direct their thinking toward the most important points more rapidly (Harvey, 1998).

Similarly, through the information conveyed by illustrations and photographs in trade books and magazines, readers can obtain a deeper meaning (Harvey, 1998). Thus, you can teach students how to comprehend the genre-specific diagrams, cross-sections, overlays, maps, tables, charts, graphs, framed texts, or boxes that will appear in a specific, upcoming chapter. In so doing, children have an anchor of specific information that they have seen before on which to tie the text. The fourth comprehension process is how to organize the text. Most children do not understand the elements that link nonfiction paragraphs together. The specific structures that an author uses in a text are taught in Comprehension Process Lesson 8 (p. 181).

A five-step instructional plan can be followed to teach students how to follow an author's train of thought. This process was described in Chapter 4 for fictional text. When teaching nonfiction, students are only asked to read the first seven sentences (or first seven pages in preprimer or primer-level text) and to discern whether on page 1 of a book, an author places the main idea as the first or last sentence in a paragraph. Next, you can ask students to identify what type of details are used in most paragraphs (i.e., does the author usually describe who, what, where, when, or why details in a paragraph?). For example, in the nonfiction, Newbery Award winning book *Volcano*, Patricia Lauber wrote her main ideas as the first sentence in each paragraph and each subsequent sentence was a "what" detail. By contrast, Diana Weir places her main ideas at the end of (and uses "when" details in) her paragraphs in *Let's Investigate Tree Frogs*.

When students have identified how sentences are related within single paragraphs, they can learn how an author links one paragraph to the next. These two steps are shown in Figure 4.4 (p. 86) and will likely be the only two that younger readers need to learn before they can effectively follow the thoughts of authors in their nonfiction texts. However, by third grade, expository texts' readability levels have increased so much that it will be important to spend a full week teaching and showing examples in numerous books, demonstrating the wide variety that authors use to summarize (step 3 of Figure 4.4) and add depth to their writing styles (step 4).

Among the most powerful lessons at grade 3 and higher involves teaching students how to predict what the next paragraph is going to be. For instance, students can learn that sometimes an author pauses to summarize all previous points; this is usually the last paragraph in a section. You can perform a think-aloud to describe this comprehension process. As you read the first sentence of a summarization paragraph, you can describe how this sentence does not follow the same pattern of sentence-to-sentence connections this author typically uses, and how the way that the author connects this paragraph to those preceeding it is different than prior connections between paragraphs. You can also teach them how the first words in the beginning sentence of many summarizing paragraphs contain "signal words" such as *in summary, to review,* or *in conclusion.* Next, you can teach that the first sentence will likely state what all former paragraphs in this section had in common. Last, you can count the number of pages or paragraphs of writing that occurs between summary paragraphs because most writers usually intersperse summarizations at predictable, regular intervals. For example, if we return to Patricia Lauber's award winning book, *Volcano,* we could teach the summary method she used by modeling each of the preceding comprehension processes in Chapter 1 "The Volcano Wakes." In this chapter, Lauber writes 5 descriptive paragraphs then 1 summary; 4 descriptive then 1 summary; and 5 descriptive then 1 summary. Although the first sentence of each summary paragraph does not contain a set of signal words, such as *in summary,* every opening sentence contains plural nouns and pronouns to demonstrate that all the single subjects of prior paragraphs would be grouped together into a summary of key ideas. Specifically, in Chapter 1 of *The Volcano,* the subjects in the descriptive paragraphs were

> The volcano
> Mount St. Helens
> The lava
> The 1800s
> The mountain
> The explosion
> Two new craters
> The bulge
> May 18
> The eruption
> The other job

By contrast, the subjects of the summary paragraphs were

> These people
> Geologists
> The answers to these questions

When students are skilled at step 3 on Figure 4.4, they can be taught how to follow an author's style of writing (step 4 on Figure 4.4). First, students can analyze and rate the level of the vocabulary as dense (V3), average (V2), or easy (V1). Second, they can rank the author's writing style by the type of sentences used most frequently (e.g., complex [S3], compound [S2], or simple [S1]), and paragraph lengths (e.g., long [P3], medium [P2], or short [P1]).

To teach students how to analyze authorial writing styles you can distribute multiple copies of the same text to students. After they have deduced the author's writing style individually, you can ask them to meet in groups to compare their results, resolve discrepancies and report back to the class. Then, you can lead a discussion about what they found to be the benefits of analyzing an author's writing style. In subsequent lessons you can make several nonfiction books on the same topic available to students and ask them to select a book by analyzing the authorial styles in each. After several exposures to step 4 of analyzing authorial writing patterns, many students come to understand, and can describe, the authorial styles that they most enjoy. Many will report to each other, for instance, that they like books with a V1-S2-P3 pattern or they most enjoy reading books with a V2-S1-P2 pattern.

The last two steps toward developing students' abilities to follow authors' thought patterns are to (1) identify common authorial characteristics between writers in the same content discipline (step 5 on Figure 4.4), and (2) create diagrams of the other types of connections an author uses in a specific text to emphasize key points, highlight important details, and illustrate the thinking in that discipline. These two steps can be taught through discussions, think-alouds, and modeling with several books you provide. Most advanced students often enjoy creating diagrams of the intratext and across text similarities that characterize the writing within specific genres.

Before learning about teaching students to comprehend specific content disciplines, four additional methods have been proven to improve students' understanding of all nonfiction texts: (1) *setting one's own purpose for reading*, (2) *the buddy beside me as I read approach*, (3) *elevating the essence of a text using summary partner questioning*, and (4) *thinking about two comprehension processes using adhesive note prompts*.

Setting One's Own Purpose for Reading.

When students are taught to read the first two pages before they set their own purpose for reading, pupils will be more likely to apply relevant background knowledge to a text, follow that specific author's train of thought, and depend on that content discipline's thinking patterns to infer deep meaning. Traditionally, students have either not been taught how to set a purpose for reading, however, or have been asked to predict what a text will be about merely by looking at its cover. The first two steps in Figure 4.4 describe the actions you can take to develop the important comprehension process of *setting one's own purpose for reading during the reading of the first two pages of fiction*, and the same two steps are applicable for nonfiction.

Buddy Beside Me as I Read.

The "buddy beside me as I read" approach is to group students together in pairs or small groups based either on student choice of with whom they want to read or the topic they select to read. When students are allowed to take turns "being the teacher" of this text, one will read a page aloud, discuss it, define unknown words, and then that reader's partner will become the teacher and duplicate the same actions. In a national study, teachers and students evaluated this method of learning nonfiction to be among the most effective that they have used (Block, Mangieri, & Johnson, in press).

Elevating the Essence Using Summary Partner Questioning.   Once students are comfortable using the "buddy beside me" approach, you can improve students' higher-level comprehension processes by helping them elevate the essence of a text using summary partner questioning. This method begins by students following the steps described in the the "buddy beside me" method. After one student has completed oral reading, discussing, and defining terms on one page, this reader's partner summarizes the most important point(s) that were conveyed by the author on that page. The reader then asks a question that he or she thinks the author will answer on the next page or within the next few pages. This process is repeated by the reader's partner who becomes the oral reader and teacher of the next page's content.

Thinking About Two Comprehension Processes.   The last methods that have proven to increase students' comprehension of content disciplines involve (1) simply reading two or more nonfiction texts related to the same topic back to back, and (2) teaching students to think about two comprehension processes as they read by placing adhesive notes at key points in a text to remind them that using a specific comprehension process at that point in the text could enrich their understanding. When students read two expository texts written by different authors on the same topic, the number of details, vocabulary words, and major concepts learned increases more significantly than if the same texts are read separately or paired with fictional text (Block et al., in press). Similarly, when students are taught to set their own purposes, they can be prompted to do so by placing an adhesive note at the top right side of page 3 in a text. On that slip of paper a sentence starter can be written that students complete: My purpose for reading this book is to. . . . After students have been taught other comprehension processes, such as inferencing, an adhesive note can be placed on the edges of pages in which the author is asking readers to make an inference before they continue reading on.

By writing their inference on adhesive notes, students develop the ability to think with an author at an inferential level continuously as they read. Then, in subsequent lessons, when students have been taught how to draw conclusions an adhesive note can be attached to a page near the end of the book (at the climax or major event in that chapter or text) to prompt to where students should begin to draw their own conclusions. As the other comprehension processes in Chapters 2 through 7 of this textbook are taught, they can be added to this lesson. You can use up to four colors of adhesive note prompts for four different processes that students should keep in mind as they read specific texts. Many teachers have found it valuable to draw simple line diagrams on these adhesive notes that depict the mental process students will experience when they use a specific comprehension process. For example, inferencing adhesive note prompts

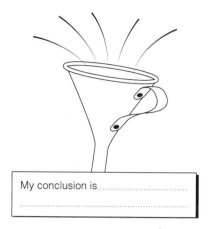

would contain this reminder of the inferential comprehension process: What I read + What I know = inference; My inference is _____. The line drawing to depict the drawing conclusions comprehension process could be a funnel, because after a reader's mind has been filled with many details, it must condense and order all data into a concise statement. The adhesive note graphic that depicts this comprehension process might look like the above illustration.

Teaching the History and Social Science Genres

Students' knowledge and appreciation of history can blossom when the following lessons are taught. Begin by locating historical topics that excite children. For example, in one sixth-grade class, Mr. Nobles found books about the roles women played in U.S. history. There had been a debate in the class the prior week as to whether women's rights increased the amount of influence that women have in the outcome of presidential elections today compared to the influence women had in influencing societal direction historically. For this study, Mr. Nobles not only identified 17 Internet sites related to the lives of famous people but also taught historical facts about each person from biographies and fictional first-person reports that appeared in government documents. As a result, his students experienced the many voices of women throughout history. Whenever his students tried to comprehend a historical text, Mr. Nobles encouraged them to read two different interpretations of those events so they could increase the contrastive cases metacognitive comprehension processes they used because they *read two nonfiction texts back to back*. This method also increased students' awareness that history is a series of people's voices, and Mr. Nobles' instruction helped them experience those voices. You can follow such lessons with student-created role plays or formal, scripted, period dramas so students can "try on historical identities." By placing themselves in someone else's shoes, a majority of students enjoy re-creating this fun-filled experience unprompted as they vicariously become historical characters in books that they read silently.

A second method of building comprehension of historical texts is to have children emphasize the present tense so that they talk and retell historical events as if they are occurring in the present. This method enables students to feel what it might have been like to have really "been there." You can end these lessons by having students write letters that express their own interpretations of history. Through these mock correspondences, students' own voices concerning specific topics of interest to them can be

TABLE 8.1   Evaluation of Live Historical Timeline Presentations

Points Scored		Possible Points
_10_	**1.** Team was well prepared for presentation.	1–10
_10_	**2.** The historical period was accurately portrayed and well researched.	1–10
	3. The script	
_10_	■ was written in the authorial style of Marilyn Nelson,* a social scientist whom we have studied.	1–10
9 features	■ included 1 to 10 features of historical writing.	1–10
_10_	■ was easy to follow and included 10 new facts about the period not learned during prior whole class lessons (10 points—1 point for each).	1–10
_10_	■ was original yet based on facts.	1–10
10 books	**4.** The group included 10 books as references in the playbill.	1–10
10 costume pieces of the period used	**5.** Costumes were historically accurate and carefully designed, based on pages read from historical texts.	1–10
8 quotes	**6.** Actors spoke loudly and clearly; all used at least one exact quote from speeches of characters that were portrayed.	1–10
_10_	**7.** Points awarded for exceptional originality of solutions, costumes, props, or presentation, indicating in-depth understanding of the era.	1–10
_97_	Total	100

*Marilyn Nelson wrote _Carver: A Life in Poems,_ a Newbery award honor book in 2001. Published by Front Street, Asheville, NC.

Source: Reason to Read, Volume 1 (p. 10) by Cathy Collins Block and John Mangieri. Copyright © 1995 by Pearson Education, Inc., publishing as Dale Seymour Publications. Used by permission.

recorded, using the same thinking patterns employed by historians. Not only will writing as if one is a historian increase one's ability to think like a social scientist but "when a person is learning history by discovering through artifacts, writing, and reading nonfiction texts, they are not going to accept simplistic explanations of the difficulties that exist in their own present lives or histories" (Graves, 1999, p. 19).

A third exciting method of teaching historical text is to divide a certain period into decades and have children explore the Internet, texts, and current events literature that describe their 10 year periods. Without revealing their findings to other people in the class until the last day of this unit's study, students' oral presentations can become **live historical timelines** as they present their findings. Table 8.1 is an evaluation checklist, in a game-like format, that can be used to evaluate how well students have learned how to read social science expository texts. This assessment combines the comprehension processes described previously and can be modified to test students' abilities using methods other than live historical timelines (for which the book list in Table 8.2 was prepared).

Books listed in Table 8.2 can be added to the classroom library. These books have been selected by students as favorites for this lesson and other methods of learning to better comprehend the social science genre.

Teaching the Math Genre

Unlike other genres, in math, most of the tables and graphs are written solely to describe facts. Children can learn to appreciate and comprehend such facts when they are given two contrasting graphs to analyze before they have to interpret a graph problem in their math textbook. These contrasting samples could be created by asking small groups of students to graph their birthdays or their favorite colors, kinds of pets, seasons, or other topics. When students construct these graphs, they begin to realize the amount of information that can be condensed into a single page. They also become more aware of the value of different graphs such as pie charts, bar graphs, line graphs, and three-dimensional forms.

A second method that increases students' comprehension of the mathematical genre is to divide the class into pairs to answer mathematical word problems written by their peers. A sample question that was generated and used by students appears in Figure 8.1 (Winograd & Higgins, 1995). As they work to answer these problems, their mathematical texts become more important to them. These hands-on activities also have been shown to become a springboard for students to start asking their own questions about statements in mathematical texts (Kennedy, 2000). When studying geometry, it is important to give students props so that they can form their own models for the questions in the books and the ones they themselves pose.

A third method that helps students comprehend mathematical concepts is called break the pattern method. It was developed by Paul Kennedy (2000). In this method,

TABLE 8.2   Children's Literature That Adds to Students' Knowledge of History and the Social Sciences

Good Books with a Lot of Pictures

Ashanti To Zulu: African Traditions by M. Musgrove, 1976, Dial

Back Home by G. J. Pinkey, 1992, Dial

A Country Far Away by N. Gray, 1989, Orchard

Darkness and Butterfly by A. Grifalconi, 1987, Little, Brown

Eating the Plates by L. Penner, 1991, Macmillan

Geography from A to Z by J. Knownlton, 1998, Scholastic

The Girl Who Loved Wild Horses by P. Goble, 1993, Aladdin

Hello Amigos by T. Brown, 1986

Ice Cream by W. Jasperson, 1989, Macmillan

John Brown by G. Everett, 1993, Rizzoli

Osa's Pride by A. Grifalconi, 1993, Little, Brown

Our Declaration of Independence by J. Schleifer, 1992, Millbrook Press

Our Money by K. Spies, 1992, Millbrook Press

Our National Anthem by S. St. Pierre, 1992, Millbrook Press

Our National Holiday by K. Spies, 1992, Millbrook Press

Rachel Parker, Kindergarten Show-Off by A. Martin, 1992, Holiday House

Take a Walk in Their Shoes by G. T. Tuner, 1989, Cobblehill Books

They Had a Dream by J. Archer, 1993, Viking

Good Books If You Are Just Beginning to Learn about History and Social Studies

Bright Fawn and Me by J. Leech & Z. Spencer, 1979, Crowell

Charles Needs a Cloak by A. Turner, 1993, MacMillan

Father of the Constitution: James Madison by K. Wilkie, 1963, Messner

The Gift of the Sacred Dog by P. Goble, 1984, Aladdin

The Goat in the Rug by C. Blood and M. Link, 1990, Aladdin

Letters from Rifka by E. Ayer, 1992, Holt

Me and Willie and Pa by F. Monjo, 1970, Harper & Row

The Milk Makers by G. Gibbons, 1985, Macmillan

Nettie's Trip South by A. Turner, 1987, Macmillan

O Canada by T. Harrison, 1993, Ticknor & Fields

One Bad Thing About Father by F. Monjo, 1970, Harper & Row

Our Flag by E. Ayer, 1992, Millbrook Press

Our National Symbols by L. C. Johnson, 1992, Millbrook Press

Teammates by P. Golenbock, 1990, Harcourt Brace

A Winter Walk by L. Barasch, 1993, Ticknor & Field

Good Books to Tell You a Lot about History and Social Studies

The Armadillo from Amarillo by L. Cherry, 1994, Harcourt Brace

Butterfly Boy by L. Yep, 1993, Farrar Straus Giroux

Cassie's Journey: Going West in the 1860's by B. Harvey, 1988, Holiday House

The Desert Is Theirs by B. Baylor, 1987, Aladdin

Faithful Elephants by Y. Tsuchiyo, 1988, Houghton Mifflin

Follow the Drinking Gourd by J. Winter, 1988, Knopf

Hiroshima by L. Yep, 1995, Scholastic

Imani's Gift at Kwanzaa by D. Burden-Palmon, 1993, Aladdin

A Long Hard Journey by P. & F. McKissack, 1989, Walker

My Name Is María Isabel by A. Ada, 1995, Aladdin

Now Is Your Time! The African-American Struggle for Freedom by W. D. Myers, 1991, Harper Collins

Our Constitution by L. Johnson, 1992, Millbrook

Tar Beach by F. Ringgold, Crown

This Place Is Dry (series) by V. Cobb, 1989, Walker

Books That Have Several Chapters about History and Social Studies

The Black Press and the Struggle for Civil Rights by C. Senna, 1994, Franklin Watts

Cowboy: An Album by L. Grandfield, 1994, Ticknor & Field

Down in the Piney Woods by E. F. Smothers, 1992, Knopf

TABLE 8.2   Continued

Every Good-Bye Ain't Gone by I. Njeri, 1990, Random House

From Sea to Shining Sea state books by D. Fradin, 1992, Children's Press

Giant Animals by T. Maynard, 1995, Franklin Watts

Pueblo Storyteller by D. Hoyt-Goldsmith, 1991, Holiday House

Puerto Rico: An Unfinished Story by D. Hauptly, 1991, Atheneum

Raney by C. Edgerton, 1985, Ballantine

The Riddle of the Rosetta Stone: Key to Ancient Egypt by J. Giblin, 1990, Crowell

The Russian Federation by D. Flint, 1992, Millbrook Press

Talking Walls by M. Knight, 1992, Tilbury House

Totem Pole by D. Hoyt-Goldsmith, 1990, Holiday House

The Underground Railroad by S. Cosner, 1991, Venture Books

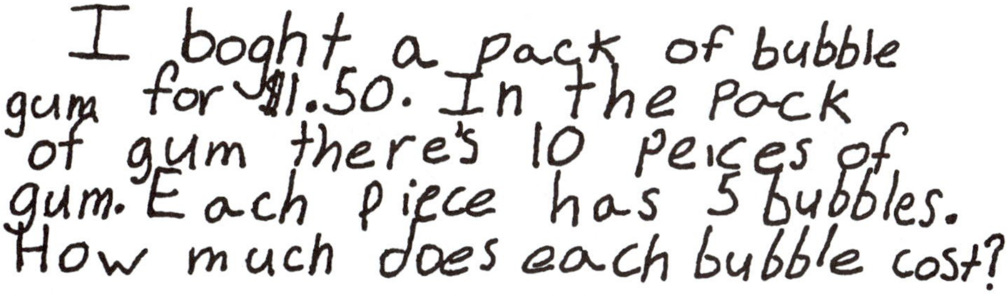

I boght a pack of bubble gum for $1.50. In the pack of gum there's 10 peices of gum. Each piece has 5 bubbles. How much does each bubble cost?

FIGURE 8.1   Barb's Bubble Gum Problem

Source: Winograd, Ken, & Higgins, Karen. (December 1994). Writing, reading, and talking mathematics: One interdisciplinary possibility. *The Reading Teacher, 48*(4), 310–318. Reprinted with permission of the International Reading Association.

students use their oral language to discover the writing/thinking patterns of mathematicians. They talk in groups as they formalize their own algebraic generalizations. Through these conversations, students begin to realize that many symbols and words in the mathematical genre do not mean the same thing as they do in fictional works. For example, an "X" in a text is pronounced "X" when it is read in a fiction murder mystery, but in a math text it is read as *times*, meaning to multiply by. Similarly, parentheses change meaning. In a fictional trade book it means that the words inside the parentheses are not as important as the other information in that sentence. In mathematical texts, however, parentheses communicate the opposite. Parentheses means that the information inside them must be the very first and most important data to which one must attend in order to satisfactorily execute the primary operation. These parenthetical data must be understood before operations outside the parentheses can be considered. These two examples, of the differences between reading math and fiction, must be taught to children, as well as others.

For example, Figure 8.2 presents a real-world problem to be solved. How many miles can a train travel in 17 hours if it is traveling at a speed of 45 miles per hour?

A train travels at
a steady rate of
45 miles per hour

Time	Distance
1	45
2	
3	
4	
5	

10	
17	

Write a sentence to
describe how to find
the distance if you
know the time.

**Lesson Plan for
Developing Algebraic Thinking**

Step 1: Give a concrete experience that
is likely to have occurred in students'
lives where the algebraic thinking
process to be taught could be used.

Step 2: Ask students to generate similar
experiences.

Step 3: Help students deduce the pattern
or common problematic features in all
examples.

Step 4: Ask students to write a sentence
about what type of events in their lives
call for use of the algebraic formula
under study. This is an informal
generalization statement.

Step 5: Students read their own
language aloud, and all of the students'
informal generalizations are collapsed
into a formal algebraic generalization.

$-3 + 2 = $ _____

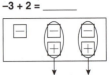

Create four other
addition problems
that have the sum -2.

$-4 + 2 =$
$-5 + 7 =$
$3 + (-5) =$
$-7 + 5 =$

$-20 + 15 =$
$15 + (-30) =$

Write a sentence to
describe how to add
integers that have
different signs.

**FIGURE 8.2   Example of How Students Can Write Sentences to Comprehend
Mathematical Discourses and Develop Algebraic Thinking**

Students discuss the problem, create a graphic, and then write a sentence that could
be used whenever in life they again have to compute the distance of something when
the only data they have available is the amount of time. As also shown in Figure 8.2,
when students are trying to learn a difficult computation, such as "how much is negative 3 plus positive 2," they can generate and discuss four other examples of this computation. Then, they can graph the solutions and write a sentence that explains what
comprehension processes the mind should follow in the future whenever students
must add integers that have different signs. The central column of Figure 8.2 summarizes this method of teaching students to comprehend the math genre: (1) provide
a concrete experience from students' lives in which a mathematical process could be
used to solve a problem; (2) ask students to talk about or write at least three other similar examples from their lives; (3) create a graph where all solutions from these examples can be written; (4) have students write a sentence that describes what they will
do in the future whenever they are faced with situations in their lives in which they
will have to use that mathematical comprehension process again; (5) after students
read their personal sentences, teachers and students can write a generalization that
encapsulates all mathematical sentences. The books listed in Table 8.3 can be used for
these lessons.

TABLE 8.3   Integrating Language Arts into the Mathematics Curriculum

Good Books with a Lot of Pictures

Adding Animals by C. Hawkins, 1997, Scholastic

A Chair for My Mother by V. Williams, 1983, Random House

Color Zoo by L. Ehlert, 1989, Lippincott

How Many Feet in the Bed? by D. Hamm, 1991, Simon & Schuster

Jumanji by C. Van Allsburg, 1981, Houghton Mifflin

Making Cents by E. Wilkensen, 1989, Little, Brown

Much Bigger Than Martin by S. Kellogg, 1976, Dial

My Very First Book of Shapes by E. Carle, 1970, Crowell

One Two, One Pair by B. McMillan, 1991, Scholastic

One, Two, Three to the Zoo by E. Carle, 1991, Picture Book Studio

Three Sides and the Round One by M. Friskey, 1975, Children's Press

The Toothpaste Millionaire by J. Merrill, 1972, Houghton Mifflin

26 Letters and 99 Cents by T. Hoban, 1987, Greenwillow

Waiting for Sunday by C. Blackburn, 1991, Scholastic

Willy Can Count by A. Rockwell, 1989, Arcade Publishers

Good Books If You Are Just Beginning to Learn about the Subject

Deep Down Underground by Oliver, 1993, Aladdin

Eating Fractions by B. McMillan, 1991, Scholastic

Fish Eyes: A Book You Can Count On by L. Ehlert, 1990, Harcourt Brace Jovanovich

How Many Is a Million? by D. Schwartz, 1985, Lothrop, Lee & Shepard

The Hundred Penny Box by S. Mathis, 1975, Viking

Just a Mess by M. Mayer, 1987, Western

Listen to a Shape by M. Brown, 1979, Franklin Watts

Moira's Birthday by R. Munsch, 1987, Annic

Mushroom in the Rain by M. Ginsburg, 1974, Macmillan

One Smiling Grandma: A Caribbean Counting Book by A. Linden, 1992, Dial

One White Sail by S. Garne, 1992, Green Tiger Press

Over in the Meadow by P. Galdone, 1986, Aladdin

Shape Space by C. Falwell, 1992, Clarion

Ten Black Dots by D. Crews, 1986, Greenwillow

Zero: Is It Something? Is It Nothing? by C. Zaslavsky, 1989, Franklin Watts

Good Books to Tell You a Lot about the Subject

All Shapes and Sizes by S. Hughes, 1986, Douglas & McIntyre

The Book of Classic Board Games by S. Sackson, 1991, Klutz Press

The Carrot Seed by R. Krauss, 1945, Harper & Row

Count on Your Fingers African Style by C. Zaslavsky, 1980

Count Your Way through India and other stories by J. Haskins, 1987–1990, Carolrhoda Books

Five Little Monkeys Jumping on the Bed by E. Christelow, 1989, Clarion

The Half Birthday Party by C. Pomerantz, 1984, Clarion

Lines by P. Yenawine, 1991, Delacorte Press

The Missing Piece by S. Silverstein, 1976, Harper & Row

Mouse Count by E. Walsh, 1991, Harcourt Brace Jovanovich

This Old Man by C. Jones, 1990, Houghton Mifflin

What Do You Mean by Average? by E. James & C. Barkin, 1998, Scholastic

What is Symmetry? by M. Sitomer & H. Sitomer, 1970, Crowell

Books That Have Several Chapters about the Subject

Angles Are as Easy as Pie by R. Froman, 1997, Crowell

Arithmetic Teacher (magazine)

Clocks: Building and Experimenting with Model Timepieces by B. Zubrowski, 1988, Morrow

A Collection of Math Lessons from Grades 1–3 by M. Burns, 1988, Math Solutions Publication

(continued)

TABLE 8.3   Continued

Making Cents: Every Kid's Guide to Money, How to Make It, What to Do with It by E. Wilkinson, 1989, Little, Brown

Ed Emberley's Picture Pie: A Circle Drawing Book by E. Emberley, 1984, Little, Brown

Esio Trot by R. Doahl, 1990, Viking

Extra Cash for Kids by L. Elliston & K. Hanks, 1989, Wolgemuth & Hyatt

The I Hate Mathematics! Book by M. Burns, 1975, Little, Brown

Sideways Arithmetic from Wayside School by L. Sachar, 1989, Scholastic

Smart Spending: A Young Consumer's Guide by L. Schmitt, 1997, Scribner

Straight Lines, Parallel Lines, and Perpendicular Lines by M. Charosh, 1970, Crowell

Where the Sidewalk Ends by S. Silverstein, 1974, Harper & Row

Teaching the Scientific Genre

Four lessons distinguish themselves as being highly successful methods of building students' comprehension of scientific materials. The first is the **attribute method.** In this approach, students increased their abilities to retain and relate details by studying pictures from specific scientific textbook chapters. When children look at the pictures they are to think about why the author may have placed each picture in that specific location and what information it was intended to convey. Then, children can read the chapter and verify if each picture's previously identified attributes were indeed those desired by the author. Next, students can be taught to list details that were depicted in tables, photographs, and graphs. As they do so, students' observation skills and retention/relational comprehension processes increase. As shown in Figure 8.3, the scientific processes of observing, classifying, measuring, collecting, communicating, and inferring depend on the ability to recall single pieces of data. You can teach each of the processes in Figure 8.3 to students by using hands-on experiments and having students write down the comprehension processes they use during the experiment. Students can write a paragraph based on each of the comprehension processes in Figure 8.3. As they read the scientific genre, students can reuse Figure 8.3 to write the page numbers and descriptions of when they initiated each comprehension process.

Another method that builds students' comprehension of the scientific genre involves using **letter probes.** A letter probe is a real letter that students write to a scientific company requesting information, samples, or products. Writing letter probes teaches students to organize scientific details. These letters contain specific facts of scientific importance and information that tells companies exactly which pamphlets, products, or brochures are desired. Companies to which children can write are found in: *Clubs for Kids, Freebies for Kids, Freebies Books: Hundreds of Things You Can Get for Free, Free and Inexpensive Learning Materials,* and *Free Things for Teachers.*

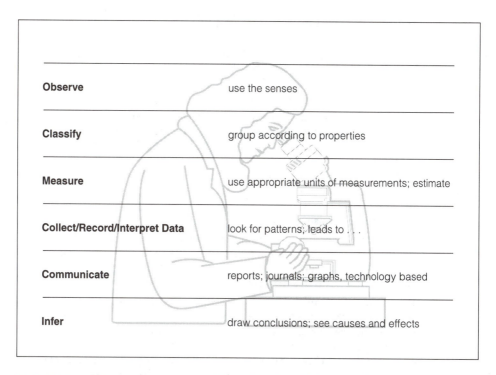

Observe · use the senses

Classify · group according to properties

Measure · use appropriate units of measurements; estimate

Collect/Record/Interpret Data · look for patterns; leads to . . .

Communicate · reports; journals; graphs, technology based

Infer · draw conclusions; see causes and effects

FIGURE 8.3   Writing Sentences and Page Numbers When Students Employed Each Thinking Process Used in Scientific Genre

Source: Created by Caryn Ellison, gifted and talented teacher, Mishaw, Indiana. Used by permission.

Two additional methods that assist students in increasing their abilities to comprehend science materials are learning logs or interactive journals and structured thinking reading activity. **Learning logs** are journals in which readers record scientific data that they have read, just as scientists have done throughout history. These entries are made at the end of a day's reading of scientific texts and materials. Students write each entry using the same thinking patterns that scientists use, which results in keen awareness of these patterns when reading scientific texts. **Interactive journals** are sections of journals that students keep privately, and ask friends, teachers, or parents to read and respond to by writing on the next page in the interactive journal.

Lastly, in the **structured thinking reading activity,** you read a main idea statement from a scientific textbook orally; now students read the paragraph silently. Then, you ask students to reread the main idea in context silently. Children enjoy pausing to reflect and discuss after three or four paragraphs have been read in this manner. During these discussions, students tell how they integrated several comprehension processes. In addition by pairing this activity with the multiple sources record keeping form (Figure 8.4) students learn to seek several sources to verify information. A list of

FIGURE 8.4   Multiple Source Record Keeping

Research team members: Suzanna, John, Clarissa, Carl
Research Book: *The Volcano* (Lauber, 1993)

Questions Team Wants to Answer

1. How long had it been since Mount St. Helens erupted?
2. What caused the volcano to erupt so suddenly without warning after having remained dormant for as long as team members had been alive?
3. How hot does lava become?
4. What is the largest volcano?
5. How many volcanoes are in the world?

Sources for and Answer to Question 1

120 years as computed by Carl from data in *Encyclopedia Britannica* CD, verified by seeking a second source in the *Volcano*, and recalculating the numbers of years by John.

Sources for and Answer to Question 2

Earthquakes and seismic vibrations of the Earth's core south of Mount St. Helens reduced the distance between the two plates beneath Mount St. Helens. This decreased space which increased the pressure on magma and forced it into the air. Source was http://volcano.und.novak.edu. Verification and names of the two plates were found in a diagram and text on pages 52 and 53 of *Volcano*. Suzanna and Clarissa worked side by side and both read all the information in both sources to provide increased verification.

Sources for and Answer to Question 3

2,000 degrees at vent decreasing in intensity *very* slowly as it mingles with the 10 to 80 degrees in the atmosphere on the mountain slopes. It takes more than 1,000 degrees to melt most rocks. Source was *Reading Rainbow Video "Hill of Fire."* Source 2 was phone call to Museum of Science and History curator, Mr. Juan Pablo. He verified the information in the video. John asked Suzanna to confirm and record the information taken during the phone call, which was made from the speaker phone in the principal's office. All team members watched the video.

Sources for and Answer to Question 4

Mauna Loa, source was Mr. Juan Pablo, in Suzanna and John's phone interview. Source 2 was http://volcano.und.novak.edu.

Sources for and Answer to Question 5

850 active volcanoes. Source was Mr. Juan Pablo, but he said "about 600 or more." Because the information was vague, Carl and Clarissa sought two additional sources for verification. Two subsequent sources reported 850, and both sources converged to verify that number. Sources 2 and 3 were *Explorapedia* CD and http://volcano.und.novak.edu.

Skills Gained by the Research Team as a Result of This Project

■ Becoming more proficient using the Internet, Explorapedia CD, and interviews with experts as sources to obtain and verify information.

FIGURE 8.4   Continued

- Vague information should be reverified with at least two sources, and we saw how gossip in people's personal lives spreads when we don't follow this principle.

- Videotapes are the best sources for experiencing large events—better than reading because our minds are freer to explore ramifications of, and pose questions about, an event immediately because we don't have to be decoding and interpreting words.

- It is important to have two people to verify.

On a separate page write the grade you think you deserve and why.

Source: Designed by Rachel Escamilla, administrative assistant, Texas Christian University, Fort Worth, Texas.

books that students appreciated in developing their comprehension of the scientific genre appears in Table 8.4.

Teaching the Fine Arts Genre

Teaching the fine arts genre

It is very interesting to note that the three countries that rank near the top of all nations in math and science scores on the National Assessments of Educational Progress also have intense, well-developed music and art programs in their elementary and middle schools. These countries—Japan, Hungary, and the Netherlands—teach students to play a musical instrument, to be involved in a choir, and/or to develop an artistic ability. Fine arts education is required because it helps develop visual thinking, problem-solving processes, and creativity, which students need to succeed in other subject areas (Jensen, 1999).

In addition, many studies suggest that students who are engaged in art and music activate more metacognitive thoughts when reading than peers who do not create artistically or musically. Fine arts activities unite emotions and meaning, a process expert readers also experience. Intense emotional involvement in artistic activities also releases the chemicals adrenaline, norepinephrine, and vasopressin. These chemicals signal that something important is occurring and when students read information relative to creative activities, the mind comprehends this information rapidly and permanently (Jensen, 1999). Without such experiences, emotions are experienced only by happenstance, on a moment-by-moment basis, as children read fiction, or only if they have learned to appreciate nonfiction texts through the methods described in this chapter.

To develop students' abilities to read artistic, musical, or other fine arts texts, it is important to recognize that many artistic pieces are written from an aesthetic

TABLE 8.4   Children's Literature That Adds to Students' Knowledge of Science

Good Books with a Lot of Pictures

Cornelius by L. Lionni, 1983, Pantheon Books

The Grouchy Ladybug by E. Carle, 1986, Harper Collins

Knots on a Counting Rope by B. Martin, Jr. & J. Archambault, 1993, Henry Holt

Mole's Hill: A Woodland Tale by L. Ehlert, 1994, Harcourt Brace

Our Yard Is Full of Birds by A. Rockwell, 1992, Macmillan

Quiet by P. Parnall, 1989, Morrow

Smelling Things by A. Fowler, 1991, Children's Press

A Tree Is Nice by J.M. Udry, 1994, Scholastic

Turtle in July by M. Singer, 1993, Macmillan

Tyrannosaurus Was a Beast by J. Prelutsky, 1992, Morrow

Vegetables, Vegetables! By F. Robinson, 1994, Children's Press

The Very Busy Spider by E. Carle, 1989, Putnam

The Very Hungry Caterpillar by E. Carle, 1994, Putnam

The X-Ray Picture Book of Dinosaurs and Other Prehistoric Creatures by K. Senior, 1995, Franklin Watts

Your Amazing Senses: 36 Games, Puzzles, and Quizzes That Show How Your Senses Work by R. & A. Van der Meer, 1987, Simon & Schuster

Good Books If You Are Just Beginning to Learn about the Subject

Bird Watch by J. Yolen, 1990, Philomel/Putnam

Discovering Butterflies by D. Florian, 1990, Aladdin

Ducklings and Polliwogs by A. Rockwell, 1994, Macmillan

Feathers by D. Patent, 1992, Dutton

Germs Make Me Sick by M. Berger, 1985, Cromwell

The Great Kapok Tree: A Tale of the Amazon River Forest by L. Cherry, 1990, Harcourt Brace

Hot and Cold by A. Fowler, 1994, Children's Press

How Does It Feel To Be Old? By N. Farver, 1988, Doubleday

Mush by P. Seibert, 1992, Millbrook Press

The New Illustrated Dinosaur Dictionary by H. Satler, 1990, Morrow

Our National Monuments by E. Ayer, 1992, Millbrook Press

Red Leaf, Yellow Leaf by L. Ehlert, 1991, Harcourt Brace

The Rock by P. Parnall, 1991, Macmillan

Timelines Flight: Fliers and Flying Machines by D. Jeffries, 1991, Franklin Watts

Turkeys That Fly and Turkeys That Don't by A. Fowler, 1994, Children's Press

The Witch's Eye by P. Naylor, 1998, Scholastic

Good Books to Tell You a Lot about the Subject

Corn—On and Off the Cob by A. Fowler, 1994, Children's Press

Carbohydrates by Dr. Alvin, R. & V. Silverstein, 1992, Millbrook Press

Dinosaurs and More Dinosaurs by J. Craig, 1999, Scholastic

Exploring the World of Animals by R. Durant, 1995, Franklin Watts

Exploring the World of Astronomy by G. Burns, 1995, Franklin Watts

Exploring the World of Plants by R. Durant, 1995, Franklin Watts

Fats by Dr. Alvin, R. & V. Silverstein, 1992, Millbrook Press

Growing Vegetable Soup by L. Ehlert, 1990, Harcourt Brace

The Legend of the Bluebonnet by T. De Paola, 1983, G. P. Putnam's Sons

Now I Know (series) by S. Peters, 1997, Scholastic

Pets of the Presidents by J. Caulkins, 1992, Millbrook Press

Proteins by Dr. Alvin, R. & V. Silverstein, 1992, Millbrook Press

Vitamins & Minerals by Dr. Alvin, R. & V. Silverstein, 1992, Millbrook Press

Who's Sick Today? by P. Durant, 1997, Franklin Watts

Books That Have Several Chapters about the Subject

Alligators, Racoons, and Other Survivors: The Wildlife of the Future by B. Ford, 1981, Morrow

TABLE 8.4   Continued

The Astronaut Training Book for Kids by K. Long, 1990, Lodestar Books	*Machines That Think* and other books by I. Asimov, 1984, Holt
The Banshee by K. Ackerman, 1999, Scholastic	*The Magic School Bus* (series) by J. Cole, 1986, Scholastic
The Big Stew by B. Shecter, 1999, Scholastic	*The Midnight Horse* by S. Fleishmann, 1999, Scholastic
A Bird's Body and other books by J. Cole, 1982, Morrow	*Norby and Yobo's Great Adventure* by J. & J. Asimov, 1993, Scholastic
Dinosaurs of North America by H. Sattler, 1981, Lothrop, Lee & Shepard	*Outer Space and All That Junk* by M. Gilden, 1999, Scholastic
Heartlight by T. A. Barron, 1990, Scholastic	*Science Facts You Won't Believe* by W. Gottlieb, 1983, Watts
If You Lived on Mars by M. Berger, 1989, Lodestar Books	*The Tunnel* by A. Browne, 1999, Scholastic
Jupiter by S. Simon, 1985, Morrow	
The Kingdom of Wolves by S. Barry, 1979, Putnam	

perspective. To develop students' interpretations and concepts of what is beautiful it is important to introduce two contrasting selections (for example, of music, art, CDs, or Web sites) and have them consider the merits of both. The "put me in the painting activity" is an effective method of teaching students how to weigh the merits in an artistic expression.

The **put me in the painting activity** can be used with any fine arts genre, including sculpture, architecture, landscaping, and city planning. This activity begins by showing two portraits of people in the same time period, two images of a similar event, two people in the same profession, or two musical selections. Prior to presenting these artisitic representations you can introduce nonfiction artistic writings to which students can refer when answering questions that are generated in class. The put me in the painting activity begins when you describe a conversation that could have occurred between two composers, two painters, or two figures in two paintings. This conversation will be based on texts that students have read concerning the people or events portrayed in the paintings or represented in the musical selections.

Another activity for fine arts comprehension is a **nonfiction author study** where a student focuses on a particular author he or she enjoys reading. Once an author is selected, the student reads books that author has written and can visit the author's Web site if one exists. Books that students have enjoyed reading about the fine arts are listed in Table 8.5.

The patterns of thought authors follow become apparent as students read more books by the same author. This activity is different for an author study involving nonfiction work from an author study using fiction work. The major difference is that you

TABLE 8.5   Children's Literature That Adds to Students' Appreciation of the Fine Arts

Good Books with a Lot of Pictures

Draw Me a Star by E. Carle, 1992, Putnam
Emma by W. Kesselman, 1980, Harper
Free Fall by D. Weisner, 1980, Lothrop, Lee & Shepard
Great Painters by P. Ventura, 1984, Putnam
I'm Dancing by A. McCarter & G. Reed, 1981, Scribner
Mr. Panda's Painting by A. Rockwell, 1993, Macmillan
Noah's Ark by P. Spier, 1977, Doubleday
No Good in Art by M. Cohen, 1980, Greenwillow
People at Work: Looking at Art by P. Conner, 1992, McElderry
The Polar Express by C. Van Allsburg, 1985, Houghton Mifflin
The Pooh Sketchbook by E. H. Shepard, 1984, Dutton
Possum Come a-Knockin' by N. Van Laan, 1990, Knopf

Books That Have Several Chapters about Fine Arts Subjects

An Artist's Album by M. B. Goffstein, 1985, Harper
Draw 50 Horses by L. Ames, 1984, Doubleday
Drawing Dinosaurs & Other Prehistoric Animals by D. Bolognese, 1982, Franklin Watts
Drawing from Nature by J. Arnmosky, 1982, Lothrop, Lee & Shepard
Jazz by L. Hughes, 1982, Franklin Watts
The Magic of Color by H. Simon, 1981, Lothrop, Lee & Shepard
Meet Matisse by N. Munthe, 1983, Little, Brown
Michelangelo by R. MacNathan, 1993, Abrams
North American Indian Masks: Craft and Legend by F. Gates, 1982, Walker
Series TV: How a Television Show Is Made by M. Drucker & E. James, 1983, Clarion
The Sky Is Full of Song by L. B. Hopkins, 1983, Harper & Row

"Sister Ann" in *A Poem for a Pickle* by R. Merriam, 1989, Morrow
Teaching Drama to Young Children by M. Fox, 1986, Heinemann
A Weekend with Matisse by F. Rodari, 1992, Rizzoli
A Weekend with Renoir by R. Skira-Venturi, 1992, Rizzoli
Winslow Homer: The Gulf Stream by E. Goldstein, 1982, Garrard

Good Books to Tell You a Lot About Fine Arts Subjects

The Art of Eric Carle by E. Carle, 1993, Picture Book Studio
A Color Sampler by K. Westry, 1993, Ticknor & Fields
Davinci by M. Venezia, 1989, Children's Press
Diego Rivera by M. Venezia, 1994, Children's Press
Fransico Goya by M. Venezia, 1991, Children's Press
Henri de Toulouse-Lautrect by M. Venezia, 1994, Children's Press
How to Make Pop-Ups by J. Irvine, 1987, Morrow
The Joy of Drawing by B. Martin, 1993, Watson-Guptill
Let's Find the Big Idea by A. Wiseman, 1979, Scribner
Lil' Sis and Uncle Willie: A Story Based on the Life and Paintings of William H. Johnson by G. Everett, 1991, Rizzoli
Making Musical Things by A. Wiseman, 1979, Scribner
Mary Cassatt by M. Venezia, 1989, Children's Press
"The Paint Box" in Scott Elledge's *Wider Than the Sky* by E. V. Rieu, 1990, Harper
The Ways to Start a Day by B. Baylor, 1986, Aladdin
What Instrument Is This? by R. Hausherr, 1992, Scholastic

introduce two to three authors' multiple book sets on the same topic. This way children can understand how the same subject, such as animals, can be viewed from different perspectives, based on an author's perspective. Nonfiction author studies not only enhance students' appreciation of the content area being studied but they also develop students' appreciation of authors' explanations of their emotions and comprehension processes, which is a powerful benefit of reading fine arts texts.

In Summary

The major objective of this chapter has been to demonstrate that students are capable of recalling content from subject matter disciplines. For them to acquire the habit and enjoyment of comprehending and referencing expository text without external prompting is another matter altogether. In this chapter, 17 methods for increasing students' comprehension of historical, mathematical, scientific, and fine arts texts were described and illustrated:

- Teaching students how to read the information in graphics
- Teaching students to set their own purpose for reading
- Teaching students how to follow an author's train of thought processes
- Teaching students to scamper and scan until they choose to stop and savor
- Having a buddy beside them as they read
- Thinking about two or more comprehension processes at once as they read using adhesive note prompts
- Helping students to elevate the essence through summary partner questioning
- Contrasting two books on the same topic
- Living historical timelines
- Graphing personal information
- Answering mathematical word problems that peers write
- Using the attribute method
- Making letter probes
- Creating learning logs or interactive journals
- Participating in structured thinking reading activity
- Using the putting me in the painting activity
- Completing author studies

These lessons help students reach deep and broad levels of literal, inferential, applied, and metacognitive comprehension. In Chapter 9, how such expansive thinking can also be achieved in technologically based environments and through culturally dominated texts is discussed.

R E F L E C T I N G   O N   W H A T   Y O U   H A V E   L E A R N E D

1. Recent research found that 32 genres are included on state assessments of reading (Gambrell, 2001). Of this number, 20 are nonfiction texts. With this in mind, what proportion of time in your reading program do you want to devote to developing students' comprehension of expository texts? Defend your decision, and be prepared to describe your reasons to your colleagues.

2. Describe four qualities of nonfiction texts that should be taught to improve comprehension instruction.

3. *Your Professional Journal: First Draft for Upcoming Oral Presentations.* Write a description that you will use to explain to parents why it is important for them to read nonfiction texts with their children at home.

4. *Making Professional Decisions.* In a paragraph describe a new action that you believe your school district should undertake to improve a student's ability to comprehend nonfiction texts.

5. Create a new method of assessing genre-specific comprehension, by altering suggestions read in previous chapters.

6. *Field Applications and Observations.* Plan and teach a lesson from this chapter, or observe a teacher implementing a lesson and evaluate its success. Be prepared to discuss the strengths and weaknesses of this lesson with colleagues.

7. *Multicultural Applications.* For a week, teach lessons from this chapter or observe a teacher teaching students to comprehend nonfiction texts. Keep a record of the activities as well as your assessment of each in a learning log or interactive journal. Decide which, if any, seemed to have maximum benefits for students from variant cultural backgrounds or minority ethnic groups. Finally, prepare a second "first draft for upcoming oral presentations" journal entry so you can organize your thoughts to share the results of your data collection with the teacher that you observed.

8. *Key Terms Exercise.* Following is a list of concepts introduced in this chapter. If you have learned the meaning of a term, place a checkmark in the blank that precedes that term. If you are not sure of a term's definition, increase your retention by reviewing the definition of the term. If you have learned seven of these terms on your first reading of this chapter, you have already learned many meanings that are important in your career.

_____ informational, expository, and nonfiction texts (p. 157)

_____ live historical timelines (p. 167)

_____ attribute method (p. 172)

_____ letter probes (p. 172)

_____ learning logs (p. 173)

_____ interactive journals (p. 173)

_____ structured thinking reading activity (p. 173)

_____ put me in the painting activity (p. 177)

_____ nonfiction author study (p. 177)

9. *Comprehension Process Lesson 8: Teaching Students to Think Metacognitively as They Read Nonfiction.* The following comprehension lesson demonstrates how students can invent their own games to practice and assess their own and peers' use of content-specific comprehension processes to learn social science, scientific, mathematical, and fine arts facts. You can use one or both of the games in Comprehension Process Lesson 8 as games students can play and/or as examples to stimulate your students' ideas about practice and assessment games that they would like to make for their classmates. When students make their own games, they have to think in ways that nonfiction writers think and invent a writing format that follows the thought pattern used by authors of that genre. Both of these thinking processes will strengthen their content-specific comprehension processes when they read nonfiction texts.

COMPREHENSION PROCESS LESSON 8

Teaching Students to Think Metacognitively as They Read Nonfiction

The following problem-solving activity for science allows students to analyze text at a deep level and then build from that analysis. As with other comprehension process lessons in this book, this activity could be easily modified to incorporate other genres including history, math, and the fine arts by simply changing the questions and the scenario. The same maze could be used as long as the questions asked in the activity are yes/no questions. This activity allows students to work independently or in groups, without the need for teacher instruction. In a follow-up lesson the teacher can ask students to explain all the negative answers as well as explaining why for all questions.

Batty's Cave
Batty needs your help! He's never left his roost and doesn't know how to get out of his cave. Help him use echolocation to find his way!

Directions: Each of the following questions corresponds to a place in the maze. For each correct answer Batty will move closer to the exit of his cave. But, if an answer is incorrect, Batty will fly into a wall. Answer each question with a YES or NO and follow the path that matches your answer on the accompanying maze.

Questions

1. The smallest known mammal is a type of bat.
2. Bats form nests like those of birds.
3. Bats are blind.
4. Bats hibernate in the winter.
5. Bats have feathers on their wings.
6. Bats produce sound with their ears.
7. Bats are the only mammals that have evolved true flight.
8. All bats feed on blood.
9. Bats use a sophisticated method called echolocation, in which they send out sound waves and listen for echoes to navigate.
10. Bats always fly left when exiting a cave.

COMPREHENSION PROCESS LESSON 8   Continued

Questions for Thought

Would a bat's sense of echolocation get confused if there were a great deal of noise?
Why or why not?

Source: Created by Andrew Farr, elementary education major, Texas Christian University, Fort Worth, Texas. Special thanks to Paige Bothwell for research and editing. Used by permission.

Technological Comprehension and Reading Culturally Dominated Texts

Anthony enjoys hypertext, interactive books, and creating his own computer comprehension assessments. His classmates look forward to Fridays, at 2:00 pm, when he unveils his newest computer creations that they are to comprehend.

TECHNOLOGICAL COMPREHENSION AND READING CULTURALLY DOMINATED TEXTS

- Differences in comprehending technology versus print

- Teaching students to comprehend with technology

- Reading culturally dominated texts

- Increasing students' comprehension of culturally dominated texts

Ms. Jiru was preparing her last reading lesson for the year. As she planned it, she continually thought about the changing world in which her students live—highly technological, culturally diverse, image driven, and sound-byte hyped. She reflected on how the majority of her students would spend their free time during the upcoming summer: walking the malls, scanning movie video covers to select favorites for home viewing, surfing the Web, sending e-mails, visiting chat rooms, watching television, and talking to friends on the telephone. Although many pupils will visit public libraries and subscribe to weekly newsletters, Ms. Jiru knew that most of her sixth graders would not spend 90 minutes each day reading as they had at school. For these reasons, she was pleased that she and her colleagues implemented the lessons in this chapter during the last 2 months of their language arts program. These lessons were designed to help her students find numerous Web sites that could be explored throughout the summer to enhance many interests, vocations, and hobbies.

She was equally pleased that these lessons had introduced her students to main characters who shared her students' cultural heritage. Many of the authors whose books they read had written additional titles, and her pupils would leave her classroom today with the knowledge of how to obtain these books at the public library. This could be the beginning of a summer habit that could last throughout her students' lives. Ms. Jiru glanced at her watch and picked up her list. She smiled with satisfaction as she carried it to the photocopying machine. She and her colleagues had prepared a list of best Web sites for their students (duplicated for your use in the Appendix of this book). These sites would provide their students with many hours of valuable reading experiences in numerous interest areas. As the bell rang marking the last day of school, her eyes filled with tears and her heart swelled. She would miss her class, but they would not miss the opportunity to build their comprehension abilities when they left her. ∎

Chapter Overview

The purpose of this chapter is to report new research concerning the advancements of comprehension instruction that enables children to process media-generated texts. A second goal is to describe the importance of knowing how to read culturally dominated texts. The chapter ends with a description of resources that can enhance students' comprehension as they grow to become adults in an ever-changing world.

By the end of this chapter you will be able to answer the following questions:

1. What practices develop students' comprehension of text presented through the Internet, hypertext, graphics, and commercially prepared communication venues (computer comprehension abilities)?
2. What is likely to occur if students' instruction does not match their cultural experiences?
3. How can we increase students' comprehension of culturally sensitive text?

Differences in Comprehending Technology versus Print

The invention of the printing press was noted as the most significant creation in the past millennium. In the new millennium, it is likely that technological literacy will become the most significant advancer of society. Statistical studies support the assertion that the computer is the most important technological development of all time. In 1994, for ex-

Differences in comprehending technology versus print

ample, for the first time in history, the number of computers sold in the United States exceeded the number of televisions purchased. With each new day, technology dominates and defines what reading comprehension is. It accelerates the pace by which people comprehend. It affects the way people gain deep knowledge because more and more information flashes instantly, electronically, and through a variety of multimedia formats (Reinking & Bridwell-Bowes, 1996). For these, and numerous other reasons, it is important to place technological literacy competence as one of the highest priorities in our schools.

Technological literacy demands that students know how to navigate around in the Internet; Web environments; and use parallel processing, pattern recognition, and strategic thinking. Experiencing multidimensional textual formats simultaneously stands in sharp contrast to traditional, linear forms of comprehending texts. For example, books are only processed from left to right, line by line, page by page, without readers' choices as to the direction or depth with which ideas will unfold.

Moreover, from their modest beginning only 30 years ago, personal computers have become central to how people define their literate selves and how they imagine they would like to live in the future. It is also today's instrument of choice for raising social consciousness and stimulating cultural change. In addition, changes that technology is creating are exponentially greater and faster than those which television (the "cultural molder" in the 1960s) created. Unlike television, it has profoundly changed people's intellectual lives. A renaissance, a highly innovative period, has begun in which people immerse themselves in reaching for new frontiers though multiple forms of comprehending. To cite only two examples, in the future, ideas will be acted on more rapidly than in the past, and they will instantly impact more lives than in previous generations. All must now develop technologically based comprehension abilities (Lanham, 1993; Negropante, 1995). Following are examples of the types of comprehension processes that students must acquire.

Hypertext is the links that appear in Web sites and split screens displayed on a computer screen. Hypertext creates a type of reading that is nonsequential. Students can view text, pictures, icons, images, and moving text to learn about a concept. More than any prior time in history, because of technologically generated text, students can bypass information that is boring and delve deep into topics that answer personally generated questions. They can also rapidly select text and images that are perfectly matched to, and provide the most up-to-date facts about, their specific reading goals. **Hypertext-based comprehension** is an understanding of dynamic, three-dimensional text, an exploration and processing of methods of presenting information in nonlinear paper and pencil format. The ramifications of hypertext-based comprehension on traditional comprehension abilities are not clear. For example, Hobbs (1997) reported that when text, video clips, and music were presented simultaneously on a computer screen, the density and variety in the information input system decreased the retention and transfer of the nonfiction text which appeared in this hypertext-formatted environment.

Another new comprehension process is the ability of readers and writers to interact with text and partially control the messages that they receive, thus reducing the boredom that often characterizes linear text reading. Electronic comprehension processes' point-and-click definitions of terms are also frequently supported by speed in data gathering, and use of other sophisticated text-processing tools.

Computer software can provide intelligent coaching to ensure that all students can problem solve with success. Computers provide tools to support students' reflection and metacognition. As an example, Intel Corporation (Spires & Estes, 2000) teaches technicians to create programs that determine when something has gone wrong with a student's comprehension. It does so by building layers and layers of information. Students continue through the layers until a problem develops. To pass through each layer of information, students must answer a question. To answer the question correctly, students perform a specific comprehension process. If the student answers incorrectly, the computer automatically sends the student to a computer-generated mini lesson designed to teach that specific comprehension process. Soon computer programs will have the capabilities to simulate difficulties that can appear in any genre, at each level of student comprehension ability.

These types of programs also prompt students as to which kind of comprehension process will be most valuable for them to use at a particularly challenging point in the text. Three of these types of comprehension process prompts are already available: (1) students can request hints from the computer before answering questions; (2) students can ask for explanations of correct and incorrect answers before or after they make selections from multiple-choice questions; and (3) students can request more instruction when they misunderstand any section of a computer-based text (Spires & Estes, 2000).

Another difference between computer-based and print-based text that could enhance some students' comprehension is the ability of computer software to saturate the mind with images and words faster than print which could enhance some students' abilities to more rapidly retrieve strongly developed comprehension processes than is possible in print-based environments. Computers can reduce students' doubts and knowledge deficits so that they build volition and persistence when facing subsequent, traditional print-based comprehension challenges. Computers provide new types of literacy. In the future, using computers, students should be less fearful of failing as comprehenders. They can access knowledge as soon as the adults in their world receive it, and enter current event literature with the same level of background knowledge as their teachers.

Young children's use of the Internet provides a final example of the values of electronic comprehension abilities. Through it, students are experiencing an increased skill for staying interconnected, keeping updated, personalizing their interactions with people, and building their abilities to comprehend more varied types of information (Carnegie Foundation, 2000). Through computers, students have also demonstrated an ability to learn with higher-quality examples than would be possible without them. Technology experts and educators outside any individual classroom require several months of concentrated work to develop each enriched example in a computer-based text program or Web site. Individual teachers do not have the time to create, or do the research connected with, such deep, high-quality creations.

Teaching Students to Comprehend with Technology

Teaching students to comprehend with technology

One of the most researched methods of building technological comprehension is having children work in pairs. Students can work together in many ways to improve their comprehension, including using word processing; working with databases; processing with voice synthesizers, spell checks, computer thesauruses, editing programs; and using branching software to provide opportunities for them to create retellings. By working in pairs, conversation strengthens long-term memory and student motivation (Ewing, 1999; Gillingham, 1993; Goldman, 1996; Haas, 1996). Working in pairs has the potential to (1) change the purpose, process, and products of students' comprehension; (2) cost no more than traditional instruction; and (3) decrease the number of literal comprehension errors (Haas, 1996).

There is also better support for higher-level comprehension when students process technologically driven text in pairs rather than alone. This appears to occur because two students are likely to have different comprehension processes engaged at any one time. By working together and dividing the labor, their separate comprehension strengths interact as they discuss what they are learning. The result is that pairs create a deeper and broader understanding than individuals working alone. When groups at the computer screen increase to three or more, however, the quality of comprehension decreases and off-task behavior increases (Alexander, 1992). A list of computer software that has been found to increase students' comprehension is shown in Table 9.1.

When computers function as tutors they can also eliminate misconceptions by observing every behavior that a child performs while reading. They have infinite patience. They also perform laborious reading tasks that students dislike. They make it easier for minds to comprehend large bodies of knowledge by collapsing many details into easy-to-read pictorial images and interactive displays. They rotate objects, dimensionalize data (particularly for nonfiction topics), categorize, and retrieve facts rapidly. Software that contains prompts to initiate certain comprehension processes at points in the text when students need them is also under development (Perfetti, 1998).

We can no longer allow children to not stay abreast of technology's changes. For example, students who know that hypertext challenges them to think during reading without textual boundaries, mobility, and limited navigation direction will become more able comprehenders of even more technologically innovative reading environments in the future than friends who are not agile hypertext comprehenders. Specifically, "at any given juncture, such able comprehenders can easily (a) transport text from one physical location to another; (b) select multiple tasks in a body of text; (c) choose to read from top to bottom, front to back and vice versa, or from page to video; (d) navigate unique paths through a network of links they create; and (e) overcome the challenges of 'on the screen reading' that readers of traditional print do not face" (Spires & Estees, 2000, p. 403).

The Internet and hypertext also put students in touch with authors quickly and there is a greater potential for direct interactions than ever before. Bolter (1998) and Levin (1999) argue that hypertext is not only nonlinear but also multilinear because it

TABLE 9.1   Software That Increases Students' Comprehension

Interactive Books

Wiggle Works (Scholastic): A total emergent reading program that contains leveled predictable books on CD-ROM. These disks also provide models for framed writing of each book.

Living Books: A set of storybooks on screen. The text is read and words are highlighted on the page so students can read along.

Discuss Books: A set of predictable stories and poems that are on CD-ROM. These books also have the added feature of action in the storybook picture and naming objects in the picture to facilitate language development.

Smart Books (Scholastic): Books on an interactive CD-ROM program arranged by themes.

Vocabulary and Comprehension Development

Phraze Craze (Macintosh Shareware): A software version of the Wheel of Fortune to help students focus on letters and letter pattern in words.

Kid Pix (Broderbund): Program that provides students a tool for visualizing concepts and then labeling them. Students can create semantic maps, outlines, or diagrams to organize thinking.

The Literary Mapper (Teacher Support Software): Program that includes predeveloped maps for character, setting, and action that students can complete as they read or write a story.

The Semantic Mapper (Teacher Supported Software): Program that allows students to create their own maps and label them.

Drafting and Editing

Bank Street Writer (Scholastic): Word processing program in which the teacher can supply customized prompts for the students' own writing.

Magic Slate II (Sunburst): Word processing program in which the teacher can supply customized prompts for the students' own writing.

Language Experience Primary Series: Teachers can record children's dictated stories. Synthesized speech available.

Story Maker (Scholastic): Assists students in learning how to construct sentences, paragraphs, and stories.

Publishing

Print Shop (Broderbund): Program that prints cards, invitations, and posters with layout and graphics.

Children's Writing and Publishing Center (The Learning Company): Desktop publishing program that includes graphics.

allows readers to force cross-connections among subtopics and to make links beyond reading in one direction, reading in one order, and reading in one predetermined pattern.

Another method of building technologically based comprehension processes is called **Internet 'n' book.** This lesson combines Internet resources with fiction and nonfiction texts. One way to do this is to provide bookmarks that have Web site addresses written on them at important points in the text where students can find more information about a specific topic described on a page. Students can add Web sites they find.

In a similar fashion, with Internet 'n' book, students can go to a Web site first, and then after they have read the Web site, reference one book that they desire to receive more in-depth information about a particular, personally interesting topic. Using this method, students develop the habit of pursuing both forms of media to integrate different types of meaning and create new venues of understanding. The goal of this method is for students to begin to seamlessly traverse between and among text-based and technologically based input systems to guide their own learning process.

Reading Culturally Dominated Texts

There are many reasons why it is important to build children's comprehension of multiculturally driven contexts. Traditionally, teachers have enlarged students' multiculture sensitivity by providing comprehension lessons that are adapted to children's language, background experiences, cultural values, and interests. Dyson (2001) however, has identified other aspects of multicultural context that have not adequately addressed the multicultural dimensions that influence children's comprehension success. Students' multicultural collective experiences, values, and cultures determine how single texts are interpreted (e.g., Alvermann & Mosie [1991] present an in-depth discussion of how a feminist perspective can interrupt one's comprehension). Students' decoding abilities and comprehension processes improve with *culturally friendly* texts (Dyson, 2001).

The social roles and responsibilities that students assume to comprehend as well as students' levels of self-efficacy affect the number of comprehension processes that they can control during meaning making. This number increased dramatically when a text includes details that relate to an individual's multicultural strengths and real-world contexts. Further, for learners to transfer meaning across texts, comprehension processes cannot be separated from the socially constructed world in which they live (Rogoff, Radzisewasak, & Masiello, 1995).

If comprehension goals are to reach beyond literal understanding, students must be allowed to share the multicultural organizational systems that they are using to make a text relevant. Doing so through teacher–reader groups (presented in Chapter 2 of this textbook) enables students to identify their own goals, relations, and organizational patterns. Moreover, culturally friendly texts can enhance learning processes that began at home. Reading printed text and electronic-based text within one's own culturally symbolic format also increases the chances that those children will become sensitive to other cultures (Block, 2000b; Nelson, 1996; Radzisewasak, 1978). This occurs because students gain the ability to link individual texts to their own experiences and to the next text-based experience.

Students learn to differentiate contrasting cases and expand their reading experiences in their lives and with the discourses of school. Such discourses include children's concerns about time, space, the geography and religion in which they were raised, their gender roles, their biological inclinations, their emotional stability, and their understanding of natural phenomena as gleaned from the nonfiction texts they read.

These understandings are overlaid, differentiated, interrelated, and elaborated every time a child reads. According to Nelson's research: "This seeming weaving together of individual, experience-based constructions, in collaboration with others, gradually molds the potential of social and cultural forms that can be learned" (1996, p. 352). Such seamless engagement of individual thinking processes can only go so far, however. Students' comprehension is filled with "gaps, loose edges, and dangling threads" (Dye, 2001, p. 1201) that must be woven together with culturally based comprehension processes familiar to a text's author and reader that must be taught to and understood by all students.

Through instruction and discussions about the cultural innuendos imbedded in an author's writing prior to reading, students can deduce more salient cultural references as they read (Bauman, Jones, & Serfert-Kessell, 1993). To give a basic, concrete example, when students were told that the foods described in an upcoming social studies chapter were indigenous to Mexico (and similar to those eaten at Mexican food restaurants), students decoded and comprehended more names of individual food items than had been the case when such clues to link cultures had not occurred. Research indicates that children who are taught such cultural subtleties also construct spontaneous links between text and their own lives that they would have never considered without such instruction (Block, 2000; Dyson, 2001; Garvey, 1990; Jenkins, 1988; Van Horn, 2000).

Teaching these culturally based factors prior to reading also makes text seem friendlier. From students' perspectives, such instruction helps make texts become vehicles that embody "shared beliefs and knowledge that define truth and goodness even when derived from different human conditions" (Dyson, 2001). Such instructional sessions prior to reading can increase a student's sensitivity to culturally based meanings most rapidly if they are framed in the child's language.

An authentic method of doing so is to use older classmates as tutors. Because adults usually write texts, the language of an older schoolmate who discusses a text will likely be closer to that of a child than the language of the author that wrote the text or a teacher. This distance is further diminished when two children interpret text in a social, cognitively rich, co-constructed lesson format, such as described in this textbook. As children begin to discuss and interpret the text, their vernacular is closer to each others' than the text vernacular. Thus, scaffolds and bridges of explanatory guidance are immediately available in words that students don't need to translate into their own multicultural context. Moreover, in lessons in which same-culture older schoolmates tutor younger readers, both students can develop a sense of belonging with friends.

As described in Chapter 8, the wider the range of genres and processes that a child has mastered, the better that child can connect a particular nonfiction text to other sources of information, even when these children have limited cultural experiences that relate to the content described in that text. Given all of the supports that sensitivity to individual multicultural-based contexts provides, it is important to develop methods that provide opportunities for children to learn how to make such connections by themselves. It is tempting to assume that if "children are taught the phonics ropes and carefully read that they'll be able to apply what they have decoded to their lives and scale any textual mountain" (Dyson, 2001, p. 23). Such skills enable readers to see the mountain, but being able to scale it requires mastery of comprehension processes that are sensitive to multifaceted, culturally based contexts. The following lessons help children on this comprehension climb.

Increasing Students' Comprehension of Culturally Dominated Texts

An effective method of helping children link comprehension and multicultural context involves paying close attention to the types of words they use in writing. You can begin by noting what the words are that students use when responding to culturally sensitive texts. The first observation to make about these words is the way they are spelled. If a spelling corresponds to students' first language, you can analyze whether it is a phonological transfer or a semantic transfer. Researchers have indicated that when children spell a word incorrectly, if teachers can detect the type of thinking process the student used to generate the error, they can begin to understand the comprehension gaps that must be filled before a literal understanding of context can be achieved (Fashola, Drum, Mayer, and Kang, 1996).

For example, if a student whose first language is Spanish writes the words "good day" and spells "day" as "d-i-a-y," the meaning of the words "buenos días" is transferring semantically to the spelling of "day." The child needs to become aware of the phonological principle in spelling that is missing. This writing analysis provides a clue that the child could be comprehending in English but needs increased decoding instruction of specific words. If the opposite is true—if the child wrote "buenos días"— he or she is thinking in Spanish and having difficulty translating the meaning of "good day" into written English words.

Developing this analytical skill as a teacher is important. When this diagnosis has been made, an unknown word can be put into a verbal riddle that the child can solve. Researchers have indicated that jokes and riddles are some of the most clearly linked contexts that can be used to help students who are having trouble comprehending (Yuill, 1999). For example, oftentimes when events occur that are not understood, people come to understand them more completely when Jay Leno, David Letterman, or Conan O'Brien makes a joke about the situation. Through the joke (hybrid riddles) the ambiguity or gaps of meaning that people were unable to understand in the written account of an event becomes clear.

To illustrate, on a television broadcast when a startling statement is made in a political speech, people may feel anger or joy during that speech, but they may not completely understand why they felt that way. It is only later, when the late night commentaries about that event occur, that through these hybrid riddles a broader perspective and context from which the rule of priority or value that the politician broke becomes apparent that you can understand the novelty that ignited your immediate emotional response. Such a cognitive response also occurs with children of non-English home language readers.

Thus, when a student does not comprehend you can have the student work with older, culturally sensitive tutors. If he or she is taught to ask a question (or to ask his or her friends to build the concept into a riddle), comprehension will improve (Block & Mangieri, 1995/1996). For instance, animal fables often vary in different cultures. When a child is reading a fable, if she or he is able to tell a similar story from her or his culture the child will understand the second-language fable better.

In addition, **readers' theater,** riddles, and jokes improve memory so that children's time for making inferences and translations increases (Block, 2000; Yuill, 1999). Riddles also develop second-language and less-able students' linguistic skills. Students can create their own riddles to challenge peers by identifying a fiction or nonfiction character about which they want to learn more. As they read, students list all the qualities that characterize and motivate that figure.

For example, Mario chooses to study the prince in *Cinderella*. He read "The charming prince bowed low, smiled kindly, and kissed Cinderella's hand. Cinderella looked as if her fairy godmother had waved her magic wand and made all her wishes come true." Mario had learned to ask himself questions and to make riddles to learn words that he did not know. He quizzed himself: "What does charming mean?" He listed all the activities of the prince in the event and added thoughts about what might have motivated the prince to be "charming." Here is his list:

bowed low

smiled kindly

kissed Cinderella's hand

made Cinderella feel like she had received a present

he wanted to make Cinderella like him

he really wanted to make Cinderella like him or to be happy because he did a lot to make her notice him

charm is a word in "lucky charm" and "charming" so charming may be actions to make people like you or to make people happy

My riddle is: Why did the prince not need to buy a magic wand? Because his charm was his "lucky charm"

Once students learn to perform this activity with riddles, they can duplicate it using longer texts, such as autobiographies and biographies of people from a wide range of cultural heritages.

Another method for increasing students' comprehension of culturally sensitive texts is for parents to verbalize the cognitive and metacognitive processes that they use while their children observe their parents reading at home. For example, mothers who participated in a study by Baker (2001) that discussed motivational and evaluative comprehension processes that they used to solve comprehension problems, and set goals with their 3-or-5-year-old children, had children who scored higher on comprehension tests than children of mothers who merely named and described the content in the book they read. Such instruction occurs when mothers of non-English home language readers describe what they are thinking and how they are controlling their comprehension.

A fourth method that builds multicultural understanding is to allow children to read in-depth texts about their hobbies. When they do so, they are improving their abilities to ask higher-level questions in content domains where they have vast background knowledge and the ability to understand very specific vocabulary terms. Each time students ask a higher-level question concerning the content read, you can write down the question. Then, you can perform a think-aloud to demonstrate how you (1) combined the details in one sentence to the next in a paragraph you are reading, (2) identified the author's writing style using the comprehension processes in Chapter 4 of this textbook, (3) made an inference by identifying the arc of information that was necessary to link two paragraphs together, or (4) used any of the other comprehension processes presented in this textbook. After you complete the think-aloud, ask students to describe what you did. Then, you could read two additional sentences (or paragraphs) and ask students to perform a think-aloud similar to yours so that you can assess whether students can perform pertinent comprehension processes at crucial points in a text when such thoughts are necessary for maximum understanding.

A fifth method that dismantles interferences to students' comprehension because of cultural-related dissonance involves using choral reading and singing to highlight ethnic textures that must be attended to for a rich comprehension of a text. Several authors attest to the power of singing and chanting to build comprehension, particularly for children from backgrounds where standard English is not the predominant language (Barclay, Benelli, & Schoon, 1999; Calkins, 1991; Fox, 1988). Students can sing along with records, tapes, and CDs that they bring from home while they read the verses from a printed page that you have made. This activity can be completed at a young age, using commercial published recordings, such as "Rock-A-Doodle-Do" sung by Steve Allen and Jane Meadows (published by Kids Matter, Ashlin, OR) or "Sing Along" sung by Oscar Bran (published by Peter Pan Industries, 88 Saint Francis Street, Newark, NJ 07105).

At an older age, children enjoy checking audio book tapes out of the library. From grades 1 through 3, checking out as many as three or four books a night to study either in hobby areas or in topics being studied at school is very beneficial. Students can hear the tape as they read about a particular historical period or subject that would be studied in history, math, reading, or science classes on the next day. Descriptions of 12 activities that can be used with each of these choral readings and recommended CD ROM talking books appear in Table 9.2. Many students who use books on tape the night before a topic is studied at school report significantly more new information orally, which they have gleaned from the previous night's tapes, than peers who did not use books on tape (Block, 2002c). After students read and hear texts, they are better able to insert new information into their schema in silent reading. This advanced associative comprehension process is akin to the advanced skill of imagery, which all readers should develop.

Dual language books, books written in both Spanish and English (or two other languages), can be read and analyzed by readers to increase the culturally influenced comprehension processes. When children read two translations of the same story, one in their

TABLE 9.2   A Dozen Things to Do with a CD Talking Book and Suggested Talking Books

1. Listen to the story first	**7.** Select words with the same sounds
2. Read along with the story	**8.** Select rhyming words
3. Echo read part of the story	**9.** Read along with a book copy
4. Read it first, then listen	**10.** Tell how one screen fits another
5. Partner read in digital readers' theater	**11.** Tell how special effects fit the story
6. Look for letters or words you know	**12.** Tell about similar stories

CD ROM Talking Books

Anasi, retold by Julie Adams and Lisa Daveck, Discis Books, Harmony Interactive Inc.

A Promise Is a Promise, by Robert Munsch & Michael Kusuzak, Discis Books, Harmony Interactive Inc.

Dr. Seuss ABC, by Dr. Seuss, Living Books, Broderbund.

Green Eggs and Ham, by Dr. Seuss, Living Books, Broderbund.

Harry and the Haunted House, by Marc Schlichting, Living Books, Broderbund.

Johnny Appleseed, retold by Susan Hughes, Discis Books, Harmony Interactive, Inc.

Paul Bunyan, retold by Susan Hughes, Discis Books, Harmony Interactive, Inc.

Pecos Bill, retold by by Susan Hughes, Discis Books, Harmony Interactive, Inc.

Sheila Rae, the Brave, by Kevin Henkes, Living Books, Broderbund.

Stellaluna, by J. Canon, Living Books, Broderbund.

The Cat in the Hat, by Dr. Seuss, Living Books, Broderbund.

The Tortoise and The Hare, Aesop's Fables, Living Books, Broderbund.

Thomas' Snowsuit, by Robert Munsch, Discis Books, Harmony Interactive Inc.

Source: Labbo, L. D. (2000). Twelve things young children can do with a talking book in a classroom computer center. *The Reading Teacher, 53* (7), 542–546.

native language and one in English, they can join in discussion by reading orally in their native language and share their responses with peers in English. Then, as second-language speakers teach peers how to comprehend the Spanish (or other language) version and what the main thesis is, they will develop these same comprehension processes themselves.

You can follow this lesson with a second approach. This second set of instructions illustrates how the cultures represented by both languages influenced the meaning portrayed in an event, sequence, and plot of the story. Dual language books that have proven valuable in these lessons are listed in Table 9.3.

Using concrete objects and hands-on activities has long been an instructional method to build the vocabulary and decoding abilities of second-language learners. By labeling objects in two languages and by using sentences rather than single words, comprehension is strengthened. For instance, instead of taping a card on the fishbowl that reads "goldfish," two sentences could be written on that card. These sentences would communicate the same message to be comprehended. One would be written in English (i.e., "Our class pet is a fish named Barney and he is swimming in the water in this fishbowl."). The second would be in Spanish (i.e., "Nuestro animal mascota es un pez que se llama Barney y él nada en el agua en esta pecera.").

Using a "buddy system" to build comprehension for second-language users has an equally long history. When two students with differing first languages read together, many cultural sensitivities develop, especially when the pair is taught to stop reading

TABLE 9.3 Dual Language Books in Spanish and English

Good Books with a Lot of Pictures

The Book of Pigericks by A. Lobel, 1986, Altea
Carlos Planta un Girasol by K. Petty, 1997, Scholastic
Family Stories/Cuandros de familia by C. L. Garza, 1990, Children's Book Press
Martha planta un rabaro by K. Petty, 1997, Barcelona, Spain: Destino
Moon Rope/Un lazo a la luna by L. Ehlert, 1992, Harcourt Brace Jovanovich
Las Navidades: Popular Christmas Songs from Latin America by L. Delacre, 1990, Scholastic
Solomon, the Rusty Nail by W. Steig, 1985, Farrar, Straus & Giroux
Tierra Amarilla: Stories of New Mexico by S. Ulibarri, 1971, University of New Mexico Press
Tortillas Para Mama and Other Nursery Rhymes/ Spanish and English by Greigo et al., 1981

Good Books If You Are Just Beginning to Learn about Spanish or English

Chicken Sunday by P. Polacco, 1992, Scholastic
The Giving Tree by S. Silverstein, 1983, Houghton/ *El arbol generoso* by S. Silverstein, 1991, Houghton
Iguana Dreams: New Latino Fiction by D. Poey & V. Suarez, 1992, HarperCollins
Mariposa by L. Fernandez, 1983, Editorial Trillas
Mrs. Frisby and the Rats of NIMH by J. Conly, 1986, Harper & Row
My First Book of Words and Mi Primer Libro de Palabras by L. Shiffman, 1992, Scholastic
My First 100 Words in English and Spanish by K. Faulkner, 1992, Simon & Schuster
My First Phrases in Spanish and English by K. Faulkner, 1993, Simon & Schuster
Noisy Nora by R. Wells, 1994, Santillana
On the Pampas by M. Brusea, 1991, Henry Holt

Good Books to Tell You a Lot in Spanish and English

Alexander and the Terrible, Horrible, No Good, Very Bad Day by J. Viorst, 1972, Antheneum/ *Alexander y el día terrible, horrible, espantoso, horroroso* by J. Viorst, 1989, Macmillan
Brave Irene by W. Steig, 1991, Farrar, Straus & Giroux/*Irene la valiente* by W. Steig, 1991, Farrar, Straus & Giroux

Bread and Jam for Frances by R. Hoban/*Pan y mermelada para Francisca* by R. Hoban, 1995
Carlota y los dinosaurios by J. Mayhem, 1998, Barcelona, Spain: Serres
Clifford the Big Red Dog by N. Birdwell, 1989, Scholastic/*Clifford el gran perro colorado* by N. Birdwell, 1989, Scholastic
The Grouchy Ladybug by E. Carle, 1991, Houghton/*La marquita malhumorada* by E. Carle, 1992
Is Your Mama a Llama? by D. Guarino, 1989, Scholastic/*¿Tu mama es una llama?* by D. Guarino, 1993, Scholastic
Me duele la lengua by A. Decis, 1997, Barcelona, Spain (Edebé)
Taking a Walk/Cominando by R. Emberly, 1990, Little, Brown
The Very Hungry Caterpillar by E. Carle, 1979, Collins/*La oruga muy hambrienta* by E. Carle, 1989, Philomel

Books That Have Several Chapters in Spanish and English

Blubber by J. Blume, 1982, Bradbury Press/*La ballena* by J. Blume, 1983, Bradbury Press
The Cricket in Times Square by G. Seldon Thompson, 1991, Scholastic/*Un grillo en Times Square* by G. Seldon Thompson, 1992, Scholastic
Diario Ana Frank by A. Frank, 1971, Plaza y Editores, S.A.
Nine Days to Christmas: A Story of Mexico by M. H. Ets & A. Labastida, 1959, Viking/*Nueve dias para Navidad* by M. H. Ets & A. Labastida, 1991, Puffin Books/Viking Penguin
Number the Stars by L. L. Lowry, 1989, Houghton Mifflin/*¿Quien cuenta las estrellas?* by L. Lowry, 1990, Espasa-Calpe
Ramona the Pest by B. Cleary, 1968, William Morrow/*Ramona la chinche* by B. Cleary, 1984, William Morrow
Roxaboxen by A. McLerran, 1991, Lothrop, Lee & Shephard/*Roxaboxen* (Spanish version) by A. McLerran, 1992, Scholastic
Tuck Everlasting by N. Babbitt, 1975, Farrar, Straus & Giroux/*Tuck para siempre* by N. Babbitt, 1992, Trumpet Book Club

and to explain to one another every time a character or event portrays cultural influence. For example, when this lesson was implemented in a second grade class the following scenario unfolded. Iowan, a Maori descendant from Australia, read a book that began with the following song to her European American friend, Wanda. "Cuccaburo sat on the old gum tree, Merry, merry King of the bush is he. Laugh, Cuccaburo, laugh, Cuccaburo. How gay your life must be." Wanda stopped Iowan's reading. "How can a tree be a bush?" Iowan then described the Australian Outback terrain and the joy that Cuccaburo brings to people who go miles without speaking to another human being. The reading continued, and Wanda became increasingly enthralled as she began to imagine herself in the Australian bush.

In Summary

As teachers begin to explore technology to improve comprehension instruction, they find that hypertext, Web site notes, Internet 'n' books, and using pairs together at the computer screen are already proving successful. When more multiculturally sensitive comprehension lessons are used, teachers are becoming more aware of the power of teaching students to ask each other questions, create riddles and jokes, and interact with CD and dual language books. Teachers are learning to carefully diagnose children's words to explain subtle meanings and culturally specific figurative language. The next chapter describes comprehension assessment, enriching parents' support for comprehension, and leading districts and individual schools toward better comprehension instructional programs and policies.

REFLECTING ON WHAT YOU HAVE LEARNED

1. Summarize the key points that you learned in this chapter. Make a graphic to depict your thought processes. It must be only one page long.

2. Based on the information in this chapter, project how the education field in the future will use technology and individual cultural context to improve comprehension skills for more students. In this projection, include a statement as to the percentage of comprehension instructional time that will be linked to both of these relatively recent advancements in curricula by the year 2010. Be prepared to defend your projection and compare it with your colleagues.

3. *Your Professional Journal: Technologically Based Journals.* In approximately one paragraph write a concise description of your philosophy for instructing and assessing technologically based comprehension. This description will help you verbalize to students, colleagues, students' parents, and administrators how you make your instructional assessment decisions concerning technologically based literacy. Before you write this description write a one-sentence reflection concerning the following: With what type of teacher did you learn to comprehend best and why? If you want to use an Internet-generated journal for this entry it would be in keeping with this chapter's theme and increase your familiarity with the wide range of journals that are available through this source.

4. *Making Professional Decisions.* Select one of the activities presented in this chapter. Design a method to evaluate an individual student's comprehension success after completing this activity. Compare your activity with the principles in the next chapter to decide how many principles you deduced yourself that would be important in the future for tailored instruction and assessment to meet an individual student's comprehension needs.

5. *Field Applications and Observations.* Using one of the activities for technologically enriched instruction, create a lesson for your class. Assess its effectiveness. Discuss its strengths and weaknesses with your colleagues by describing your objective; the steps you took in implementing the lesson; the materials used including CDs, Web sites, Web links, or other sources of text to be read; and the evaluation that you used to determine the success for your class. If you are not presently teaching, design an ideal program that systematically incorporates technology and culturally sensitive lessons into the comprehension instruction that you want to deliver.

6. *Multicultural Application.* Select a book from those listed in Tables 9.4 to 9.7 that contains main characters from a culture that is different from those of the students in your class. Use that book as you teach one of the lessons from this chapter to students from a minority cultural background. After you complete the lesson, write about the adaptations that you had to make, or will make in the future, to meet the special needs of students from minority cultures.

TABLE 9.4   Children's Literature That Represents Asian Cultures

Grades K–2

Crow Boy by T. Yashima, 1955, Viking
The Funny Little Woman by A. Mosel, 1972, Dutton
How My Parents Learned to Eat by I. R. Friedman, 1984, Houghton
Japanese Children's Favorite Stories by F. Sakade, 1958, Tuttle
Our Home Is the Sea by R. Levinson, 1988, Dutton
Tuan by E. Boholm-Olsson, 1988, Farrar
The Wave retold by M. Hodges, 1964, Houghton Mifflin

Grades 3–4

The Brocaded Slipper retold by L. D. Vuong, 1982, Addison-Wesley
The Crane Wife by S. Yagawa, 1981, Morrow
The Dragon Kite by N. Luenn, 1982, Harcourt Brace Jovanovich
Elaine, Mary Lewis, and the Frogs by H. Chang, 1988, Crown

The Emperor and the Kite by J. Yolen, 1967, World
First Snow by H. Coutant, 1974, Knopf
The Happy Funeral by E. Bunting, 1982, Harper
In the Land of Small Dragon by A. N. Clark, 1979, Viking
Magic Animals of Japan by D. Pratt & E. Kuls, 1967, Parnassus
Sadako and the Thousand Paper Cranes by E. Coerr, 1977, Putnam
The Tongue-Cut Sparrow by M. Ishii, 1987, Lodestar
Yeh-Shen by A.-L. Louie, 1982, Philomel

Grades 5–6

The Land I Lost: Adventures of a Boy in Vietnam by Q. N. Huynh, 1982, Harper
The Leaving Morning by A. Johnson, 1990, Putnam
Separations by R. Lehrman, 1994, Viking

TABLE 9.5   Children's Literature That Represents Native American Cultures

Abenaki Captive by M. L. Dubois, 1994, Carolrhoda [Abenaki]

Artic Memories by N. Ekoomiak, 1990, Holt [Inuit Eskimo]

Baby Rattlesnake by T. Ata, 1989, Children's Book Press [Chickasaw]

Fox Song by J. Bruchac, 1993, Philomel [Abenaki]

The Huron Carol by F. J. de Brebeuf, illustrated by F. Tyrrell, 1990, Dutton [Huron]

The Incredible Journey of Lewis and Clark by R. Blumberg, 1987, Lothrop, Lee & Shepard [Native American]

In My Mother's House by A. N. Clark, 1991/1941, Viking [Tesuque Pueblo]

Ladder to the Sky by B. J. Esbensen, 1989, Little, Brown [Anishinabe/Ojibway]

The Legend of the Bluebonnet by T. dePaola, 1983, Putnam [Comanche]

The Legend of the Indian Paintbrush by T. dePaola, 1988, Putnam [Plains]

Maii and Cousin Horned Toad by S. Begay, 1992, Scholastic [Navajo]

The Mud Pony by C. L. Cohen, illustrated by S. Begay, 1988, Scholastic [Skid/Pawnee]

Navajo Code Talkers by N. Aaseng, 1992, Walker [Navajo]

A Picture Book of Sitting Bull by D. Adler, 1993, Holiday [Hunkpapa Sioux]

Powwow by G. Ancona, 1993, Harcourt Brace [Native American]

Quillworker: A Cheyenne Legend by T. Cohlene, 1990, Watermill [Cheyenne]

Seven Little Rabbits by J. Becker, 1994/1974, Walker [Native American]

Weasel by C. DeFelice, 1990, Macmillan [Shawnee]

The Whistling Skeleton: American Indian Tales of the Supernatural by J. Bierhorst, 1982, Four Winds [Pawnee, Blackfoot, and Cheyenne]

Source: Prepared by Peggy K. Ford and Susan L. Ford Carr, Tarrant County Junior College.

TABLE 9.6   Children's Literature That Represents Hispanic Cultures

Primary	**Intermediate**
Amigo by B. Baylor, 1963, Macmillan	*Baseball in April and Other Stories* by G. Soto, 1990, Harcourt Brace Jovanovich
Arroz con leche by L. Delacre, 1989, Scholastic	*Cuentos! Tales from the Hispanic Southwest* by J. G. Maestas & R. A. Anaya, 1980, Knopf
Dance of the Animals by P. Belpre, 1965, Warne	*Felita* by N. Mohl, 1979, Dial
Hello Amigos! by T. Brown, 1986, Holt	*Going Home* by N. Mohl, 1986, Dial
The Lady of Guadalupe by T. dePaola, 1980, Holiday	*Hispanic Americans* by M. Meltzer, 1982, Crowell
Las Navidades by L. Delacre, 1990, Scholastic	*In Nueva York* by N. Mohl, 1977, Dell
Once in Puerto Rico by P. Belpre, 1973, Warne	*The Most Beautiful Place in the World* by A. Cameron, 1988, Knopf
Perez and Martina by P. Belpre, 1960, Warne	*Stories from el Barrio* by P. Thomas, 1978, Knopf
Santiago by P. Belpre, 1969, Warne	*Taking Sides* by G. Soto, 1991, Harcourt Brace Jovanovich
Tonight Is Carnaval by A. Dorros, 1991, Dutton	
Uncle Nacho's Hat by H. Rohmer, 1989, Children's Book Press	
Yagua Days by C. Martel, 1976, Dial	

TABLE 9.7   Children's Literature That Represents African American Cultures

Anthony Burns: The Defeat and Triumph of a Fugitive Slave by V. Hamilton, 1988, Knopf

Baby Says by J. Steptoe, 1988, Lothrop, Lee & Shepard

Cornrows by C. Yarbrough, 1979, Coward-McCann

Cousins by V. Hamilton, 1990, Philomel

The Drinking Gourd by F. N. Monjo, 1970, Harper

Flossi and the Fox by P. McKissack, 1986, Dial

The Friends by R. Guy, 1973, Bantam

The House of Dies Drear by V. Hamilton, 1968, Macmillan

I Am the Darker Brother by A. Adoff, 1968, Macmillan

In the Beginning: Creation Stories from around the World by V. Hamilton, 1988, Harcourt Brace Jovanovich

Jackie Robinson by D. Adler, 1989, Holiday House

Jafta by H. Lewin, 1981, Carolrhoda

Justin and the Best Biscuits in the World by M. P. Walters, 1986, Lothrop, Lee & Shepard

The Lucky Stone by L. Clifton, 1979, Dell

M. C. Higgins, the Great by V. Hamilton, 1974, Macmillan

Malcolm X by A. Adoff, 1970, Crowell

Mary McLeod Bethune by E. Greenfield, 1977, Crowell

Matthew and Tilly by R. Jones, 1991, Dutton

Mirandy and Brother Wind by P. McKissack, 1988, Knopf

Mufaro's Beautiful Daughters by J. Steptoe, 1987, Lothrop, Lee & Shepard

My Daddy Is a Monster . . . Sometimes by J. Steptoe, 1980, Lippincott

Nathaniel Talking by E. Greenfield, 1989, Black Butterfly

Nettie Jo's Friends by P. McKissack, 1989, Knopf

The Orphan Boy by T. Mollel, 1991, Clarion

The People Could Fly by V. Hamilton, 1985, Knopf

Peter's Chair by E. J. Keats, 1967, Harper

The Planet of Junior Brown by V. Hamilton, 1971, Macmillan

Ragtime Tumpie by A. Schroeder, 1989, Little, Brown

Rosa Parks by E. Greenfield, 1973, Crowell

Shimmershine Queen by C. Yarbrough, 1989, Putnam

Sidewalk Story by S. Mathis, 1971, Puffin

Spin a Soft Black Song by N. Giovanni, 1985, Farrar, Straus & Giroux

Stevie by J. Steptoe, 1969, Harper

The Stories Julian Tells by A. Cameron, 1981, Pantheon

Tailypo! by J. Wahl, 1991, Holt

The Talking Eggs by R. San Souci, 1989, Dial

Tar Beach by F. Ringgold, 1991, Crown

Under the Sunday Tree by E. Greenfield, 1988, Harper & Row

We Keep a Store by A. Shelby, 1990, Orchard

What a Morning! The Christmas Story in Black Spirituals by J. Langstaff, 1987, Macmillan

When I Am Old with You by A. Johnson, 1990, Orchard

Whistle for Willie by E. J. Keats, 1964, Viking

Willie Bea and the Time the Martians Landed by V. Hamilton, 1983, Greenwillow

Zeely by V. Hamilton, 1967, Macmillan

---

7. *Key Terms Exercise.* Following is a list of concepts introduced in this chapter. If you have learned the meaning of a term place a checkmark in the blank that precedes that term. If you are not sure of a term's definition, increase your retention by reviewing the definition of the term. If you have learned four of these terms on your first reading of this chapter, you have constructed many meanings that are important for your career.

_____ technological literacy (p. 185)	_____ Internet 'n' book (p. 188)
_____ hypertext-based comprehension (p. 185)	_____ readers' theater (p. 192)
	_____ dual language books (p. 193)

8. *Comprehension Process Lesson 9: Teaching Students the Comprehension Process of Translating Their Understanding into Visual or Technologically Based Retellings.* The following comprehension lesson demonstrates how to implement technology and multiculturally sensitive comprehension processes to increase students' retention. Comprehension Process Lesson 9 contains six steps that enable students to increase their retention of material through creative, innovative, and technological retellings. Technological and poetic retellings have proven to significantly increase the retention of less able students from various cultural backgrounds.

COMPREHENSION PROCESS LESSON 9
Visual and Technologically Based Retellings

Students can develop visual and technologically based comprehension by practicing research skills that they have been taught. This comprehension process lesson includes using the Internet for culturally relevant research, videotaping creative retellings of an episode learned during the study of a specific culture, and making an oral presentation to the class that incorporates the perspectives of different cultural groups.

1. It may be helpful at first to show students several episodes of *Reading Rainbow* so they will understand the format of the show. (Ordering information may be found at http://gpn.unl.edu\rainbow.)
2. Each group of four to five students chooses a topic for their episode. This may be a topic related to one the students have studied in science, social studies, or another content area.
3. The students choose one culturally relevant book that will be the centerpiece of their episode. This should be an interesting nonfiction book that gives lots of information about a particular cultural heritage. One student prepares to read this book aloud during the episode.
4. The team does additional research using the Internet. As a team, students decide how to present the extra information they learn about their topic in their episode. They may choose taped interviews, charts and diagrams, on-site visits (such as at a zoo or museum), or monologue-type segments narrated by a member(s) of the team.
5. Each student chooses an additional trade book that gives information on some aspect of the topic, then prepares a short book review for the episode, incorporating technology or their own culturally based perspectives.
6. Students share all they have learned by presenting their episodes to classmates, parents, or students in other classes. Audience members ask questions from Table 1.3 following the presentation.

Source: Adapted from an idea co-created by Courtney Jones, elementary education major, Texas Christian University, Fort Worth, Texas. Used by permission.

CHAPTER 10

Assessment of Comprehension

Ms. Whalen is volunteering to do repeated readings with three students who have not demonstrated exceptionality in metacognitive processes. She is also the president of the Parents to Advance Reading Achievement Group at Rockdale Elementary. Her group has contributed more than 2,000 hours of assistance to teachers and raised $4,000 to buy Reading is Fundamental books for every child to take home to begin their own libraries.

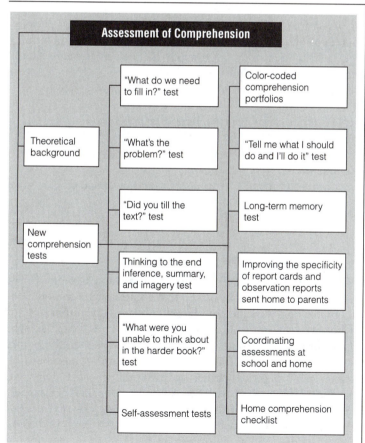

Assessment of Comprehension

- Theoretical background
- New comprehension tests
  - "What do we need to fill in?" test
  - "What's the problem?" test
  - "Did you till the text?" test
  - Thinking to the end inference, summary, and imagery test
  - "What were you unable to think about in the harder book?" test
  - Self-assessment tests
  - Color-coded comprehension portfolios
  - "Tell me what I should do and I'll do it" test
  - Long-term memory test
  - Improving the specificity of report cards and observation reports sent home to parents
  - Coordinating assessments at school and home
  - Home comprehension checklist

As the last bell rang to end the school year, Ms. Whalen at St. Mary of the Mills School (Baltimore, Maryland), hugged all students in the fifth grade and said good-bye. Jeanette Montgomery was the last in line. After she told Ms. Whalen how much she would miss her, she reached in her pocket and handed her beloved teacher the following note: "I liked how you tested my comprehension by asking me to write an advertisement, and how we read out loud, and I thought that was something I could improve. I was scared to read out loud because I'm so shy but I liked that best of all. I liked our other new comprehension tests. They were really good. I have read four times as much as I used to. I think that we should stick with these tests. This is the best class I've had in all my 5 years at Saint Mary's School. I love you."

How can comprehension be measured? This question has been asked for several decades. Unfortunately, educational tests have not changed as rapidly as desired. Most do not incorporate the principles discussed in this book. Instead, many comprehension evaluations are based on brief paragraphs. Such tests often only assess pupils' background experiences rather than their ability to comprehend a novel piece of text. How often do students image? How often do students infer? How often do students engage effective, metacognitive processes? How motivated are students to overcome confusion? Do they use what they read to make their lives better? ■

Chapter Overview

This chapter reports new research and methods of assessing comprehension. It draws upon community resources to build a more effective comprehension assessment program. The chapter begins with a description of principles that new assessments should embody. It then describes new assessment measures.

By the end of this chapter, you will be able to answer the following questions:

1. How can the assessment of reading comprehension be improved?
2. What improvements are needed?
3. What methods can be used to assess comprehension at the primary, intermediate, and middle school levels?
4. What can administrators, teachers, and students use as evidence of individual comprehension successes?

Theoretical Background

Theoretical background

The National Reading Panel (1999) and the Rand Reading Study Group (Sweet & Snow, 2002) agreed that additional professional development beyond a bachelor's degree is especially important for those who wish to teach reading comprehension. These scientists synthesized prior research studies and found that the elementary school years are the most critical for diagnosing students' comprehension competencies. This is true because by third grade most students will have developed defense strategies to camouflage weaknesses in their abilities to make meaning from text. Only precise, effective assessment instruments can disarm them. When these comprehension weaknesses are detected and eliminated, the chances for developing richer interactions among cognitive processes can begin. If they are not detected, many pupils begin to develop even more effective methods of masking their reading failures (Block, 2002b).

Many studies are under way to examine new staff development programs designed to enhance teachers' assessment abilities. These are entitled the Best Comprehension Practices Consortium and are sponsored by the Institute for Literacy Enhancement in Charlotte, North Carolina. These training programs are creating new assessment initiatives that enable teachers to "get inside the heads" of students' independent silent reading processes. The work at this institute has also documented that teachers want new comprehension tools that not only assess what they have taught about comprehension but how much students are *actively* engaged in making meaning. When such measures are developed, children's zones of proximal development (Vygotsky, 1978) and their rates of learning can be assessed, which are crucial to planning the pace of comprehension instruction. Building on this perspective and Vygotsky's (1978) theory, assessments should measure how rapidly a child can acquire new comprehension processes when these are modeled by more advanced comprehenders.

Dark and Gilmore (1999) challenge educators to address another need in comprehension assessment, **assisted performance evaluations.** These tests measure a student's engagement in the process of comprehending when a second person challenges this reader beyond his or her independent reading level.

> These forms of assisted performance that are common place in everyday life are seldom used by teachers in classrooms. Instead, since the last century, teaching comprehension in North America has consisted of only providing tasks and assessing individual development. This must change. Students cannot be left to learn on their own. Teachers cannot be content to merely provide opportunities to learn and then assess outcomes. Recitation must be de-emphasized. Responsive assertive interactions must become commonplace in the classroom. Minds must be roused to life. (p. 116)

In support of this position, Tierney (1998) delineated the following principles to assess comprehension:

1. Assessments must contain a variety of comprehension experiences, including nonfiction.
2. Effective testing requires teacher professionalism with teachers as learners; teachers should establish goals for what they are assessing and tie them to learning.
3. Assessments should lead from behind and help students assess themselves with instruction after they have been assessed. Scores and grades only give the illusion of accuracy and authority. "Conversations connected to portfolios or other forms of more direct assessment unmask the basis of decision making and spur the conversation toward a consideration of the evidence and appreciation of the assumption and the negotiation of goals" (Tierney, 1998, p. 378).
4. Assessment should be done judiciously with teachers as advocates for students, ensuring their due process.

5. Assessment should extend beyond improving present tests to making new tests that are more conceptually valid.

6. Diversity should be embraced, not slighted, in comprehension assessment. Assessments must use culturally based texts to discern students' multicultural sensitivity. Unfortunately, in the past, test developers have tried to make tests culture free, which is impossible. "Cultural free assessments afford, at best, only a partial, perhaps distorted, understanding of a student's comprehension ability" (Tierney, 1998, p. 381).

7. Future comprehension tests must allow for different students to have differing amounts of encouragement and support to measure the degrees that they are interrelating comprehension processes. Some students have the potential to reveal their inner thoughts accurately, others do not, and still others do not process meaning as they read. When future tests are developed, individual performance assessments that tap into this knowledge processing component more directly must be considered.

8. Some things that are worth assessing cannot be evaluated unless students self-assessed (e.g., self-questioning, level of reported engagement, and degrees of interpretation). The interaction between speed, factual literal recall, vocabulary development, inference accuracy, and metacognitive depth must be evaluated. Presently, few tests measure such indicators. Educators need data that will help advance instruction at each level of comprehension competence.

9. Assessment should be developmentally sensitive and involve sustained reading rather than "dipstick approaches" to assessment. For example, instead of measuring all children's ability in one day using only a few paragraphs or page-length passages, tests should continue for several days and be calculated from longer-term engagements.

10. Assessments must be viewed as ongoing and suggestive rather than "fixed or definitive" (Tierney, 1998, p. 385).

11. Assessment must be differentiated by the quality of material to be read and the methods used in instruction.

According to Tierney's (1998) review of the current status of reading assessment, there are three specific actions that can be taken. First, culturally sensitive assessments must be developed that are directly related to the teaching process. Second, these assessments should be ongoing, involve students in goal setting, and be related to students' developmental stages. Third, these data can be used to make better instructional decisions. Teachers should not have to repeat the same lessons several times; they should evaluate growth effectively so that comprehension becomes active and exciting for students. To do this correctly, collaborative planning with students is essential. Teachers can use assessment sessions to scaffold, support, and coach students. Such assessments become complementary and supplementary, more tools than final outcomes. Individual tests can be refined as prototypes that use new resources to address the complexity of comprehension, through a lens of individuality, which can project clear evidence of progress for groups and individuals.

New Comprehension Tests

There are eleven new comprehension assessment tools that can serve as models. They are discussed in the following sections.

Assessment 1: "What Do We Need To Fill In?" Test. Based on the research of Oakhill and Yuill (1999), one of the most effective comprehension assessments is a test that allows students to resolve the inconsistencies that they see in printed text. This test allows children to tell us what needs to be "fixed" in a particular passage so that the information in adjacent sentences is connected. Children who need more work in integrating their inferences with literal comprehension will not perform well on this test. By administering it, teachers hope to find out which two types of information (literal or inferential) will need to be developed for particular students.

An example of this new assessment can be found in Oakhill and Yuill's research. This example allows students to describe what they need to fill in to create a complete comprehension. This test begins by asking children to come to the teacher's desk to read a passage similar to the following:

> A scarecrow was dressed by someone else. A scarecrow is tied down to a pole forever. He is not allowed to turn his head at all. He must stand in the rain without an umbrella all day long. When the winter comes, no one lends him a coat. But a scarecrow's life is all his own. (Modified from *Scarecrow* by Cynthia Ryland [1998])

When they finish, they tell what they read in a retelling. Then, a question is asked: "What do we need to fill in to make this story more complete for others to read?" When children read and tell what needs to be added where to make the text easier for others to comprehend, students are revealing what it is that they need to comprehend better. As they answer this question, you can write down as many of their comments as possible. When students return to their seats and the next pupil comes to read the same passage, teachers can summarize their diagnoses of the next type of instruction that child needs in each column of the form in Figure 10.1. During the next week, teachers can place children into groups based on the types of strategies that individual pupils need to be taught.

Assessment 2: "What's the Problem?" Test. This test is designed to measure students' imagery and metacognition. To conduct this assessment, you can create two passages that children are to read aloud. In

FIGURE 10.1   "What Do We Need to Fill In?" Test

Directions: (1) Put names of group members above each column. (2) Put a tally mark in the appropriate box each time a group member contributes that comprehension process in writing or orally. (3) Make notes on the back when interesting things happen that are not captured by the categories.

	Student A	Student B	Student C	Student D	Student E	Totals
1. Contributes ideas from other sources						
2. Describes feelings and makes connections						
3. Paraphrases main ideas						
4. Recalls sequence						
5. Makes inferences						
6. Summarizes						
7. Images						
8. Uses authorial writing pattern; is determined						
9. Draws conclusions and summarizes						

each of the passages, you substitute "X"s (using the same number of "X"s as letters in the correct word) for a word that could be visually imaged. You continue to make one substitution in alternating sentences: There would be one correct sentence, followed by one sentence that had a nonsense word inserted, then a correct sentence, and then a non correct sentence. The words to be removed are vivid verbs and thick nouns. For example, if you were to use sentences from *My Chinatown: One Year in Poems*, written by Kam Mak, published by Harper Collins in 2002, you would rewrite the underlined word into a nonsense word or insert "X"s in the two sentences that follow:

> "I pass the cobbler everyday sitting and working on shoes. I stop and watch him cutting the leather in small curves, pulling the needle, tugging the thread tight" (Mak, 2002, p. 7).

The reason that "thread" was chosen to be rewritten as "XXXXX" was because if students were imaging as they read, the visual image of "thread" must be present in their mental pictures. So many context clues had been given that thread would be the only word that could have appeared in that testing passage. Therefore, if a student read this passage and did not recognize that "XXXXX" stood for thread, you could deduce that this student needed additional catch-up lessons on how to image.

This assessment would not be based on only two sentences however. Because new comprehension tests should use more than one page of text to assess comprehension, the text a child reads should have at least 10 words removed and 20 sentences. Such a length will ensure that students have several opportunities to demonstrate their imagery abilities. However, if a student misses the first three words you can stop the test as this student would not be able to score 80 percent proficiency even if he or she was to continue.

On a subsequent day, using paragraphs in which a key detail sentence is removed give students 10 such paragraphs from the same text. Allow students, 9 years of age or older, to read these paragraphs. When they finish, ask them if they noticed anything that did not make sense in the text. According to Oakhill and Yuill (1999), "67% more skilled comprehenders commented on problems than did less-skilled comprehenders (17%)" (p. 78). Then, in a second set of 10 paragraphs, tell the students in advance that there will be something wrong in every paragraph. Tell them as they read they are to stop and tell you if they find something that doesn't make sense. According to Oakhill and Yuill's research, both skilled and nonskilled readers are equally able to detect problems in text when told to do so in advance. If students detect all errors in both testing experiences, they are able to fully engage their metacomprehension processes continuously with texts at the level of difficulty at which the testing passage was written. If a student scored higher on the second set of paragraphs than the first, the difference in these scores suggests that the student may know that he or she is to be thinking about the text while reading, but is unable to initiate these processes without additional instruction. Similarly, if a student detects only a few problems in one or both sets of passages, these scores indicate that the student may need to learn from several additional metacognitive development lessons described in Chapter 7.

"Did you till the text?" test

Assessment 3: "Did You Till the Text?" Test.   Oakhill and Yuill (1999) also explored the effectiveness of creating an inconsistent text to identify whether students noticed inconsistencies separated by several sentences. According to their research, a significant interaction occurs between students' abilities to till a text and to retain literal information. Less skilled comprehenders were more affected by the distance that existed between incongruent information than were more skilled students. To create a "Did you till the text?" test, you can identify a passage whereby a sentence is inserted on every other page that does not make sense and needs to be changed. Then, you can ask children to read and determine if the passage does or does not make sense.

This kind of test will not only enable the determination of which children can till a text, but also which ones can follow an authorial writing pattern so carefully that they notice clues which alert them that new information is about to be presented by the author. The error pattern on this test can also help you to understand students' memory loads and how much information they can retain. Short-term memory is needed to store and integrate information, whereas long-term memory is necessary for this information to become permanent and serve as background knowledge in making future inferences. Poor readers are less able to monitor texts, detect anomalies, and make inferences when information in different parts of a text is inconsistent. Integration is especially difficult if unusually large portions of memory must be allocated to decoding (Oakhill & Yuill, 1998; Perfetti & Lesco, 1979; Stanovich, 1986; Tergeson & Wagner, 1987). A sample of comprehension processes to assess at the fourth-grade level appears in Figure 10.2.

Thinking to the end inference, summary, and imagery test

Assessment 4: Thinking to the End Inference, Summary, and Imagery Test. This evaluation can be administered after students have been taught the process of thinking to the end of paragraphs, stories, and pages. After students read a paragraph or page, you can ask them what they did when they were trying to comprehend, inference, or image. When they describe what they were doing—whether

FIGURE 10.2 "Did You Till the Text?" Test

Name: _____ Grade: _____ Date: _____

Circle the appropriate numbers to describe your most recent silent reading.

Guide Myself through Text	Always Do By Myself				Can't Do
1. Set my purpose for reading	5	4	3	2	1
2. Make predictions	5	4	3	2	1
3. Use subtitles	5	4	3	2	1
4. Read sections and find summaries	5	4	3	2	1
Know How Text Works					
5. Story grammar	5	4	3	2	1
6. Draw inferences	5	4	3	2	1
7. Used authorial writing patterns of nonfiction texts	5	4	3	2	1
Think Metacognitively					
8. Raise questions about unknown information	5	4	3	2	1
9. Identify the arcs of unknown information between sentences	5	4	3	2	1
10. Recognize the types of details and main idea statements in paragraphs	5	4	3	2	1

they were putting single facts together, putting themselves in the text, or accepting new pieces of information in the ongoing story—their answers will provide clues as to what children can do and what can be improved in their inferring, summarization, and imagery processes.

Figure 10.3 is an assessment tool that can be used for this purpose. Students write their answers to each direction in the space that follows that instruction. When an answer is incorrect, this error suggests that the specific step in the summary process that was missed is not being used by that student. For younger students, instead of asking what they are thinking in their minds (which Pressley [1976] determined to be a very difficult task), ask them to play school and teach someone else to read. You can also have

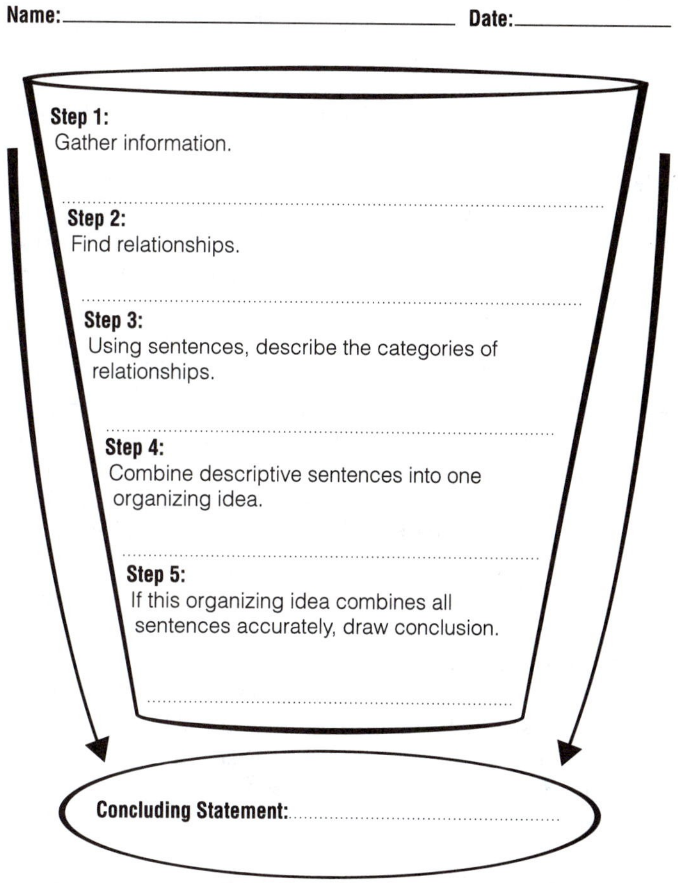

Name:_____   Date:_____

Step 1:
Gather information.

Step 2:
Find relationships.

Step 3:
Using sentences, describe the categories of relationships.

Step 4:
Combine descriptive sentences into one organizing idea.

Step 5:
If this organizing idea combines all sentences accurately, draw conclusion.

Concluding Statement:..

FIGURE 10.3   Thinking to the End Imagery Test

Source: Reason to Read, Volume 1 (p. 128) by Cathy Collins Block and John Mangieri. Copyright © 1995 by Pearson Education, Inc., publishing as Dale Seymour Publications. Used by permission.

younger students draw pictures to depict the end of what they read. As the children draw, you can deduce what they are thinking and assess the quality of their imagery abilities.

Assessment 5: "What Were You Unable to Think about in the Harder Book?" Test.   For children ages 9 and older, their metacognition can be assessed by giving them one book that is at their grade level and another book on a different topic that is above their grade level. Both books should be selected by the child to ensure that the affective domain is equal in both testing situations. Students read two consecutive pages from each book. You then can ask the children what they thought about while they read the more difficult book. Inquire as to what they were unable to think about as they read the more difficult book that they were able to think about while they read the easier book. Finally, ask what they thought about when they read the easier book and what they would like to learn to think more about whenever they read more difficult books. For instance, the type of answers you may receive could include: "I want to be able to remember more of the details." "I want to think more about where the author's going. I can't follow what's being said." Or "I want to learn how to remember more of what I read from harder books." The answer students give can assist you to place them in the exact strand 3 lesson group in which many methods of reaching each student's specific comprehension goal can be learned. This assessment is based on the principle of using familiar and challenging literacy experiences with children so that they can determine (for themselves) how to become better comprehenders.

Assessment 6: Self-Assessment Tests.   These assessments enable students to measure their own comprehension. At the end of the book, in the "Learners Choices" sheet are sample self-assessment tests. Students can also select the self-assessment format they like best, which can be (1) a checklist in which they list the comprehension processes taught that week and give themselves a 5, 4, 3, 2, or 1 rating as to how well they learned each, (2) essay form in which they describe what they want to learn next, or (3) work samples that they grade, stating the criteria they used to determine their grade in comprehension. Allowing them to do so will increase their motivation as they use it (Guthrie, Cox, Knowles, Buehl, Mazzoni, & Fassulo, 2000). Students should use one form each 6 weeks (at the beginning of the year), and no more frequently than once every 3 weeks in the second half of the year. Children should store these forms in their portfolios or reading folders and share them during discovery discussion meetings.

Assessment 7: Color-Coded Comprehension Portfolios.   In this assessment, students are allowed to choose the comprehension process for which they want to be evaluated. Students insert examples of text that demonstrate that they used a process correctly in a color-coded folder. For example, when teaching students how to let main ideas find them, you can use a yellow highlighter to mark each paper that stu-

dents use in independent application of the process. Then, when they are reading magazines or computer pages that can be printed and stored in folders, students can mark a yellow strip across the top when they found the main idea and would like to prove that the main ideas were located.

Then, these papers can be placed in a yellow folder. When you are ready to assess that student's ability to discern main ideas, you can reference that folder and ask the student to describe how the main ideas in the passage he or she selected became vivid. When you teach another process, you would highlight the papers to be used for pupils' independent practice with a different color. The benefits of color-coded comprehension folders are that students learn processes fast because of the color reference tool, and they can be assessed using passages for which they know they have achieved mastery of a comprehension process. In so doing, you can strengthen their motivation, self-efficacy, and abilities to choose wisely. Color-coded folders set higher expectations than is possible using other forms of paper and pencil assessments, such as multiple-choice.

Assessment 8: "Tell Me What I Should Do and I'll Do It" Test. This assessment measures metacognition, fluency, and abilities to process variant writing styles found in expository and narrative texts. In the past, many teachers have not modeled frequently enough for students to understand what their minds should be thinking when they are comprehending well. For instance, some teachers do not demonstrate how to understand phrases, how to connect meanings between paragraphs, and how to put single pieces of information together in different genres' writing formats. Some do not talk about how minds read faster with topics for which a reader has a large data bank of past experiences. To do so, you can read orally to children and allow them to do an assisted reading, or a repeated reading afterward.

But to make this a test for comprehension, you need to add an initial step first. Take a passage that has been written by a child and type it or have the child type it as a final draft. When the child has finished writing a final draft of her or his work, you can read that work silently to understand where to pause when comprehending it to model what your mind is doing. Then, you read the passage orally demonstrating to the child how to stop after phrases to make the passage memorable and build into the passage a flow of the beauty and rhythm of the English language.

Immediately after reading it, ask the child to read her or his own writing orally mimicking the manner in which you read. After this step, you can then ask the child to describe what was different in his or her mind, the speed, or the thinking during his or her reading that occurred this time than from prior reading experiences. For some students who are unable to describe this process another step is necessary. This step must precede all others. All steps are tape-recorded. You ask the child to read his or her writing before you read it. Then, you read it silently, and then you read it aloud. You allow the child to listen to how he or she read it first, how you read, and the child's reading mimicking what you read. Next, you can ask the pupil to describe any differences that he or she heard. Last, you teach the child how to think while reading in the future to make the differences that he heard.

Long-term memory test

Assessment 9: Long-Term Memory Test.   To assess pupils' long-term memory, you can ask children to list all the books that they have read (or all of the stories that have been taught within the past 2 weeks from the literature anthology). When you review this list, you can identify gaps in long-term memory (e.g., the title of a story you know the child has read during the past 2 weeks is not listed). Then you can ask the child to tell you about that story, jotting down the specific things that the child says. You then pass out Figure 10.4 and ask the child to fill it out concerning the most memorable book that she or he has read. When the child has finished, you can hold a discovery discussion and

FIGURE 10.4   Long-Term Memory Test

Dear Reader,
The book I have just read is the best thing I have read. I would now like to write you this letter to let you know why I think it is the best.

Sincerely,

ask the child to tell you the difference as to how much was remembered and comprehended from both of the books in this assessment and why those differences exist. These thoughts can be recorded on Figure 10.4 and used to guide the instruction provided in the coming week.

Assessment 10: Improving the Specificity of Report Cards and Observation Reports Sent Home to Parents. It is important to communicate an expanded vision of comprehension instruction to parents and to children. This can be accomplished by listing the types of processes that have been taught in school on report cards and observation forms. This method was described by Block (in press a). You can observe children to ascertain whether they demonstrate these processes always, usually, or occasionally. Doing so will ensure that your plans for the next 6 weeks of comprehension instruction will contain each of the steps necessary to enhance all children's full abilities.

Assessment 11: Coordinating Assessments at School and Home. Often observations are used to assess comprehension. It is important to increase the value of these observations. The following evaluations can help improve comprehension assessments. Following this chapter, an Appendix contains samples that can be used to coordinate home and school assessments. The directions for their use are described on each page so that an assessment can be made based on the needs of individual students. Each of the processes that have been reported in this book can be listed.

Book sharing assessments are one example of how to coordinate comprehension assessment so it mirrors work that the child does at home and at school. Harwayne (2000) provided a list of ten books that could be recommended to parents as benchmarks for each grade level to assess book sharing experiences at home. These books could be used by parents at the beginning and at the end of the school year, so that they can begin to hear the progress in comprehension, fluency, and decoding skills that their children are making. Parents can also be shown how to use these books by sending home instructions in which you describe the strengths and weaknesses parents can observe as their children read silently and orally.

The specific books recommended by Harwayne (2000) for first graders entering second grade are *Town Mouse and Country Mouse* by Val Biro and *Morris Goes to School* by B. Wisemen. For second graders entering third grade she recommends *Nate the Great* by Margerie Weiman Sharmat and *The Growing Up Feet* by Beverly Cleary. For third graders entering fourth grade she recommends *Busybody Nora* by Johanna Horwtz and *Teddy Bear's Scrapbook* by Debra and James Howe. For fourth graders entering fifth grade she recommends the *Trumpet of the Swan* by E. B. White and *Absolutely Normal Chaos* by Sharon Creech.

Home comprehension checklist

Another method of assisting parents to build on the instruction that children receive at school is to ask them to complete the **home comprehension checklist** shown in Comprehension Process Lesson 10 (p. 216). When this information is acquired from the parent, you can use it to communicate at school to students about how proud you are of the steps the students are taking at home and use it to plan new instruction so any gaps are filled. Last, there is a Web site that can help parents to reinforce the comprehension instruction given at school. This site offers home tutorials that are correlated to state comprehension standards. It also helps parents find books geared to their child's interest level: www.home.II.sch.

In Summary

All of the assessments discussed in this chapter are graphically depicted in Figure 10.5. This chapter was designed to describe new comprehension tests. Each is intended to demonstrate comprehension processes in action. Many are performance based, such as (1) assisted performance assessments, (2) "what do we need to fill in" tests, (3) "what's the problem" tests, or (4) "did you till the text" tests. Others assess students' abilities to

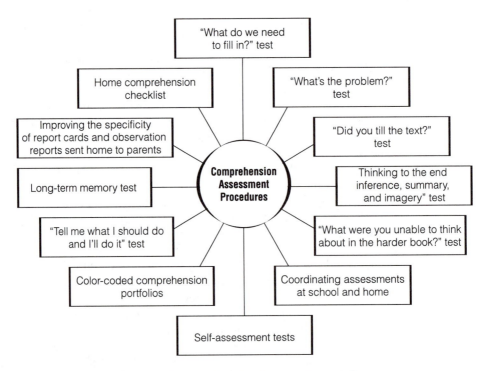

FIGURE 10.5 Summary of Comprehension Process Approach Assessment Procedures

reflect on their own comprehension processes, such as (1) the thinking to the end imagery test, (2) the "what were you unable to think about in the harder book" test, (3) the "tell me what I should do and I'll do it" test, and (4) the long-term memory test. Many involve parents' participation or written forms, folders, and multiple work samples (e.g., self-assessment systems, color-coded comprehension portfolios, report cards or observations, integrating assessments at home and school, and the home comprehension checklist). By using these evaluations, teachers can provide valuable comprehension instructional experiences for students because they can identify specific limitations in individual students' past comprehension experiences.

REFLECTING ON WHAT YOU HAVE LEARNED

1. List as many of the assessment tools as you can remember without referring back to the textbook. When you have finished compare your list to the one in Figure 10.5. What does your list tell you about your comprehension ability? Why did you not remember some of the assessments covered? This type of assessment is similar to one that you would give to children (assessment 10 as described in this chapter) about the books that they have read. Once you have completed this assessment, you can understand how powerful assessment 10 is.

2. Select the type of self-assessment system that you want to administer once every 3 weeks (or once every 6 weeks based on the age of your students). Make a list of these and describe why you want to use them.

3. Select one assessment method that you would like to use to coordinate school and home assessments of comprehension. What will your first step be in using this instrument and how can this information be used to more frequently include parents in the development of their children's comprehension?

4. *Your Professional Journal: Drawing Conclusions.* Summarize the key principles of assessment that were presented in this chapter. What do these principles have in common with the principles that were cited relative to instruction in Chapters 1 through 9?

5. *Making Professional Decisions.* In approximately one paragraph, write a concise description of your philosophy for instructing and assessing comprehension. Describe how you will tell students, parents, and administrators about the processes you use to make your assessment decisions.

6. *Multicultural Application.* Select the assessment in this chapter that you most appreciated. Modify it to better meet the needs of students from a minority culture. Specify the adaptation that you recommend, prepare an example, and share it with colleagues. In addition, what advice can you give to teachers at your school (or future school) concerning the information that you have read in this chapter that could help them improve their comprehension assessment? What is the first step that your school must take in your opinion?

7. *Key Terms Exercise.* Following is a list of concepts introduced in this chapter. If you have learned the meaning of a term, place a checkmark in the blank that precedes that term. If you are not sure of a term's definition, increase your retention by reviewing the definition

of the term. If you have learned 10 of these terms on your first reading of this chapter, you have constructed many meanings that are important for your career.

_____ assisted performance evaluations (p. 203)

_____ "what do we need to fill in?" test (p. 205)

_____ "what's the problem?" test (p. 205)

_____ "did you till the text?" test (p. 207)

_____ thinking to the end inference, summary, and imagery test (p. 208)

_____ "what were you unable to think about in the harder book?" test (p. 210)

_____ self-assessment tests (p. 210)

_____ color-coded comprehension portfolios (p. 210)

_____ "tell me what I should do and I'll do it" test (p. 211)

_____ long-term memory test (p. 212)

_____ improving the specificity of report cards and observation reports sent home to parents (p. 213)

_____ coordinating assessments at school and home (p. 213)

_____ home comprehension checklist (p. 214)

8. *Comprehension Process Lesson 10: Teaching Students the Process of Assessing Their Own Comprehension Processes at Home and When They Select Their Own Books.* Comprehension Process Lesson 10 demonstrates how students can assume the responsibility of assessing their own comprehension at home and when they select a book. You can use this lesson in your classroom to improve conversations about self-assessment of comprehension. Students' answers to these questions will assist them to become more active participants in increasing their own abilities to make meaning.

COMPREHENSION PROCESS LESSON 10
Self-Assessing Reading at Home and Choosing the Best Book to Read

Home Comprehension Checklist

Readers can evaluate their home study by reading each sentence in the checklist and putting an *X* on the line under the appropriate column: *Always, Sometimes, Never.*

	Always	Sometimes	Never
1. I have a quiet, private place to read at home.	____	____	____
2. My home comprehension place has good light.	____	____	____
3. My study place has a comfortable temperature.	____	____	____
4. There is a desk or table large enough to hold all of the materials in my home study place.	____	____	____
5. There is a comfortable chair to sit in at my home comprehension place.	____	____	____

6. I keep all the required work and reference
   materials in my home study place that I will need
   to complete my content assignments.   _____   _____   _____
7. There are no distractions of any kind at my
   home comprehension study place.   _____   _____   _____
8. My home comprehension place is kept private
   from my brothers or sisters who disturb me.   _____   _____   _____
9. I can use my home comprehension place
   whenever I need or want to.   _____   _____   _____
10. I enjoy studying at my home comprehension place.   _____   _____   _____

Choosing the Best Book to Read

Step 1: Expert readers know that they can read more advanced books in topics about which they have read extensively in the past. Therefore, students identify the topic about which they want to read based on how much and what they want this particular reading experience to achieve: learning, relaxing, reviewing, or escaping into another person's world. As students approach a set of books, the purpose of their reading goals will determine the thickness of the book that they will examine. For example, if they want to relax, they may choose a shorter book than if they wanted to learn very specific information about a topic.

Step 2: Expert readers read books by authors that they enjoy. Students then survey the authors and titles of book that are about the length that they desire. If a favorite author or captivating title attracts their attention, they should examine that book first.

Step 3: Students thumb through the book to determine the density of the text and the amount of effort that they will have to exert to enjoy this author's writing. They then select a single page near the middle of the book to read to determine whether they know the majority of words. As they read that page students can press one finger down on the opposite page for every word that they do not know. If students press down all five fingers on one hand before they finish reading a single page, they will know that this book may cause frustration in decoding and interfere with their comprehension and enjoyment. Students should return to Step 1 in this case.

Appendix

Checklist of Actions Teachers Can Take to Increase Students' Comprehension

	Name	Strategies	Goals
Goal 1 Giving choices during scaffolding	Pivotal point scaffolding and avoiding the slight rejection phenomenon	Advanced scaffolds: Model, co-create with student, take the first step in a process yourself, and name the process	Giving students a choice of which suggestion you gave that they want to use
Goal 2 Discovery discussions	PAR	Discovery discussions	Filling in the text
Goal 3 Avoid merely giving instructions			
Goal 4 Becoming the contributor	Respond to centered questions	Handling incorrect answers	
Goal 5 Seeking deep understanding	Power of three		

Story Frame Form

Setting: (When and where does the story take place?) _____

_____

I know this because the author uses these words: _____

_____

Main characters: (Who are the important people in the story?) _____

_____

I know they are important because: _____

_____

The problem starts when: _____

_____

or

The main character's goal is: _____

_____

The plot: (What happened?)

Event 1: _____

_____

After that . . .

Event 2: _____

_____

Next . . .

Event 3: _____

_____

Then . . .

Event 4: _____

_____

Turning point: (How I know the plot is reaching a solution)

The resolution: (How did it end?) _____

_____

I know this because the author uses these words: _____

Author's moral or purpose (or, purpose for me): _____

_____

I think this is the moral because: _____

_____

_____

Learner's Choices: Self-Assessments That Occurred
Each Month as Chosen by the Student

Teacher	K	1	2	3	4	5
September — Self-portrait						
October — Writing sample						
November — Continuums						
December						
January — Photograph						
February — Content area						
March — Writing sample						
April — List of books						
May — Self-evaluation						
June — Math card continuums progress report						

Source: Adapted from Hill, Bonnie Campbell, & Ruptic, Cynthia A. *Authentic Assessment.* Copyright ©
1994 Christopher-Gordon Publishers, Inc. Used by permission.

Form for Parents to Evaluate Their Child as a Learner

Name _____

Grade _____

Date _____

Indicate your observation of your child's learning in the following areas.
Please comment where appropriate.

	Yes/No	Comments/Examples
1. My child likes to listen to me read to him/her.		
2. My child likes to read to me.		
3. My child tries to read in everyday situations (street signs, cereal boxes, store signs).		
4. It is clear from the way my child talks that a book has been understood.		
5. My child sometimes guesses at words but they usually make sense.		
6. My child tries to figure out new words for him/her when reading.		
7. My child sometimes chooses to write.		
8. My child likes to talk about and share what was written.		
9. My child voluntarily tries out new words or forms of writing.		
10. My child listens and thinks better this year.		
11. My child has become a more discriminating viewer.		
12. My child's speaking abilities improved.		

Source: Adapted from Hill, Bonnie Campbell, & Ruptic, Cynthia A. (1994).
Authentic Assessment, p. 171. Copyright © 1994 Christopher-Gordon Publishers,
Inc. Used by permission.

Sample of a Parent Evaluation Calendar

Sunday	Monday	Tuesday	Wednesday	Thursday	Friday	Saturday
			Ⓐ 1 B C D ☺	A 2 B C Ⓓ ☺	A 3 B Ⓒ D ☺	A 4 Ⓑ C D ☺
A 5 B C D ☺	A 6 B Ⓒ Ⓓ ☺	A 7 Ⓑ C Ⓓ ☺	Ⓐ 8 B C Ⓓ ☺	A 9 B Ⓒ D ☺	A 10 Ⓑ C Ⓓ ☺	A 11 B C Ⓓ ☺

Source: Fredricks, Anthony D., & Rasinski, Timothy V. (1990, December). "Working with Parents: Involving Parents in the Assessment." *The Reading Teacher*, *44*(4), 346–349. Reprinted with permission of the International Reading Association.

Reading Incentive Program Time Sheet

For the week of _____ to _____ .

Date							
Day	Monday	Tuesday	Wednesday	Thursday	Friday	Saturday	Sunday
Number of minutes							
Parent's initials							

Student's name _____ (Parent's signature) _____

Grade: _____

Keep track of time spent reading daily and initial each day. Your goal is to read 20 minutes a night, 5 nights a week for a total of 100 minutes a week (1 hour and 40 minutes).

Source: Fredricks, Anthony D., & Rasinski, Timothy V. (1990, December). "Working with Parents: Involving Parents in the Assessment." *The Reading Teacher*, *44*(4), 346–349. Reprinted with permission of the International Reading Association.

Web Sites

To obtain more information about children and adolescent nonfiction and fiction authors for summer readings and author studies consult the following sources.

www.learn2.com

www.acs.ucalgary.ca/~dkbrown

www.scils.rutgers.edu/special/kay/author.html

www.friend.ly.net/scoop/biographies

www.bdd.com/index.html

www.harpercollins.com/authors/index.htm

http://pathfinder.com/twep/lb_childrens/author

www.penguinputnam.com

www.randomhouse.com/kids/catalog

www.acs.ucalgary.ca/~dkbrown/k6/aliki.html

www.xensei.com/users/newfilm/homelsk.htm

www.indiana.edu/~eric_rec/ieo/bibs/lauber.html

www.ala.org/alsc/children_links.html

www.educ.ucalgary.ca/litindex

www.ed.gov/pubs/parents/reading.html

www.readin.org

www.sdcoe.k12.ca.us/score/cyberguide.html

www.readin.org/Authors/Blume/blume.htm

www.learn2.com/08/0888/08882.asp

www.readin.org/Educator/Lessons/4-6/lpgamesh.htm

References

Adams, M. (1990). *Beginning to read*. Cambridge, MA: Harvard University Press.

Afflerbach, P. (1996). Engaged assessment of engaged reading. In L. Baker, P. Afflerbach, & D. Reinking (Eds.), *Developing engaged readers in school and home communities* (pp. 191–214). Hillsdale, NJ: Erlbaum.

Alexander, P. A. (1992). Domain knowledge: Evolving themes and emerging concerns. *Educational Psychologist, 27*, 33–51.

Alexander, P. A., & Murphy, P. K. (1998a). Profiling the differences in students' knowledge, interest, and strategic processing. *Journal of Educational Psychology, 90* (3), 435–447.

Alexander, P. A., & Murphy, P. K. (1998b). The research base for APA's learner-centered psychological principles. In N. M. Lambert & B. L. McCombs (Eds.), *How students learn: Reforming schools through learner-centered education* (pp. 25–60). Washington, DC: American Psychological Association.

Allington, R. (1996 December). What we need instructionally. Presidential address at the National Reading Conference, Charleston, SC.

Allington, R. L. (2001). *What really matters for struggling readers: Designing research-based interventions*. New York: Longman.

Alvermann, D. & Mosie R. (1991 December). Sociological perspectives on literacy in content areas. Paper presented at the annual meeting of the National Reading Conference. Austin, TX.

Ambruster, B. B. (1991). Silent reading, oral reading, and learning from text. *The Reading Teacher, 45*, 154–155.

American Library Association, (1996). *Report on book distribution in American homes*. Washington, DC: ALA.

American Medical Association. (l996). *Principles of professional practice in psychological analyses*. Washington, DC: AMA.

Ames, W. (1992). Children's motivation. *Review of Research in Education, 23*, 156–174.

Applebee, A. N., & Langer, J. A. (1983). Instructional scaffolding: Reading and writing as natural language activities. *Language Arts, 60*, 168–175.

Ashton-Warner, S. (1966). *The teacher*. New York: Macmillan.

Au, K. (1993). *Literacy instruction in multicultural settings*. Fort Worth, TX: Harcourt.

Baker, L. (1984a). Children's effective use of multiple standards for evaluating their comprehension. *Journal of Educational Psychology, 76*, 588–597.

Baker, L. (1984b). Spontaneous versus instructed use of multiple standards for evaluating comprehension: Effects of age, reading proficiency, and type of standard. *Journal of Experimental Child Psychology, 38*, 289–311.

Baker, L. (1994). Fostering metacognitive development. In H. Reese (Ed.), *Advances in child development and behavior* (Vol. 25, pp. 201–239). San Diego, California: Academic Press.

Baker, L. (2001). Metacognition in comprehension instruction. In C. Block & M. Pressley (Eds.) *Comprehension instruction: Research based practices* (pp. 274–289). New York: Guilford Press.

Baker, L., & Anderson, R. I. (1982). Effects of inconsistent information on text processing: Evidence for comprehension monitoring. *Reading Research Quarterly, 27*, 281–294.

Baker, L., & Brown, A. L. (1984a). Metacognitive skills and reading. In P. D. Pearson, M. Kamil, R. Barr, & P. Mosenthal (Eds.), *Handbook of research in reading* (pp. 353–395). New York: Longman.

Baker, L., & Brown, A. L. (1984b). Metacognitive skills and reading. In P. D. Pearson, R. Barr, and L. Kamil (Eds.) *Handbook of reading research* (pp. 491–572). New York: Longman.

Baker, L., & Cerro, L. (2001). Assessing metacognition in children and adults. In G. Schraw (Ed.), *Issues in the measurement of metacognition*. Lincoln, Nebraska: University of Nebraska Press.

Baker, L., & Zimlin, L. (1989). Instructional effects on children's use of two levels of standards for evaluating their comprehension. *Journal of Educational Psychology, 81*, 340–346.

Baker, S., Gersten, R., & Keating, T. (2000). When less may be more: A 2-year longitudinal evaluation of a volunteer tutoring program requiring minimal training. *Reading Research Quarterly, 35,* (4), 494–520.

Bakhtin, M. M. (1993). *Toward a philosophy of the act* (V. Liapunov & M. Holquist, Eds.; V. Liapunov, Trans.). Austin University of Texas Press.

Bales, R. & Gambrell, L. (1985). *Visual imagery and the comprehension monitoring performance of fourth and fifth grade poor readers.* Unpublished paper. University of Maryland.

Bandura, A. (1986 April). Achievement goal orientations: research for choice must have challenge. Paper presented at the annual meeting of the American Educational Research Association. San Francisco, CA.

Barclay, K., Benelli, D., & Schoon, S. (1999). Making the connection: Science and literacy. *Childhood Education, 75,* 146–149.

Barrows, A. (1985). *How to design a problem-based curriculum for the preclinical year.* New York: Springer.

Baumann, J. F., Jones, L. A., & Seifert-Kessell, N. (1993). Using think alouds to enhance children's comprehension monitoring abilities. *The Reading Teacher 54* (5), 235–241.

Beal, C. R. (1996). The role of comprehension monitoring in children's revision. *Educational Psychology Review, 8,* 219–238.

Beck, I. L. & Dole, J. (1994). Comprehension schema in science and social studies content areas. In C. Block & J. Mangieri. (Eds.), 72–89. *Teaching thinking: An agenda for the twenty-first century.* Hillsdale, NJ: Erlbaum.

Beck, I. L., McKeown, M. G., Hamilton, R. L., & Kucan, L. (1997). *Questioning the author: An approach for enhancing student engagement with text.* Newark, DE: International Reading Association.

Beck, I. L., Omanson, R. C., & McKeown, M. G. (1982). An instructional redesign of reading lessons: Effects on comprehension. *Reading Research Quarterly, 17,* 462–481.

Bereiter, C., & Bird, M. (1985). Use of thinking aloud in identification and teaching of reading comprehension strategies. *Cognition and Instruction, 2,* 131–156.

Bereiter, C., & Scardamalia, M. (1989). Intentional learning as a goal of instruction. In L. B. Resnick (Ed.), *Knowing, learning, and instruction: Essays in honor of Robert Glaser.* pp. 361–392. Hillsdale, NJ: Erlbaum.

Beyer, B. (1986). *Overcoming blocks to creativity.* New York: Wiley/Jossey Bass.

Blachowicz, C. & Ogle, D. (2001). *Comprehension Instruction.* New York: Guilford Press.

Blair, Larson S. & Williams, K. (1999). *The balanced reading program.* Newark, DE: International Reading Association.

Blanton, W. E., Wood, K. D., & Moorman, G. B. (1990). The role of purpose in reading instruction. *The Reading Teacher, 43,* 486–493.

Block, C. C. (1992). Improving reading and thinking: From teaching or not teaching skills to interactive interventions. In M. Pressley, K. Harris & I. Guthrie (Eds.). *Promoting Academic Competence & Literacy in Schools,* 149–167. San Diego: Academic Press.

Block, C. C. (1993). Strategy Instruction in a literature-based reading program. *Elementary School Journal, 33,* 123–147.

Block, C. C. (1997a). *Literacy difficulties: Diagnosis and instruction.* Ft. Worth, TX: Harcourt Brace.

Block, C. (1997b). *Teaching the language arts, 2nd ed.* Boston, MA: Allyn & Bacon.

Block, C. C. (November 19,1998). New millennium reading. Presentation to the Nobel learning communities' biannual board meeting. Educational advisory board member, Nobel Learning Communities, Inc.

Block, C. (1999). The case for exemplary teaching especially for students who begin first grade without the precursors for literacy success. *National Reading Conference Yearbook, 49,* 71–85.

Block, C. C. (2000). *How can we teach all students to comprehend well. Research Paper.* NY: Scholastic.

Block, C. C. (2001a). Teaching the language arts: Expanding thinking through student-centered instruction, Third edition. Boston, MA: Allyn and Bacon.

Block, C. C. (2001b). A spotlight on exemplary practices that significantly increase students' literacy even when they enter first grade without the precursors for literacy success. In T. Shananan (Ed.). *National Reading Conference Yearbook* pp. 43–55. Chicago, IL: National Reading Conference.

Block, C. C. (May 2001c). Reading to learn: Comprehending non-fiction. Paper presented at the Annual Meeting of the International Reading Association. New Orleans, Louisiana.

Block, C. C. (May 2001d). Effects of teacher change on student achievement. Paper presented at the Annual Meeting of the International Reading Association. New Orleans, Louisiana.

Block, C. C. (2002a). Effects of books on tape on students' comprehension abilities. Paper presented at the thirtieth plains regional conference of the International Reading Association. Topeka, KS.

Block, C. C. (2002b). *Literacy Difficulties: Diagnosis and Instruction for Reading Specialists and Classroom Teachers.* (2nd ed.). Boston, MA: Allyn & Bacon.

Block, C. C. (in press). Teaching non-fiction: What we know, what we still need to learn, and what we can do now. *California Reader.*

Block, C. C. (in preparation). Teacher Change: Effects on Student Achievement.

Block, C. C. & Beardon, P. (1997 April). Student initiative in literacy instruction. Paper presented at the anual meeting of the American Educational Research Association. San Francisco, CA.

Block, C. C. & Cavanagh, C. (1998). Teaching thinking: How can we and why should We?" In Bernhardt, R., Hedley, C. N., Cattaro, G., & Svolopooulous, V. (Eds.). *Curriculum.*

Block, C. C., Gambrell, L., & Pressley, M. (2002) (eds.). Improving comprehension: Rethinking research, theory and practice. San Francisco, CA and Newark, DE: Jossey-Bass and International Reading Association.

Block, C. C. & Johnson, R. (2002). Teaching the comprehension process approach. In C. C. Block, L. Gambrell & M. Pressley (eds.). *Improving comprehension: Rethinking research, theory & practice.* San Francisco, CA & Newark, DE: Jossey-Bass and International Reading Association, pp. 17–40.

Block, C. C. & Mangieri, J. N. (1994). *Increasing thinking abilities of teachers and students: Diverse perspectives.* Fort Worth, Texas: Harcourt Brace.

Block, C. C. & Mangieri, J. N. (1995/1996 a, b, & c). *Reason to read: Thinking strategies for life through literature.* Vols. 1, 2, & 3. Palo Alto, CA: Addison Wesley.

Block, C. C. & Mangieri, J. N. (2003). *Exemplary literacy teachers: What have we learned from them.* New York: Guilford Press.

Block, C. C., & Mangieri, J. N. (in press). Are you the best teacher you can be? *Instructor.*

Block, C. C., Mangieri, J. Rodgers, L., and Johnson R. (in press). *Teaching Comprehension in Kindergarten to Grade 3.* NY: Guilford Press.

Block, C. C., Oakar, M., Hurt, N. (2002). Exemplary literacy teachers: A continuum from preschool through grade 5. *Reading Research Quarterly.*

Block, C. C. & Pressley, M. (2002). *Comprehension instruction: Research based practices.* NY: Guilford Press.

Block, C. C. & Pressley, M. (2003). Comprehension instruction. In L. Gambrell, L. Morrow & M. Pressley (eds.). *Best practices in literacy instruction.* New York: Guilford Press.

Block, C. C., Schaller, J., Joy, J., & Gaines, P. (2002). Teaching students to think about comprehension as a process and more than strategies. In C. Block, & M. Pressley (Eds.). *Comprehension instruction: Research based practices.* New York: Guilford Press. (pp. 33–56).

Bloome, D.(1986). Building literacy and the classroom community. *Theory Into Practice, 15.* 71–6.

Bolter, J. D. (1998). Hypertext and the question of visual literacy. In D. Reinking, M. McKenna, L. Labbo & R. Kieffer (Eds.), *Handbook of literacy and technology: Transformations in a post-typographic world.* (pp. 3–13). Mahwah, NJ: Erlbaum.

Borkowski, J. G., Carr, M., Rellinger, E., & Pressley, M. (1990). Self-regulated cognition: Interdependence of metacognition, attributions, and self-esteem. In B. F. Jones & L. Idol (Eds.), *Dimensions of thinking and cognitive instruction* (pp. 53–92). Hillsdale, NJ: Erlbaum.

Britton, B. K., & Graesser, A. C. (1996). *Models of understanding text.* Mahwah, NJ: Erlbaum.

Broudy, H. S. (1989). Types of knowledge and purposes of education. In R. C. Anderson, R. J. Spiro, & W. E. Montague (Eds.), *Schooling and the acquistition of knowledge,* (pp. 1–17). Hillsdale, NJ: Erlbaum.

Brown, A. L. (1978). Knowing when, where, and how to remember: A problem of metacognition. In R. Glaser (Ed.), *Advances in instructional psychology.* (pp. 56–71). Hillsdale, NJ: Erlbaum.

Brown, A. L. & Campione, J. C. (1998). Designing a community of young learners: Theoretical and practical lessons. In N. M. Lambert & B. L. McCombs (Eds.), *How students learn: Reforming schools through learner-centered education* (pp. 153–186). Washington, DC: American Psychological Association.

Brown, A. L., Collins, A., Duguid, D. (1989). Metacognition: Effects on academic achievement. *Journal of Educational Psychology, 81* (3), 403–419.

Brown, R. (2002). Straddling two worlds: Self-directed comprehension instruction for middle schoolers. In Block, C. & Pressley, M. (Eds.). *Comprehension instruction: Research based practices.* NY: Guilford.

Bruner, J. (1985). The model of a learner. *Educational researcher, 14*(6), 5–8.

Cain-Thoreson, C., Lippman, M. Z., & McClendon-Magnuson, D. (1997). Windows on comprehension: Reading comprehension processes as revealed by two think-aloud procedures, *Journal of Educational Psychology, 89*(4), 579–590.

Caine, R. N., & Caine, G. (1997). *Education on the edge of possibility.* Alexandria, VA: Association for Supervision of Curriculum and Development.

Calkins, L. (1991). *Whole language classrooms.* Portsmouth, NH: Heinemann.

Calkins, L. (1997). *Whole language classrooms: (2nd ed.).* Portsmouth, NH: Heinemann.

Cameron, J., & Pierce, W. D. (1994). Reinforcement, reward, and intrinsic motivation: A meta-analysis. *Review of Educational Research, 64,* 363–423.

Carnegie Foundation. (1995). *Understanding: New developments.* New York: Carnegie Foundation.

Carnegie Foundation. (2000). What is the new generation "Y"? (Research report 31). New York: Carnegie Foundation.

Carr, K. (May 1998). *Implications for inferencing and interpreting.* Paper presented at the annual meeting of the International Reading Association. New Orleans, LA.

Carroll, J. B., & Freedle, R. O. (Eds.). (1972). *Language comprehension and the acquisition of knowledge.* Washington DC: V. H. Winston.

Carver, R. (1994 December). Can all of the variance in word identification be explained by cipher knowledge? Paper presented at the annual meeting of the National Reading Conference, Austin, TX.

Carver, R. (1995). *Can all of the variance in word identification be explained by cipher knowledge and lexical knowledge?* (Handout). Austin, TX: National Reading Conference.

Cazden, C. (1991). *Balancing whole language.* Portsmouth, NH: Heinemann.

Chall, J. (1998). *Teaching children to read.* Cambridge, MA: Brookline.

Chambliss, M. (1993 December). *Science textual awareness.* Paper presented at the annual meeting of the National Reading Conference, Miami, FL.

Chi, M. T. H., Slotta, J. D., & deLeeuw, N. (1994). From things to processes: A theory of conceptual change for learning science concepts. *Learning and Instruction, 4,* 27–43.

Children's Defense Fund; (1992). *Impact of literacy achievement on future earning potential* (Report 122) New York: Children's Defense Fund.

Chipman, S., & Segal, E. (April 1985). *Literacy achievement: Effects of decoding and comprehension instruction for at-risk students.* Paper presented at the annual meeting of the American Educational Research Association. New York, NY.

Christie, F. (1987). Genres as choice. In I. Reid (Ed.), *The place of genre in learning: Current debates.* (22–34). Melbourne and Geelong, Australia: Deakin University, Centre for Studies in Literary Education.

Clark. H. H., & Clark, E. (1984). *Psychology and language.* NY: Harcourt Brace.

Clark, H. H., Deshler, D., Shoemaker, M., Alley, R., & Warner, T. (1984). Understanding what is meant from what is said: A study of conversationally conveyed requests. *Journal of Verbal Learning and Verbal Behavior, 14,* 56–72.

Clay, M. (1979). *Observation survey.* Portsmouth, NH: Heinemann.

Colizar, M. (1993). Literacy discourse analysis. NY: Macmillan.

Collins, C. (1991). Reading instruction that increases thinking abilities. *Journal of Reading, 34,* 510–516.

Congressional Record. (March 7, 2001). Comprehension Emphasis. p. 9.

Cornoldi, C., Debeni, D., & Pazzaglia, P. (1998). Metacognitive control processes and memory deficits in poor comprehenders. *Learning disability quarterly, 13,* 245–255.

Cornoldi, C., & Oakhill, J. (1998). Constructive processes and pronoun resolution in skilled and less-skilled comprehenders: Effects of memory load and inferential complexity. *Language and Speech, 29,* 25–37.

Council of Exceptional Children. (1997). *Reading instruction through infusion in regular classrooms.* (Research and Policy Report 56). Washington, DC: Council of Exceptional Children.

Craig, G. & MacGuire, K. (1998 April). *Metacognitive development and impact on literal comprehension for youth.* Paper presented at the annual meeting of the American Educational Research Association, Toronto, Canada.

Cullinan, B. (1999). Imagery is of the essence. *Instruction/ UMI* [online]. Available: www.texshare.edu.

Culp, M. (1985 April). Comprehension research: Review of research. Paper presented at the annual meeting of the American Educational Research Association, Washington, DC.

Daniels, H. A. (1996). Developing a sense of audience. In T. Shanahan (Ed.), *Reading and writing together: New perspectives for the classroom* (pp. 99–125). Norwood, MA: Christopher Gordon.

Dark. L., & Gilmore, J. (1999 April). *Assessment of comprehension in this internet society.* Paper presented at the annual meeting of the American Educational Research Association, New Orleans, LA.

Delisle, R. (1997). *How to use problem-based learning in the classroom.* Alexandria, VA: Association for Supervision and Curriculum Development.

Diamond, B. (1999). Students' role. *Educational Leadership, 79,* 381–394.

Doane, S. M., McNamara, D. S., Kintsch, W., Polson, P. G., & Clawson, D. M. (1992). Prompt comprehension in UNIX command production. *Memory and Cognition, 20,* (4), 327–343.

Dole, J. A., Duffy, G. G., Roehler, L. R., & Pearson, P. D. (1991). Moving from the old to the new:

Research on reading comprehension instruction. *Review of Educational Research, 61,* 239–264.

Donnantuono, M. (2000 May). *Teaching comprehension during content area instruction.* Paper presented at the annual meeting of International Reading Association, Orlando, FL.

Dorfman, N., & Brewer, L. (1994 December). *Metacomprehension: Review of research.* Paper presented at the annual meeting of the National Reading Conference, San Diego, CA.

Dowhower, S. L. (1999). Supporting a strategic stance in the classroom: A comprehension framework for helping teachers help students to be strategic. *The Reading Teacher, 52,* (7), 672.

Duin, G., & Graves, M. (1987 December). *Detail retention through main idea schema imagery.* Paper presented at the annual meeting of the National Reading Conference, San Diego, CA.

Duke, N. K. (2000). 3.6 minutes per day: The scarcity of informational texts in first grade. *Reading Research Quarterly, 35* (2), 202–224.

Duke, N. K., & Kays, J. (1998). "Can I say 'once upon a time'?" Kindergarten children developing knowledge of information book language. *Early Childhood Research Quarterly, 13,* 295–318.

Durkin, D. (1978/1979) What classroom observations reveal about reading comprehension. Instruction. *Reading Research Quarterly, 14,* (4), 481–533.

Durkin, D. (1981). Reading comprehension instruction in five basal reading series. *Reading Research Quarterly, 16,* 515–544.

Dye, R. (2001 December). *Comprehension instruction: Advancements at the elementary school level.* Paper presented at the annual meeting of the National Reading Conference, Austin, TX.

Dymock, E. (1993 April). *Literal interpretations: Review of research.* Paper presented at the annual meeting of the American Educational Research Association. San Francisco, CA.

Dyson, A. H. (2001). Transforming transfer: Unruly children, contrary texts, and the persistence of the pedagogical order. Manuscript prepared for A. Iran-Nejad & P. D. Pearson, (Eds.), *Review of Research in Education, 24,* 23–49.

Edwards, M. (1999). The aim is metacognition: For teachers as well as students. In J. Hancock (Ed.), *The explicit teaching of reading* (pp. 80–96). Newark, DE: International Reading Association.

Elbaum, S., Vaughn, S., Hughes, M., & Moody, S. W. (1999). Grouping practices and reading outcomes for students with disabilities. *Exceptional Children, 65* (3), 145–172.

Elley, W. (1992). Acquiring literacy in a second language: The effect of book-based programs. *Language Learning, 41*(3), 375–411.

Elster, J. (2000 December). *Inferencing for at-risk adolescents.* Paper presented at the annual meeting of the National Reading Conference, Miami, FL.

Euler, R., & Hellekson, B. (1993 April). *Imagry training and effect on retention.* Paper presented at the annual meeting of the American Educational Research Association. San Francisco, CA.

Ewing, J. M. (1999). Learning using the World Wide Web: A collaborative learning event. *Journal of Educational Multimedia and Hypermedia, 8,* 3–22.

Fashola, O. S., Drum, P. A., Mayer, R. E., & Kang, S. J. (1996). A cognitive theory of orthographic transitioning: Predictable errors in how Spanish-speaking children spell English words. *American Educational Research Journal, 33* (1), 825–843.

Fisher, J. B., Schumaker, J. B., & Deshler, D. D. (2002). Improving the reading comprehension of at-risk adolescents. In C. C. Block & M. Pressley (Eds.). *Comprehension instruction: Research based practices.* (pp. 310–329). New York: Guilford Press.

Fitzgerald, J., & Spiegel, D. (1983). Teaching main ideas and the effect on student achievement. *National Reading Conference Yearbook, 14,* 116–129.

Flavell, J. C. (1976). Metacognitive aspects of problem solving. In L. B. Resnick (Ed.), *The nature of intelligence.* Hillsdale, NJ: Erlbaum.

Fleckenstein, F. (1991 April). *Inferencing and impact on comprehension.* Paper presented at the annual meeting of the American Educational Research Association, Toronto, Canada.

Fletcher, C. R., van den Broek, P., & Arthur, E. J. (1966, 2000). A model of narrative comprehension and recall. In Britten, B. K. & Graesser, A. C. (Eds.) *Models of understanding text.* (2nd ed.). (pp. 13–31). Mahwah, NJ: Erlbaum.

Fountas, I. C., & Pinnell, G. S. (2001). *Guided reading for third through sixth graders.* Portsmouth, NH: Heinemann.

Fox, M. (1988 April). *Content area instruction: Influence upon comprehension achievement.* Paper presented at the annual meeting of the American Educational Research Association, Chicago, IL.

Frederiksen, C. H. (1981). Structure and process in discourse production and comprehension. In M. A. Just & P. Carpenter (Eds.), *Cognitive processes in comprehension.* (pp. 156–170). Hillsdale, NJ: Erlbaum.

Freire, P. (1999). *Pedagogy of the Heart.* New York: Continuum.

Galda, L. (1998). Mirrors and Windows: Reading as transformation. In T. E. Raphael & K. H. Aw, (Eds.). *Literature-based instruction: Reshaping the curriculum.* Norwood, MA: Christopher-Gordon. (pp. 23–33 & 39–52).

Gambrell, L. (1982). Induced mental imagery and the text prediction performance of first and third graders. In J. A. Niles and L. A. Niles (Eds.), *New inquiries in reading research and instruction* (pp. 131–135). Rochester, NY: The National Reading Conference.

Gambrell, L. (2001 May). *Non-fiction instruction and comprehension achievement.* Paper presented at the annual meeting of the International Research Association. Indianapolis, IN.

Gambrell, L., & Koskinen, P. (2001). Imagery: A strategy for enhancing comprehension. In M. Pressley, & C. Block, (Eds.). *Teaching comprehension.* (pp. 219–240). New York: Guilford Press.

Gillingham, M. (1993). Effects of question complexity and reader strategies on adults' hypertext comprehension. *Journal of Research on Computing in Education, 26,* 1–15.

Glaubman, R., Glaubman, H., & Ofir, L. (1997). Effects of self-directed learning, story comprehension, and self-questioning in kindergarten. *Journal of Educational Research, 90,* 361–374.

Golden, R., & Rumelhart, D. (1993). A parallel distributed processing model of story comprehension and recall. *Discourse Processes, 16*(3), 203–237.

Goldman, S. R. (1996). Reading, writing, and learning in hypermedia environments. In H. van Oostendorp & S. de Mul (Eds.), *Cognitive aspects of processing electronic texts,* (7–42). Norwood, NJ: Ablex.

Goldman, S. R., Varma, S., & Cote, N. (1996). Extending capacity-constrained construction integration: Toward "smarter" and flexible models of text comprehension. In B. K. Britten, & A. C. Graesser, *Models of understanding text.* (pp. 291–329). Mahwah, NJ: Erlbaum.

Goodman, K. (1973). *What's whole in whole languge.* Portsmouth, NH: Heinemann.

Gorsline, M., & Gorsline, D. (1977). North American Indians. New York: Random House.

Gowan, J. (1980). *The divergent thinking theory of creativity.* New York: Basic Books.

Graesser, A. C., Lang, K. L., & Roberts, R. M. (1991). Question answering in the context of sories. *Journal of Experimental Psychology, 120* (3), 254–277.

Graham, M. & Block, C. C. (1994). Elementaary students as co-teachers and co-researcher. *Greater Washington Journal of Literacy, 12,* 34–48.

Graves, D. (1999). *Bringing life into learning.* Portsmouth, NH: Heinemann.

Graves, M., Cook, T. & Laberge, G. (1983 December). *Literal comprehension research.* Paper presented at annual meeting of the National Reading Conference, Austin, TX.

Gray, B. (1999 December). *Teacher's impact of student achievement.* Paper presented at the annual meeting of the National Reading Conference, Austin, TX.

Greene, M. (1998 April). *Imagination, passion, and intelligence.* Paper presented at the annual meeting of the Teaching for Intelligence Conference, New York.

Greene, R. L., Thapar, A., & Westerman, D. L. (1998). Effects of generation on memory for order. *Journal of Memory Language, 38,* 255–264.

Guilford, J. (1978). *The Structure of intellect.* New York: Columbia University Press.

Guthrie, J. T. (1981). (Ed.). *Comprehension and teaching: Research reviews.* Newark, DE: International Reading Association.

Guthrie, J. T., Cox, K. E., Knowles, K. T., Buehl, M., Mazzoni, S. A., & Fasulo, L. (2000). Building toward coherent instruction. In L. Baker, M. J. Dreher, & J. T. Guthrie (Eds.), *Engaging young readers: Promoting achievement and motivation* (pp. 209–236). New York: Guilford Press.

Haas, C. (1996). *Writing technology: Studies in the materiality of literacy.* Mahwah, NJ: Erlbaum.

Haberlandt, K. F., & Graesser, A. C. (1985). Component processes in text comprehension and some of their interactions. *Journal of Experimental Psychology, 114,* 357–374.

Hacker, D. J. (1998). Self-regulated comprehension during normal reading. In D. J. Hacker, J. Dunlosky, & A. C. Graesser (Eds.), *Metacognition in educational theory and practice* (pp. 165–191). Mahwah, NJ: Erlbaum.

Haenggi, D., Kintsch, W., & Gernsbacher, M. (1995). Spatial Situation Models and Text Comprehension. In J. R. Anderson (Ed.), *The architecture of cognition.* (pp. 198–213). Cambridge, MA: Harvard University Press.

Hansen, J. (1980 May). When writers read for comprehension development. Paper presented at the annual meeting of the International Reading Association, New Orleans, LA.

Hansen, J., & Pearson, P. D. (1983). An instructional study: Improving the inferential comprehension of good and poor fourth-grade readers. *Journal of Educational Psychology, 75,* 821–829.

Hapgood, J., Palinscar, A., & Magnusson, J. (2000). The role of dialogue in providing scaffolded instruction. *Educational Psychologist, 21,* 211–225, 229.

Harvey, S. (1998). Reading nonfiction: Learning and understanding in *Nonfiction matters,* (pp. 67–87). York, ME: Stenhouse Publishers.

Harwayne, S. (2000).Providing Safety Nets for Struggling Students in *Lifetime guarantees toward ambitious literacy teaching*, (pp 287–350). Portsmouth, NH: Heinemann.

Heath, S. B. (2000). Linguistics in the study of language in education. *Harvard Educational Review, 70*, (1), 49–59.

Hiebert, E. (1991). Patterns of literature-based reading instruction. *The Reading Teacher, 43*, 14–19.

Hiebert, E. (1999). Creating communities of teachers and learners across school districts. Reading Research 99. International Reading Association, San Diego, CA.

Hobbs, R. (1997). Literacy for the information age. In J. Flood, S. B. Heath, & D. Lapp (Eds.) *Handbook of research on teaching literacy through the communicative and visual arts.* (pp. 7–14) New York: International Reading Association.

Holmes, A. (1987 April). *Predictive thinking and its development.* Paper presented at the annual meeting of the American Educational Research Association, San Francisco, CA.

Holmes, B. (1981). *The world's first baseball games.* Cleveland, OH: Modern Curriculum.

Horne, J. (2000 December). *Reading instruction: From the past to the future.* Paper presented at the annual meeting of the National Reading Conference, Scottsdale, AZ.

Hunt, M. A., & Vipond, R. (1985). *A multimedia approach to children's literature.* Chicago, IL: American Library Association.

Invernez, M., Mendon, B., & Juel, C. (1999 December). *Building students' vocabulary through book buddies.* Paper presented at the annual meeting of the National Reading Conference, San Diego, CA.

Iser, W. (1978). *The act of reading: A theory of aesthetic response.* Baltimore, MD: Johns Hopkins University Press.

Jacobs, S. E., & Paris, S. G. (1987). Children's metacognition about reading: Issues in definition, measurement, and instruction. *Educational Psychologist, 22*, 255–278.

James, W. (1890). *Elementary Reading Instruction.* New York: World.

Jenkins, J. J. (1988). Remember that old theory of memory? Well, forget it! *American Psychologist, 29*, 785–95.

Johnson, D. W. (1985). *Learning together and alone: Cooperative, competitive, and individualistic learning.* Boston: Allyn & Bacon.

Johnston, J., Invernizzi, M., & Juel, C. (1998). *Book buddies.* New York: Guilford Press.

Johnston, P. & Winograd, P. (1985). Comprehension instruction. In P. D. Pearson, R. Barr, M. L.

Kamil, & P. Mosenthal. (Ed.). *Handbook of reading research* (pp. 237–265). NewYork: Macmillan.

Keene, E. O. & Zimmerman, S. (1997). *Mosaic of thought: Teaching comprehension in a reader's workshop.* Portsmouth, NH: Heinemann.

Kennedy, P. (2000). *Mathematical and Literacy Interactions.* Presentation to the School of Education, Texas Christian University, Fort Worth, TX.

King, A. (1994). Guiding knowledge construction in the classroom: Effects of teaching children how to question and how to explain. *American Educational Research Journal, 31*(2), 338–368.

Kintsch, W. (1991). A theory of discourse comprehension: Implications for a tutor for word algebra problems. In M. Pope, R. J. Simmons, J. I. Poso, & M. Caretero (Eds.), *Proceedings of the 1989 EARLI conference* (pp. 235–253). London: Pergamon Press.

Kintsch, W. (1993). Information accretion and reduction in text processing: Inferences. *Discourse Processes, 16*, 193–202.

Kintsch, W. (1994). Learning from text. *American Psychologist, 49*, 294–303.

Kintsch, W. (1998). *Comprehension: A paradigm for cognition.* New York: Cambridge University Press.

Kintsch, W. (2000 April). *Coherence memory: Theoretical perspectives.* Paper presented at the annual meeting of the American Educational Research Association, San Francisco, CA.

Kintsch, W. (2001 April). Nodes of memory. Paper presented at the annual meeting of the American Educational Research Association. St. Louis, MO.

Kintsch, W., & Otera, O. (1992). *Inference: A model for understanding.* Paper presented at the annual meeting of the American Educational Research Association, Washington, DC.

Kintsch, W., & van Dijk, T. A. (1978). Towards a model of text comprehension and production. *Psychological Review, 85*, 363–94.

Kirby, M. (1994). *Mind matters.* New York: Holt.

Kletzien, L. (1991). Strategy used by good and poor comprehenders. *Reading Research Quarterly, 26* (1), 70–94.

Koslyn, A., Brunn, B., Cave, T., & Wallach, S. (1984 May). *Metacognitive thinking and its effect on literal comprehension abilities.* Paper presented at the annual meeting of the International Reading Association, New Orleans, LA.

Langer, J. (1999). Reading comprehension. *Research in the Teaching of English, 55*–88.

Lanham, G. P. (1993). *Hypertext: The convergence of contemporary critical theory and technology.* Baltimore: Johns Hopkins University Press.

Lauber, P. (1985). *Volcano: The eruption and healing of Mount St. Helens.* New York: Macmillan.

Lehr, S. & Thompson, D. (2000 March). Comprehension: Semantic maps revisited. *Reading Teacher, 53* (6), 480.

Leslie, L., & Allen, L. (1999). Factors that predict success in an early literacy intervention project. *Reading Research Quarterly, 34* (4), 404–424.

Leslie, L., & Caldwell, J. (2001). *Qualitative reading inventory.* Boston: Allyn & Bacon.

Leu, D., & Kinzer, C. (1995). The convergence of literacy instruction with networked technologies for information and communication. *Reading Research Quarterly, 35,* 108–127.

Levin, J. R. (1991). A comparison of semantic and mnemonic-based vocabulary learning strategies. *Reading Psychology, 5,* 1–16.

Levin, J. R., Barry, I. K., Miller, G., & Bartel, R. (1982 April). *Metacognition and key word method.* Paper presented at the annual meeting of the American Educational Research Association, St. Louis, MO.

Levin, J. R., & Pressley, M. (1981). Improving children's prose comprehension: Selected strategies that seem to succeed. In C. M. Santa & B. L. Hayes (Eds.), *Children's prose comprehension* (pp. 44–71). Newark, DE: International Reading Association.

Lin, X. D., Bransford, J. D., Kantor, R., Hmelo, C., Hickey, D., Secules, T., Goldman, S. R., Petrosino, A., & the Cognitive Technology Group at Vanderbilt. (1995). Instructional design and the development of learning communities: An invitation to a dialogue. *Educational Technology, 35* (5), 53–63.

Linden, L. & Wittrock, R. (1981). Vocabulary Development. In Pearson, P. D., et al (Eds.). *Handbook of Reading Research.* (pp. 566–690). NY: Macmillan.

Lion, R., & Betsy, B. (1996 December). *Teacher improvement: Research concerning student achievement.* Paper presented at the annual meeting of the National Reading Conference. Miami, FL.

Lipson, M. Y. & Wixson, K. K. (1997). *Assessment and instruction of reading and writing disability: An interactive approach* (2nd ed.). New York: Longman.

Locken, R. (1981 December). *Literal comprehension: Influenced by decoding abilities.* Paper presented at the annual meeting of the National Reading Conference, Austin, TX.

Long, G. (1994). *Spatial learning strategies: Techniques, applications, and related issues.* New York: Academic Press.

Loxterman, J. A., Beck, I. L., & McKeown, M. (1994). The effects of thinking aloud during reading on students' comprehension of more or less coherent text. *Reading Research Quarterly, 29* (4), 353–366.

Lysaker, J. T. (1997). Learning to read from self-selected texts: The book choices of six first graders. In C. K. Kinzer, K. A. Hinchman, & D. J. Leu, (Eds.), *Inquiries in literacy theory & practice: National reading conference yearbook* (pp. 399–407). Chicago, IL: National Reading Conference.

Mackey, M. (1997). Good-enough reading: Momentum and accuracy in the reading of complex fiction. *Research in the Teaching of English, 31* (4), 428–458.

Mackey, M. (1998 April). *Erasing good-enough reading forever.* Paper presented at the annual meeting of the American Educational Research Association, New Orleans, LA.

MacKenzie, A. (1972). *The time trap.* New York: Macmillan.

Maduram, I. (2000). "Playing possum": A young child's response to information books. *Language Arts, 77* (5), 391–397.

Mak, K. (2002). *My Chinatown.* New York: Harper Collins.

Mangieri, J. N., & Block, C. C. (1994). *Creating powerful thinking for teachers and students: Diverse perspectives.* Fort Worth, TX: Harcourt Brace.

Mangieri, J. N., & Block, C. C. (1996). *Power thinking for success.* Cambridge, MA: Brookline.

Martinez, M., Roser, N., & Strecker, J. (1990 December). *Readers' theatre: Method to improve fluency and vocal qualities.* Paper presented at the annual meeting of the National Reading Conference. Austin, TX.

Marzana, R. (2001). Teaching for understanding. *Educational Leadership, 87,* 12–20.

Maslow, B. (1968). *Human nature and man's hierarchy.* New York: Teachers College Press.

McKay, D., Thompson, E., & Schabuh, R. (1970). Effect of imagery upon retention. *Journal of Educational Psychology, 52,* 118–126.

McKenna, M. C., Robinson, R., & Miller, J. (1993). Whole language and research. In D. Leu & C. Kinzer, (Eds.), *Examining central issues in literacy research.* National reading conference yearbook (pp. 141–152). Chicago, IL: National Reading Conference.

McNamara, D. S., & Kintsch, W. (2000). Learning from texts: Effects of prior knowledge and text coherence. *Discourse Processes, 22*(3), 247–288.

Means, B., & Knapp, M. (1991). Introduction: Rethinking teaching for disadvantaged students. In B. Means, C. Chaiemer, & M. Knapp (Eds.) *Teaching advanced skills to at-risk students.* San Francisco: Jossey Bass, pp. 333–369.

Meichenbaum, P., & Biemiller, A. (1990, May). *In search of student expertise in the classroom: A metacognitive analysis.* Paper presented at the conference on Cognitive Research for Instructional Innovation, University of Maryland, College Park, MD.

Melo, T. (1994 December). *Metacognition and effects on student achievement.* Paper presented at the annual meeting of the National Reading Conference, San Diego, CA.

Meyer, B. J. F. (1975). *The organization of prose and its effect on memory.* Amsterdam: North-Holland.

Mezynski, W. (1983). *Literal comprehension instruction and the correlations with detail versus main idea retention.* Unpublished dissertation, University of Wisconsin, Madison.

Miholic, V. (1994). An inventory to pique students' metacognitive awareness. *Journal of Reading, 38,* 84–86.

Miller, G. E. (1985). The effects of general and specific self-instruction training on children's comprehension monitoring performance during reading. *Reading Research Quarterly, 20,* 616–628.

Miller, G. E. (1987). The influence of self-instruction on the comprehension monitoring performance of average and above average readers. *Journal of Reading Behavior, 19,* 303–317.

Miller, G. E. (1999 April). *Metacognitive comprehension monitoring performances of below average readers.* Paper presented at the annual meeting of the American Educational Research Association, Seattle, WA.

Moll, L. (Ed.). (1997 March). *Cultural bearings upon early literacy development.* Paper presented at the School of Education, Texas Christian University, Fort Worth, TX.

Moss, E. F. (1989). *Macroprocessing in expository text comprehension.* Unpublished dissertation. University of Colorado, Boulder.

Myers-Briggs, J. (2001). *Myers-Briggs Personality Trait Assessment, Battery 7 Research Manual.* San Antonio, TX: The Psychological Corporation.

Nagy, W., & Herman, P. (1987). Incidental vs. instructional approaches to increasing reading vocabulary. *Educational Perspective, 23,* 16–21.

National Reading Panel. (Febuary 22,1999). Progress report to the National Institute on Child Health and Development. Washington, DC: NICHD.

National Reading Panel. (2001). *Teaching children to read: Report of the comprehension instruction subgroup to the National Institute on Child Health and Development.* Washington, DC: NICHD.

National Research Council. (1998). *Preventing reading difficulties in young children.* Washington, DC: National Academy Press.

Negropante, I. (1995). *Expository text analysis versus schematic analysis.* Unpublished dissertation, University of Oklahoma, Norman.

Nell, A. (1988). Teaching themes: Effects on student comprehension. Unpublished dissertation. University of New York, Albany.

Nelson, K. R. (1978). *Differences in the thinking processes of expert and novice teachers.* Unpublished dissertation, Louisiana State University, Baton Rouge.

Nelson, K. R. (1996) *Thinking processes, management routines and student perceptions of expert and novice physical education teachers.* Research Report, School of Education, Louisiana State University, Baton Rouge.

Noordman, L. G., & Vonk, W. (1998). Readers' knowledge and the control of inferences in reading. *Language and Cognitive Processes, 7,* 373–391.

Norman, D. A. (1981). The trouble with UNIX. Datamation, 139–150.

Oakhill, J., & Yuill, N. (1999). Higher order factors in comprehension disability: Processes and remediation. In C. Cornoldi, & J. Oakhill, (Eds.). *Models of effective educational assessment,* (pp. 111–135). Hillsdale, NJ: Erlbaum.

Ogle, D. M. (1986). K-W-L: A teaching model that develops active reading of expository text. *The Reading Teacher, 39,* 564–570.

O'Flahavan, J. O. (1989). *Second graders' social, intellectual, and affective development in varied group discussions about narrative texts: An explanation of participation structures.* Unpublished doctoral dissertation, University of Illinois, Urbana-Champaign.

Omanson, R., Warren, R., & Trabasso, T. (1978 April). *Comprehending text through strategies.* Paper presented at the annual meeting of the American Educational Research Association, New Orleans, LA.

Optiz, M. & Rasinski, T. (1999). *Goodbye round robin reading.* Portsmouth, New Hampshire: Heinemann.

Otero, J., & Kintsch, W. (1992). Failures to detect contradictions in a text: What readers believe versus what they read. *Psychological Science, 3* (4), 229.

Palincsar, A. S. (1986). The role of dialogue in providing scaffolded instruction. *Educational Psychologist, 21,* 73–98.

Palincsar, A. S., & Brown, A. L. (1984). Reciprocal teaching: Explicit strategy instruction in literature groups. *Cognition and Instruction, 1,* 11–27.

Pappas, C. C. (1991). Young children's strategies in the "book language" of information books. *Discourse Processes, 14,* 203–225.

Pappas, C. C. (1993). Is narrative "primary"? Some insights from kindergartners' pretend readings of stories and information books. *Journal of Reading Behavior, 25,* 97–129.

Pardo, L. S. (1997). Criteria for selecting literature in upper elementary grades. In T. Raphael, & K. Au,

(Eds.), *Literature-based instruction: Reshaping the curriculum.* (pp. 187–209). Norwood, MA: Christopher-Gordon.

Paris, S. G. (1986). Teaching children to guide their reading and learning. In T. E. Raphael (Ed.), *The contexts of school-based literacy* (pp. 115–130). New York: Random House.

Paris, S. G. (1991). Assessment and remediation of metacognitive aspects of children's reading comprehension. *Topics in Language Disorders, 12,* 32–50.

Paris, S. G., Wasik, B. A., & Turner, J. (1991). Portfolio assessment for young readers. *The Reading Teacher, 44,* 680–682.

Paris, S. G., & Winograd, P. (1990). How metacognition can promote academic learning and instruction. In B. F. Jones & L. Idol (Eds.), *Dimensions of thinking and cognitive instruction* (pp. 15–51). Hillsdale, NJ: Erlbaum.

Payne, B. D., & Manning, B. H. (1992). Basal reader instruction: Effects of comprehension monitoring training on reading comprehension, strategy use and attitude. *Reading Research and Instruction, 32,* 29–38.

Pearson, P. D., Hansen, J., & Gordon, C. (1979). The effect of background knowledge on young children's comprehension of explicit and implicit information. *Journal of Reading Behavior, 9* (3). (pp. 509–534).

Pearson, P. D., & Johnson, D. (1978). *Teaching comprehension.* Fort Worth, TX: Harcourt Brace.

Perfetti, C. (1998). The limits of co-occurrence: Tools and theories in language research. *Discourse Processer, 25* (2–3), 363–377.

Perfetti, C. & Lesco, R. (1979). Sentences, individual differences, and multiple texts: Three issues in text comprehension. *Discourse Processes, 23,* 337–355.

Perfetti, C. A., Marron, M. A., & Foltz, P. W. (1999). Sources of Comprehension Failure: Theoretical Perspectives and Case Studies. In S. Cornaldi & J. Oakhill (Ed), *Learning disabilities: New models of instruction.* Mahwah, NJ: Erlbaum.

Piaget, J., (1963). *Play, dreams, and imitation in childhood.* New York: Norton.

Piaget, J., & Inhelder, B. (1971). *Mental imagery.* New York: Basic Books.

Poltrock, A., & Brown, A. L. (1984). Reciprocal teaching of comprehension-fostering and comprehension-monitoring activities. *Cognition and Instruction, 1,* 117–125.

Prawatt, G. (2001 April). *Theoretical models for comprehension development.* Paper presented at the annual meeting of the American Educational Research Association, Seattle, WA.

Preia-Raldeanne, J. A. (1997). Development and validation of a self-report measure of reading strategy use. *Reading Psychology, 18,* 185–235.

Presseisen, B. (1987). *Teaching thinking: Piagetian influences.* Paper presented at the annual meeting of the American Educational Research Association, Chicago, IL.

Pressley, M. (1976). Mental imagery helps eight-year olds remember what they read. *Journal of Educational Psychology, 68,* 355–359.

Pressley, M. (1998). *Balanced Reading Instruction.* New York: Guilford Press.

Pressley, M. (1999). *Reading Instruction that Works.* New York: Guilford Press.

Pressley, M. (2000). Comprehension instruction in elementary school: A quarter century of research progress. In B. M. Taylor, M. F. Graves, & P. van den Broek (Eds.), *Reading for meaning: Fostering comprehension in the middle grades* (pp. 32–51). New York: Teachers College Press.

Pressley, M., & Afflerbach, P. (1995). *Verbal protocols of reading: The Nature of constructively responsive reading.* Hillsdale, NJ: Erlbaum.

Pressley, M., Almasi, J., Schuder, T., Bergman, J., Hite, S., El-Dinary, P. B., & Brown, R. (1994). Transactional instruction of comprehension strategies: The Montgomery County, Maryland, SAIL program. *Reading and Writing Quarterly: Overcoming learning difficulties, 10,* 5–19.

Pressley, M., Goodchild, F., Fleet, J., Zajchowski, R., & Evans, E. D. (1989). The challenges of classroom strategy instruction. *Elementary School Journal, 89,* 301–342.

Pressley, M., Harris, K., & Guthrie, J. (1995). Mapping the cutting edge in primary level literacy instruction for weak and at-risk readers. In D. Scrubles & M. Mastropileri (Eds.), *Advances in learning and behavioral disabilities,* (447–482). Greenwich, CT: JAI Press.

Purcell-Gates, V. (1996). Stories, coupons and the *TV Guide:* Relationships between home literacy experiences and emergent literacy knowledge. *Reading Research Quarterly, 31* (4), 406–430.

Radzisewsak, R. (1978). *The technological revolution.* New York: Free Press.

Raphael, T. & Au, K. (Eds.). (1997). *Literature-based instruction: Reshaping the curriculum.* Norwood, MA: Christopher-Gordon.

Reinking, D., & Bridwell-Bowles, L. (1996). Computers in reading and writing. In *Handbook of Reading Research, 1,* 310–340. Mahwah, NJ: Erlbaum.

Rhodes, L. K. (Ed.). (1993). *Literacy assessment: A handbook of instruments.* Portsmouth, NH: Heinemann.

Richgels, D. J., Mackey, M., Lomax, S., & Shepard, S. (1997). Invented spelling ability and printed word learning in kindergarten. *Reading Research Quarterly, 30,* 96–109.

Rogoff, B., Radzisewasak, W., Masiello, M. (1995). *Apprenticeship in thinking.* New York: Oxford University Press.

Roller, G. M. (1994). Commentary: The interaction of knowledge and structure variables in the processing of expository prose. *Reading Research Quarterly, 25* (2), 7–10.

Rose, D. (2001 April). Brain research and its implications for comprehension instruction. Paper presented at the annual meeting of the American Educational Research Association, Seattle, WA.

Rosenblatt, L. M. (1978). *The reader, the text, the poem: The transactional theory of the literary work.* Carbondale: Southern Illinois University.

Rosenshine, B., & Meister, C. (1997). Cognitive strategy instruction in reading. In S. A. Stahl & D. A. Hayes (Eds.). Instruction of learning by doing in text editing. Mahwah, NJ: Erlbaum.

Rowler, J. (1990). The importance of comprehension abilities. *English Journal, 79,* 623–630.

Ruffman, M. (2000 December). *Literal comprehension of details and the effect on retention of causal relationships and inferences.* Paper presented at the annual meeting of the National Reading Conference, Scottsdale, AZ.

Rylant, C. (1998). *Scarecrow.* New York: Scholastic.

Rylant, C. (2000). *The Whales.* Vero Beach, FL: Rourke.

Sachar, L. (2000). *Holes.* New York: Scholastic.

Sadoski, M. (1985). The natural use of imagery in story comprehension and recall: Replication and extension. *Reading Research Quarterly, 20,* 658–667.

Sadoski, M., & Paivio, A. (1994). A dual coding view of imagery and verbal processes in reading comprehension. In R. B. Ruddell, M. R. Ruddell, & H. Singer (Eds.), *Theoretical models and processes of reading* (4th ed. Pp. 582–601). Newark, DE: International Reading Association for learning effects on memory and cognition, *Journal of Experimental Psychology, 23,* (4) 173–180.

Sander, E., & Richard, J. (1997). Analogical transfer as guided by an abstraction process: The case for learning effects on memory and cognition. *Journal of Experimental Psychology, 23* (4), 173–180.

Santa, C. M., & Hoien, R. (1999). An assessment of Early Steps: A program for early intervention of reading problems. *Reading Research Quarterly, 34* (1), 54–79.

Schmitt, M. C. (1988). The effects of an elaborated directed reading activity on the metacomprehension skills of third graders. In J. E. Readance &

R. S. Baldwin (Eds.), *Dialogues in literacy research* (Thirty-seventh yearbook of the National Reading Conference) (pp. 167–181). Chicago, IL: National Reading Conference.

Schmitt, M. C. (1990). A questionnaire to measure children's awareness of strategic reading processes. *The Reading Teacher, 43,* 454–461.

Schmitt, M. C., & Hopkins, C. J. (1993). Metacognitive theory applied: Strategic reading instruction in the current generation of basal readers. *Reading Research and Instruction, 32,* 13–24.

Schunk, J., & Rice, R. (1991). *Scripts, goal attainment and understanding: An inquiry into human comprehension.* Hillsdale, NJ: Erlbaum.

Schwartz, D. L., & Bransford, J. D. (2001). A time for telling. *Cognition and Instruction 41* (4), 291–321.

Scott, J. A., Jamieson, D., & Asselin, M. (1999). Instructional interactions in upper elementary classrooms: An observational study. In T. Shanahan et al. (Eds.), *National Reading Conference yearbook, 48,* 167–177.

Sebaros, B. (1985). Imagery drawings. New York: Scholastic.

Shoemaker, M., & Deshler, D. (1992). Effects of strategy instruction on at-risk students' comprehension. *Journal of Educational Psychology, 98,* 668–679.

Singer, M., & Ritchot, K. F. M. (1996). The role of working memory capacity and knowledge access in text inference processing. *Memory and Cognition 24,* 733–743.

Singer, M., Graesser, W., & Trabasco, T. (2001). Sequential thinking models as relates to retention. *Journal of Educational Psychology, 98,* 334–346.

Smey-Richman, B. (1988). *Involvement in learning for low-achieving students.* Philadelphia: Research for Better Schools.

Smolkin, L. (2002). Comprehending expository text. In C. C. Block and M. Pressley (Eds.), *Comprehension instraction: Research based best practices,* (pp. 173–194). New York: Guilford Press.

Spires, R., & Ester, T. (2000 April). *Comprehension and teacher-made assessments.* Paper presented at the annual meeting of the American Educational Research Association, New Orleans, LA.

Stanovich, K. E. (1986). The Matthew effects in reading: Some consequences for individual differences in the acquisition of literacy. *Reading Research Quarterly, 21,* 360–407.

Stein, R., & Kirby, W. (1992). The effects of text absent and text present conditions on summarization and recall of text. *Journal of Reading, 24,* (2), 217–222.

Stiles, J. (1991). *Sequential thinking and retention of main ideas.* Paper presented at the annual meeting of the American Educational Research Association, Chicago, IL.

Sweet, A. & Snow, C. (2002). The RAND Corporation: New perspectives on comprehension. In C. C. Block, L. Gambrell, & M. Pressley, (Eds.). *Comprehension instruction: Building on the past to influence the future.* (pp. 7–230). San Francisco: Jossey Bass/International Reading Association.

Taylor, B. M. (1980). Text structure and children's comprehension and memory for expository material. *Journal of Educational Psychology, 74,* 323–340.

Taylor, B. M., & Beach, R. W. (1984). The effects of text structure instruction on middle-grade students' comprehension and production of expository texts. *Reading Research Quarterly, 19,* 134–146.

Taylor, B., Graves, M., van de Broek, P. (2000). *Reading for meaning, fostering comprehension in the middle grades.* New York: Teachers College, Columbia University.

Tergeson, J. K., Wagner, J. (1987). What it means to learn to read. *Child Development, 56* (5), 1134–1144.

Terman, L. (1961). *Measuring Intelligence.* New York: Harper & Row.

Tharp, R. G., & Gallimore, R. (1988). Assessment and not reading. *Language Arts 14* (1), 26–330.

Thorndike, R., & Woodworth, R. (1901). *Reasoning and comprehension.* New York: World.

Tierney, R. J. (1998). Literacy assessment reform. *The Reading Teacher, 51* (5), 371–393.

Torrance, P. (1981). *The Study of Creativity.* Athens: University of Georgia Press.

Torrance, P. & Sisk, D. (2001). *Spiritual intelligence.* Association for gifted students. Washington, DC.

Trabasso, T., & Bouchard, E. (2002). Teaching readers how to comprehend text strategically. In C. C. Block, & M. Pressley (Eds.), *Comprehension instruction: Research based practices.* New York: Guilford Press, 156–177.

Trimble, S. (1994). The scripture of maps, the names of trees: A child's landscape. In G. P. Nabhan & S. Trimple (Eds.), *The geography of childhood: Why children need wild places* (pp. 15–32). Boston: Beacon Press.

Van Dijk, T. A. (1980). *Macrostructures.* Hillsdale, NJ: Erlbaum.

Van Dijk, T. A., & Kintsch, W. (1983). *Strategies of discourse comprehension.* New York: Academic Press.

Van Horn, L. (2000). Sharing literature, sharing selves: Students reveal themselves through read-alouds. *Journal of Adolescent and Adult Literacy, 43,* (8), 752–763.

Vye, N. J., Schwartz, D. L., Bransford, J. D., Barron, B. J., & Zech, L. (1998). SMART environments that support monitoring, reflection, and revision.

In D. J. Hacker, J. Dunlosky, & A. C. Graesser (Eds.), *Metacognition in educational theory and practice* (pp. 305–346). Mahwah, NJ: Erlbaum.

Vygotsky, L. S. (1978). *Mind in society.* Cambridge, MA: MIT Press.

Way, B., Buxton, R., & Kelly, J. (1999). Effects of dramatic engagement on development. *Educational Psychologist, 67,* 344–356.

Weaver C. A., III, & Kintsch, W. (1996). Expository text. In *Handbook of reading research* (pp. 230–245). Mahwah, NJ: Erlbaum.

Weinberger, N. M., (1998). "The Music in Our Minds." *Educational Leadership: How the Brain Learns, 56,* (3). November 1998, 36–43.

Wertsch, J. (1991). *Voices of the mind.* Harvard University Press. Cambridge, MA.

Wigfield, A., Eccles, J. S., & Rodriguez, D. (1999). The development of children's motivation in school contexts. *Review of Research in Education, 23,* 73–118.

Wiley, J., & Voss, J. F. (1999). Constructing arguments from multiple sources: Tasks that promote understanding and not just memory for text. *Journal of Educational Psychology, 91* (2), 301–311.

Winograd, K., & Higgins, K. M. (1995). Writing, reading, and talking mathematics: One interdisciplinary possibility. *The Reading Teacher, 48* (4), 310–318.

Wittrock, M. C. (1998). Students' thought processes. *Educational Psychologist, 35,* 76–87.

Wood, D. J., Bruner, J. S. & Ross, G. (1976). The role of tutoring in problem solving. *Journal of Child Psychology and Psychiatry, 17,* 89–100.

Yuill, N. (1999). A funny thing happened on the way to the classroom: Jokes, riddles, and metalinguistic awareness in understanding and improving poor comprehension in children. In J. Oakhill, & N. Yuill, (Eds.). *Children's comprehension difficulties, (pp. 136–162).* Cambridge, England: Cambridge University Press.

Yuill, N., & Oakhill, J. (1991). *Children's problems in reading comprehension.* Cambridge, England: Cambridge University Press.

Zecker, L. B., Pappas, C. C., & Cohen, S. (1998). Finding the "right measure" of explanation for young Latina/o writers. *Language Arts, 76* (1), 49–60.

Zimmerman, B. J., & Bonner, S. (2000). Models of self-regulatory learning and academic achievement. In B. J. Zimmerman & D. H. Schunk (Eds.). *Self-regulated learning and academic achievement: Theory, research, and practice* (pp. 1–25). New York: Springer-Verlag.

Index